T0392987

Cyber-Physical Systems in the Construction Sector

Editor

Wesam Salah Alaloul

Department of Civil and Environmental Engineering
Universiti Teknologi PETRONAS, Malaysia

CRC Press
Taylor & Francis Group
Boca Raton London New York

CRC Press is an imprint of the
Taylor & Francis Group, an **informa** business

A SCIENCE PUBLISHERS BOOK

First edition published 2022
by CRC Press
6000 Broken Sound Parkway NW, Suite 300, Boca Raton, FL 33487-2742

and by CRC Press
2 Park Square, Milton Park, Abingdon, Oxon, OX14 4RN

© 2022 Taylor & Francis Group, LLC

CRC Press is an imprint of Taylor & Francis Group, LLC

ISBN: 978-1-032-03992-3 (hbk)
ISBN: 978-1-032-03993-0 (pbk)
ISBN: 978-1-003-19013-4 (ebk)

DOI: 10.1201/9781003190134

Typeset in Times New Roman
by Innovative Processors

Preface

Open spectrum technological trends in modern construction projects are taking over the construction sector at an elevated pace. One such technological space is being created by Cyber-Physical Systems (CPSs). A CPSs is a mechanism that is monitored and controlled by computer-based algorithms. In the construction sector, CPSs can help to increase the efficiency of construction projects with reduced costs, time, and better management approaches. This book aims to develop the fundamental concepts of construction project management which are associated with the CPSs and their applications within modern construction projects aligned to the scope of Industry Revolution (IR) 4.0.

The target audience of this book are academicians, such as students and faculty, and construction sectors prime stakeholders such as clients, consultants, and contractors. The book covers the overall concept and major applications of CPSs in the construction sector, starting from the basic fundamental model of CPSs to its important aspects, domains, future revolutions, and challenges. A general preview for CPSs technologies in the construction sector was illustrated to the reader under IR 4.0 umbrella, which will motivate the researchers and practitioners towards its adaptability in future projects.

Wesam Salah Alaloul

Contents

Fundamentals of Construction Project Management

Syed Saad, Wesam Salah Alaloul and Syed Ammad

Introduction

Construction project management can be defined as the process of planning, organizing, and managing the response to an event or other demands (Love et al. 2002). This process is also known as project management when its goal is discreet production. The end products are typically a facility, product, or structure upon which no construction work has been yet performed. In managing a construction project, the importance of managing technical approaches and performance specifications with contractual requirements between construction organisations is very important. This is because, without such consideration, coordination may not be able to function properly. Without any coordination, its success will undermine the efficiency of the job. Construction project management is required to ensure that all construction projects have a high level of coordination among different project stakeholders (Maqbool et al. 2017). It's considered to be shrewd and wise when tasks are completed on time, on budget, and the mission or vision has been reached. The goal of construction project management is always the safety and success of the vision (Park et al. 2015). Construction project management skills are required for every profession in construction. It requires professionals with construction organisations to have an emphasis on different levels of expertise, from architects to engineers. Quality analysts can provide valuable insight into the constructions' complexities around materials and risks. In some scenarios, large-scale construction organisations are needed to complete the complex work; therefore, project management is necessary due to all the different tasks required (Adam et al. 2018). Organisations work closely with architects and designers to ensure project goals are achieved as they involve a detailed understanding of what needs to be done in order for them to come together for the best possible outcome. Construction project management began in the late 1940s when the first continuous cast-in-place zipper slab was erected. This slab became known as "Gertie" and is used to this day on portions of the Bay Bridge close to Yerba Buena Island. The first planner hired specifically for a construction project was Everette Ward. Ward managed the construction of Wickes College in 1942. Originally, "construction managers were designated as the engineer's assistant by participating in preparing design calculations and drawings" to give engineers a break from their intensive work, in the hope towards producing an excellent outcome. Since this time, they have aided in other parts of many projects besides design. Today's construction project managers may not be like before, but the key part to their accomplishment is able to see the vision and product of construction that still necessitates an excellent outcome (Berg and Karlsen 2007).

What is a Project?

Projects are temporary in nature, and the temporary nature of such undertakings underline that projects have definite beginnings and ends. Projects, by their characterization, have defined starting and ending points in time. Furthermore, project objectives should be finite, measurable, and achievable (Artto et al. 2008). When we are assessing whether something is a project, we often ask ourselves, "Is it a temporary event?" If the answer is yes, then we can conclude that it is, in fact, a project. A project comes to an end when its objectives have been achieved, or when it must be terminated because its objectives cannot be met, or when its usefulness has ceased. Each project is unique, so the output differs depending upon the endeavour involved. The output may be either tangible or intangible in nature (Dwyer et al. 2000). The largest challenge that many projects' managers face is uncertainty. An unknown factor encompasses any project, so time-based goals cannot be attained (Heagney 2016). When an element of an endeavour changes or a project manager makes an error, the project and its objectives change. One of the most important things that project managers need to have is a thorough understanding of their organisations' philosophy (Pinto and Slevin 1987); this will provide them with the motivation to complete the objectives of the project. Effective goals and timeline management as a whole, careful management of resources, effective communication with stakeholders, and establishing a realistic budget are also necessities for project management. The term "project status" can refer to the phases of a project or "progress towards completion." A project is traditionally very distinct phases such as an initiation, management and governance, planning, execution, monitoring and control, closing, and closing phases (Marcelino-Sádaba et al. 2014).

One example of a project is a "building construction" project. The outputs here are what is being achieved in the project, such as a new building. Activities here are what takes place in creating the project, such as finishing up the blueprint drawings. Inputs here are all the resources that are used in the project, such as tools and labours. A building construction project includes any in-progress structure that is not yet able to be used or sold. In the planning phase, a team of people makes plans for a project, creates a timeline of when the phases will happen, and works through risks and identifies resources needed (Johnson et al. 2002). There are five stages for a project to be successful:

1. "Planning activation" includes defining the project, developing a timeline and creating a system for team communications.
2. "Execution" includes managing the process of carrying out the project (e.g., checking on resources and supplies needed).
3. "Monitor," includes the process by which the progress and risks assessment of the project are analysed to see which changes need to be made.
4. "Control" includes coordinating the project teams involved in carry out the project, as well as addressing all changes to the timeline.
5. "Closure," concluding the project by documenting what happened and by creating an audit report.

Project Quality Management

In any project, the quality of the product is of key importance; therefore, a need of project quality assessment is needed. Project quality management measures the ability of the project lead to produce quality products on time with pre-defined resources (Anderson et al. 1994). This process includes making design mistakes with the highest available quality, achieving the highest level of quality that will not exceed budget and rendering a project management schedule within the scope which meets a company or organisations' expectations. Ultimately, increasing the overall quality of a project for use leads to its success. Construction projects are prone to mistakes and delays when project management uses faulty methods (Shrivas and Singla 2020). The quality of a construction project is determined by planning, defining the finish goal, and goal measurement and hence there are some guidelines to ensure the quality of project management. In construction, the following guidelines on project management are (Schrapers 2018):

1. Create realistic but achievable goals by clarifying what success means.
2. Identify project stakeholders and get their participation.
3. Keep stakeholders informed about the progress made.
4. Create a realistic and detailed project schedule.
5. Ask for help when faced with decisions.
6. Measure the success of the project.

Quality Control and Construction Management

Quality control is necessary for construction management as all stakeholders want products to exceed expectations. Quality control measures the ability to carry out the quality requirements (Shewhart and Deming 1986). This includes inspecting the correspondence between the product quality and customer requirements, inspecting that the customer requirements are still met, the quality of the products are corresponding to the delivery date, and making the seller's name immaculate and not touching it. It also includes the probability that stores will be chaotic and constructed with the highest product and most cost-effective manner. Quality control thus articulates the construction management with the ability to release quality products and systems without the threat of a lawsuit or customer dissatisfaction, internally and externally.

Classifications of Construction Project Management

Construction project management is a process that poses risks, rewards, and opportunities. As a consultant, the quality of one's decisions could along determine the success or failure of projects (Jaafari 2001). A lot goes into managing construction projects and its risks, rewards, and opportunities. The process to introduce construction project management by discussing how it is very time consuming, along with a back-and-forth dialogue between architects, designers' generators, and site managers to assure work is progressing accordingly. The process of construction consists of designing and building buildings, roads, bridges, etc., according to drawings produced by architects or civil engineers (Halfawy and Froese 2005). The management aspect can be difficult because the team needs to be informed with updates on time remaining and progress on projects that may alter a design. For example, the team have to decide how to adjust the foundation when they learn that heavier traffic than anticipated and wider and longer than what is expected might be the norm. Meeting with clients or management committees is also a needed activity before construction begins to ensure that all parties are on the same page with timelines and costs. Maintaining productive and enjoyable relationships with construction subcontractors by being open to their input as well as noticing when they need help or ordering materials will also be needed. Without consideration to the other aspects of construction project management, decisions could ruin a process that seems relatively easy on paper in the first place (Patel and Jha 2015). Whilst considering company and public safety while developing a master plan that will be coherent with any set policies for land-use classification (Chan et al. 2018). Lastly, overseeing all aspects of the project to come up with the best possible solutions and make sound decisions according to stakeholders' interest are also integral when discussing Construction Project Management (Zhou et al. 2013). The following sections introduce the discussed in the form of classifications based on construction project management. This chapter provides a brief overview of the fundamentals of construction project management, Figure 1.1 below shows the classification breakdown of different disciplines.

Figure 1.1 shows the construction technology tools and technology inclusive of a few points as mentioned i.e. mobile internet connectivity, GPS system security measures and field force automation etc. It also describes causes of accidents on the site as well as design and contract management between client and contractor. The structure of regional practices is already defined in different frameworks e.g.

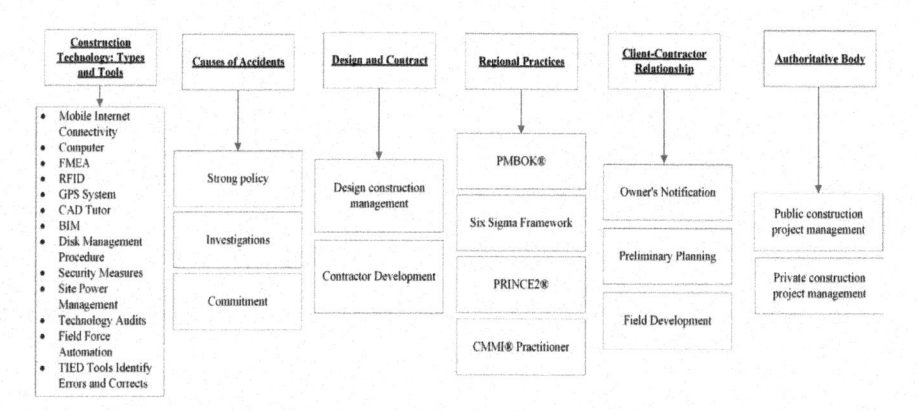

Figure 1.1: Classification Breakdown

PMBOK® and six sigma framework, which conveniently have been brought into account when dealing with different stages of construction project management such as owner's notification, preliminary planning or field development stage.

Authoritative Body

On the basis of authority, the construction project management can be classified into public and private (Ng et al. 2007). Public construction project management is the one which any public department or agency carries out, including that done by governments, local authorities, state government departments, legislatures etc. The other classification of construction project management is private, which is done without the involvement of those aforementioned entities but in full cooperation with them for example projects including sewer or water underground (Abu Samra et al. 2018).

Public Construction Project Management

This is the kind which any public department or agency carries out, including that done by governments, local authorities, state government's departments, legislatures etc. Several public bodies oversee it, such as the government, including civil departments, local authorities, state government's departments and legislative bodies, these include regulations, statutory orders, and statutory regulations by parliament.

Private Construction Project Management

The other classification of construction project management is private, which is done without the involvement of those aforementioned entities but in full cooperation with them like sewer or water underground. For example, if a company develops and provides housing (apart from the limited facilities such as sewers and water pipes), it is private.

Client-Contractor Relationship

Based on the client-contractor relationship, the construction project management can be classified into three sectors: Owner's Notification, Preliminary Planning, and Field Development (Wong Zhang 2013).

Owner's Notification

The major responsibility is to collect the budgeting information and ensure that all requirements are met for adequate funding, develop, and insert any changes of the contract documents as required by the owner, analyse and review bids for works.

Preliminary Planning

One oversees situation-flan development; establishes site condition records and develops sequence drawings; selects equipment requirements, specifies all contract specifications, and creates construction documents.

Field Development

The field development makes necessary revisions of an engineered plan design for the work and directs it for their correction prior to requesting bids, manages field resources, estimates material take-offs, and coordinates mobilization and demobilization of equipment and personnel as required to satisfy customer requirements or individual projects.

Regional Practices

The construction project management can also be classified into two regions: from the point of view of management practices and project types, as well as global regions (Marcelino-Sádaba et al. 2015). The first classification is based on construction project management's practices such as PMBOK®, Six Sigma Framework, PRINCE2®, and CMMI® Practitioner. The first classification divides PMBOK® construction project management from Six Sigma Framework, PRINCE2®, and CMMI® Practitioner classification, respectively (Bergstroem et al. 2009). The second classification is divided based on the location of the region as it includes different regions such as the USA, E.U, the Middle East and Africa.

PMBOK®

Defines systems that can be implemented when managing a construction project. It includes the work processes of needs assessment, project planning, executing the work according to plan, monitoring progress of the work, managing change and risk, integrating project requirements, and finally closing out all of the processes.

Six Sigma Frameworks

Similar to PMBOK®, the Six Sigma Framework requires an organisation to set objectives that should be measured objectively, communicate the framework's key successes for quick end-user adoption every time a Six Sigma project is accomplished, and have a defined Six Sigma Champion.

PRINCE2®

It can be classified into two subcategories that are the following: PRINCE2® Foundation, this level provides basic knowledge of the participants in construction project management such as project coordinator, project sponsor, project director, project team leader and consultant. PRINCE2® practitioner which means that this level is used when there is more involvement in executing the project requirements and all the information for a project audit. This includes documentation compliance, information accuracy, change control satisfaction, and management's objectives.

CMMI® Practitioner

This level provides a project manager with more in-depth knowledge of the construction project management practices and output skills to manage large and complex projects successfully.

The second classification is based on region, including the USA, European Union, The Middle East, and Africa. The location is also based on regions which are again classified as USA, European Union, Middle East and Africa. The locations for these classifications are organized according to the country where it includes all of the countries that are located within that specific region. For example, European Union classifies all the European countries in one region.

Design and Contract

Design and contract construction project management are classified into two parts: design construction management and contractor development (Al Haadir and Panuwatwanich 2011).

Design Construction Management

Design construction management comprises of making sample graphics, architectural plans, and detailed drawings so that the construction agency can follow it for one project or do away with alteration while executing a project. It is the profession of managing all construction projects from the early stages of design through completion and hand-over to their owners. It encompasses a wide range of skills with experience and understanding of the process of construction. It likewise focuses on sorting out staff members' needs and schedules, gathering data concerning delivery of supplies, equipment, and materials, escalating deals to resolution, and writing a construction administration plan.

Contractor Development

It is the estimation and management of projects' work points for different sectors. It includes orientation to contractual commitments, managing cash flow for construction projects, estimating costs and postponing effects on charges generated amid advancement, along these lines enhancing contract quality and contractual obligation fulfilment. Contract development is to help contractors stay in good standing with their contracts. There are many ways to keep contractors accountable, but the point of contractor development is to ensure the happiness of the contractors by incentivizing them to work responsibly and meet deadlines while retaining their resources. Contract development first analyses the resources of the contractor for a particular project, assesses their ability, and then suggests accurate charges for the different job elements of the project. The contractor can then choose to accept the charges or not. If they sign, then they have an incentive to be responsible and complete the project. In any contract development, it is important for contractors to have an incentive that ensures that the contractor is carefully motivated and bounded to accept the task. The five activities of contractor development are: estimating and projecting probable work outcomes, estimating project costs, delivering asset development and building contract charges, distributing expenses with firms and groups from areas that use them, likewise, managing cash flow for building charges.

Issues in Construction Industry

In the day-to-day life of the construction industry, there are predicaments of construction that may arise because of the building's geographic area or quality and authenticity problems. Following are some modern issues connected to the construction industry (Brett 1996).

Quality Control

The main issues related to the quality control in the construction industry are the quality control planning, management and fabrication (Chen and Jin 2013). The steps taken for the quality control can include preconstruction drawing reviews, engineered production drawings review, on-site workshops around waste disposal logistics and design options analysis during plan development. The goal here is to understand regional environmental services and materials interface through service inspections and cost analysis for materials through life cycle studies (Nematchoua et al. 2020). Finally, production inspections are take place on the site before and after to confirm quality. The person in control of quality control varies according to the company culture but generally, a team leader manages all or most areas and staff are either solely assigned tasks or split between teams (Hedlund 1994). Quality controllers, also known as QC, can often be found inspecting a process or operation. Quality control has weaknesses just like any other review-based or as-built system, including incomplete or inaccurate documentation and procedures. Lack of compliance with current standards for quality assurance practices and conflicts between operations can alter plans. The day-to-day management of the business that changes objectives without communication, etc. (Talebi et al. 2016).

Project Delivery Systems

The main issue of project delivery systems in construction is the sequencing of project delivery systems, which affects overall performance and quality. Short term projects create their own incentive structures, which lead to building fewer but oversized buildings that result in asymmetric budgeting (Tabassi and Bakar 2009). For example, some companies are compensating for low short-term profitability through higher long-term rates of return or through the sale of under-priced land to the government. These issues result in excess of shops, warehouses and service chain stores that are seldom used. Non-compliant materials result in a high number of projects abandoned on the ground before being completed because phase developers cannot afford the livelihood costs required to finish them. Physical immobilization is another issue facing third-world legislators. A good project delivery system in the construction industry uses a computerised database system to include all relevant information. This prevents duplicate payments, overpayments and fraudulent expenses through electronic fund transfer (Hager et al. 2006).

Construction Technology

The lack of construction technology waste time and money. Construction labour is paid for by the hour, meaning that downtime affects profits (Golden 2012). Contractors using outdated technology can only use a fraction of the resources on hand or cannot overcome technological setbacks. A large number of problems with digitally powered solutions create deadlines problems on a daily basis, wasting time and money to return to the issue (Toor and Havlick 2004). One problem is that construction input data is often entered manually, which is intensive and prone to human error. Furthermore, some digital solutions are not building trade-specific and do not understand the way in which a job site can be dangerous for workers and all the inherent safety requirements based on their job site (Ammad et al. 2021b).

Types and Tools for Construction Technology

Construction technology involves how project data is linked with construction operations thereby displaying the entire lifecycle of a project (Robichaud and Anantatmula 2011). Connecting panels to create "big picture" perspectives to provide insights into processes, problems and improve productivity from lessons learned on past projects. Construction technologies change based on individual needs, available resources, and the size of the project (Gann and Salter 2000). There are many speciality constructions tools for any given tasks, including:

Mobile Internet Connectivity: This device becomes crucial when bidding or managing outside of work time frames.

Computer: The best equipment for storing 3D models, sketches, blueprints, and other project progress documents.

FMEA: To reduce the cost of operational and repair costs in their budget for emergency response repairs.

RFID: Used for tagging and storing equipment identification numbers.

GPS System: Improve workforce safety, accuracy and accounting of materials, work procedures, site logistics.

CAD Tutor: An effective strategy for fast-learning new software to reduce supply chain delays.

Web Capture Techniques: Picture exports for solutions such as building construction process analysis, which evaluates construction drawings to identify potential problems with a building design and anticipating potential difficulties.

Building Information Modelling (BIM): Data and drawings integrate data across disciplines such as 3D modelling, engineering, and construction management to oversee and coordinate construction projects.

Disk Management Products: Optimize raw storage technologies with the management of the digital data for better performance.

Security Measures: Secure data with password protection, encryption, and a personal firewall.

Site Power Management: Technology that creates access to power in remote difficult to reach areas of site.

Technology Audits: Using devices such as PCR's, ARENs or Particle counters to test for problems early on in the construction process.

Field Force Automation: Field force automation software includes tools that automate the process of managing mobile workers, and streamlines routes for premade deliveries and cuts the time footprint down. These products integrate with a company's supply chain management (SCM) platform to demonstrate a level of efficiencies.

TIED Tools Identify Errors and Correct: Uses Artificial Intelligence to remove undesirable influences in data process management.

Collaboration and Connectivity

Collaboration and connectivity problems can include lack of communication and data sharing between facets or entities working on the same project, not understanding deliverables, gaps in timelines, absence of alignment between design phases delivered by different stakeholders, and lack of alignment in the final stage of the construction processes. Data can consist of drawings, renderings, models, or other specifications (Hodell 2013). A lack of connectivity also affects the slower adoption of innovative practices. One example is being able to capture 360-degree views on a vertical building, drones commonly capture such images.

Another issue regarding the lack of connectivity between different entities like drawings and sell sheets is that in the construction industry, aligning design phases directly impacts the implementation of sustainable practices. A lack of alignment can lead to missed opportunities for implementing photovoltaic (PV) solar panels, geothermal heating and cooling systems, and green roofs/walls (Pandey et al. 2018). Often, delays in becoming fully connected to these types of sustainable design can quickly escalate before they've even begun. Innovation presents an enormous opportunity for construction firms looking to address client demands in the areas of sustainability. But, achieving sustainability requires close coordination among trades and business consulting firms. For example, in construction, renewable materials for construction such as bamboo are quickly becoming mainstream however, when considering a sustainable design that considers renewable materials matched with PV solar panels and geothermal heating/cooling systems an organisation must fully understand the impact of their input in order to make effective resource management. The solar panels must face south-southwest in the northern hemisphere and north-northwest in the southern hemisphere; otherwise, they won't harness all of the sun's energy. The geothermal heating and cooling systems can create a cost avoidance of $250,000 over 35 years (Drake 1988). This looks at first glance like it requires teamwork. However, if gaps exist, the building's sustainability case will diminish in benefits, and innovation may never happen. One illustrative example of how a lack of collaboration and connectivity among construction players within a project does not necessarily lead to better sustainability outcomes occurred in New York City during Hurricane Sandy. With a missed opportunity to alter construction practices in areas badly hit by the storm, builders continued their construction, albeit in a more urgently and rushed manner. This ultimately did not improve sites connectivity nor reduce vulnerabilities to future storms. Integrating new construction techniques can provide opportunities for a breakthrough in the field of sustainable design, where collaboration and connectivity among trades and business consulting firms (building service companies) are getting much-needed attention (Steiner 2014). This allow organisations to understand the impact they have on sustainability goals-whether it's sourcing/using sustainable construction materials (e.g. bamboo) or implementing green technologies (e.g., solar panels, geothermal heating/cooling systems).

Safety

Safety is an important issue and especially a concern in the construction industry due to the risk of unfortunate accidents (Ammad et al. 2021a. Construction workers are subjected to bodily harm because of repetitive movements, hazardous materials, uncertain weather conditions, and faulty equipment (Ammad 2020). Hazards that do not necessarily present a direct threat to people can still translate into chronic health issues for those workers with complications that arise later in life (Ammad et al. 2021b). If workers are not properly trained, equipping them with tools or complying with regulations set by governing safety standards, they may soon turn into an accident waiting to happen (Qureshi and Altaf 2020). Concerns about safety in construction sector will not be rectified as long as these issues continue to plague the industry (Alaloul et al. 2021).

Causes of Construction Accidents

Construction sites are known for rubble, tight spots and cracks in roofing, all hazards which can produce debilitating injuries. There are more than 30,000 people injured in construction site accidents annually and about 300 fatalities each year (Approach et al. 2020). Workers can be subjected to potentially fatal hazards because they are not in compliance with safety or precautionary regulations to safeguard them against potential risks (Cheng et al. 2010). The most common causes of accidents stem from the following:

1. Engineering errors.
2. Fall protection system not being in place.
3. Lack of Project management and/or safety plan.
4. Damaged or faulty equipment to withstand congested conditions.
5. Missing warnings.
6. Damaged or defective workwear.
7. Lack of coordination in the working area.
8. Defects in equipment such as electric cables, pipelines.
9. Lack of knowledge on how to handle materials appropriately.
10. Working on rotting structures.
11. Power grid overload.

An accident can occur due to inadequate training, lack of knowledge on how to handle materials in an appropriate manner, structural defects or any other hazard that puts the worker in danger. It is clear that to have construction sustain their key functions; it is imperative for not only the workers but also everyone involved to embrace a culture of responsibility and ask questions about workplace safety (Alruqi and Hallowell 2019). There are a few avenues in which construction project management can help make construction sites safer (Alruqi and Hallowell 2019).

Commitment

Outlining the requirement and showing accuracy when it comes to safety standards for construction can be successful if there is a higher level of commitment by every role involved in the planning and management process (Manzoor et al. 2021). Levelling out more expectations ensures that safety becomes mainstream, and no one will scrutinize its importance (Karakhan et al. 2019).

Investigations

Construction accidents are difficult to trace because they are caused under different circumstances in different sectors that can sometimes involve more than one culprit, increasing the probability of accidents in areas known for other work content. Activities like checking on project managers and investigating whether there are any irregularities related to work.

Strong Policy

Establishing a higher level of accountability and giving them the power to follow-up was introduced in almost all construction investigations that were done over the past ten years. People in charge of investigating accidents coordinate regulatory bodies and interview those responsible for the organisations or anyone who might have significant knowledge on what factors are to be blamed for an accident.

Construction Management using CPSs

Design-Build

The phrase design-build refers to a concurrent development process in which the designer and the contractor collaborate on the end product specification (Gil et al. 2001). In many cases, design information is relayed to manufacturing facilities for specific material deliveries prior to work commencing. Companies utilizing this contracting strategy typically direct these operations with office engineers who work with architects and have company-designated responsibility for construction. Using this process, rather than having the different parties deliver their design and then have the other groups modify their efforts as each phase are built, there is a close collaboration between the two sides from beginning to end (Wikström 1996).

CPSs embodied in intelligent, shared Autonomous Machine Fabrication (AMF) machines that have the capability of self-adapting intelligence during operation. Furthermore, CPSs is emerging as a way to think about future manufacturing and the production processes instead of old school shop floor simulations (Thoben et al. 2017). Modular technologies that are composed of reusable, interchangeable ISO 10m modules form highly agile digital fabrication "factories for things". CPSs encompass the use of new quantum mechanical or properties of photons that sensor's measure and respond to process quality (Passian and Imam 2019). Artificial Intelligence (AI) and machine learning algorithms can be improved through the automation of design tasks, in which intelligence is built into the fabric of hardware. Moreover, CPSs is often manifested through big data and machine learning technologies (i.e. Julia Morgan) while enabling the logical, cause-effect relationships that increase our comprehension of complex phenomena so that a "sense" for new conditions could be anticipated. Integrating CPSs in the construction industry can be done by synchronizing higher bandwidth broadband networks with the more pervasive use of miniaturized sensors or photonics and faster data and wireless transmission speeds. This can be done by linking databases, archives and even file systems into region-wide knowledge repositories in much bigger ways than were possible a few years ago (Bissett

2015). The outcome is intelligent and predictive shared semantic spaces. Big data algorithms could be embedded directly within products, which might link in automated manufacturing facilities for clothes to complex fabrication systems for the architecture, urban design and construction (Kolarevic and Klinger 2013).

Sustainable Green Environment

The sustainable green environment in the construction industry is where contractors focus on optimizing reductions in environmental and overall construction waste (Jalaei et al. 2019). This initiative promotes non-toxic, low VOC paints and adhesives, mandates recycling policies, use of renewable materials, no Xylene or other hazardous chemicals in painting rules. Limiting hydrocarbon emissions by utilizing the practice of pulling pipe and power cords when moving buildings, recycling wooden form wood scraps into mulch or fuel pellets. The conservation in a sustainable green environment pertains to companies that reduce the company's environmental footprint by using renewable energy or reducing carbon emissions and production. They also commit not to use production methods that pollute soil, water, or air (Naidoo and Gasparatos 2018).

The CPSs in the sustainable green environment are networks of sensors that measure atmospheric pollution, human behaviors, and weather changes in cities (De et al. 2017). These systems can help governments forecast environmental disasters previously unknown or unreachable. This information can lead to more innovative, sustainable policies. The CPSs can be both invasive and non-invasive. The invasive sensors are typically more accurate in measuring air pollution, heat or other environmental changes in the environment. Non-invasive CPSs measure heat or other emissions with fewer sensors. There are more companies currently supporting better efficiencies with environmental measures. Increasingly more companies are initiating an environmental management system, systemizing environmental as integral data and performance indicator for assessing sustainability (Zorpas 2010). The construction project management practices need to design buildings that comply with living building criteria, which would be met. These must cover some or all the building's energy needs and clean up or offset hazardous materials to a net-zero means by 2026. The living buildings systems also have nourishment business, photovoltaic systems, waste disposal systems, and more (Salameh et al. 2020). In conclusion, sustainable practices in the sustainable green environmental domain will become a primary concern for a number of different economic sectors. Excellent ethical and environmental responsibility practices today with integrated technologies are needed to continue and increase prosperity for the country now and in the future.

Interoperability and BIM

BIM is an emerging technology that aims to improve management of projects from the very beginning of the design process. It is a holistic, collaborative approach to the design, construction, and operation of a building, facility, or other complex process. It provides a systematic approach to building information, utilizing advanced computer-aided design tools to allow offline coordination of industrial, contractual, and business information with an online presence and collaboration. BIM involves all members of the project team and scales to suit the size of the project. It creates the opportunity for increased self-assembly of part/component designs in order to reduce overall construction cost and maximizes productivity of the workforce on site. BIM is a technical process to include digital models, documented descriptions of the construction project and their underlying design in all stages, i.e., inverse modelling, geometry modelling, and detail model. They are done as a gathering of information during the design stage (Crotty 2013). The 3D models, surface modelling, structure model are converted into construction documents such as plots, sections, elevations drawings. Semantic description in the case of BIM is necessary to link different catalogues needed to design and describe all aspects of a project. The semantic description links different catalogues and helps describe all aspects of a project and communicate its information in detail to multiple stakeholders within the design process. Internally, interoperability deals with the communication between a company's software (Pauwels et al. 2017). Externally, this deals with the exchange of information across company boundaries. In this sense, it means including links from another system into your own. The two main areas of interoperability are intelligence collaboration and the exchange of information.

CPSs is a hybrid of virtual and physical. Although there are currently no standards set for the interoperability between software in the construction industry. Standardized measurement allows for interoperability (Rojas and Garcia 2020).

Intelligence Collaboration

Intelligence collaboration is the intelligence combined with collaboration when groups do problem-solving or design together. The group being addressed has its own content and participates in the group work generated by the development team (Paulus 2000). Suppose there is an organisation supplying support in the construction sector, such as IT or surveying. In that case, they are often ready to help another organisation in the same sector on a complimentary basis. The level of work envisioned can be as little as internet research or as extensive as constructing and designing the entire project. Technology tools and intelligence can mutually assist each other to get the objectives of each party completed, and it is thought that the more tools and the more intelligence that is utilized, the project will become more productive. Technology tools become smarter and useable whenever they are combined with intelligence. Some types of technology tools which are used on the intelligence work in construction include computer generated image, 3D virtual reality, and information gathering software. 3D building simulations are used to gather information on the preservation of sites and buildings. Tools like sketch up and three-dimensional modelling allow surveyors to get an idea of where unwanted hazards disrupted to be hidden and monitored for the sake of the building's foundation. Computer-generated image allows the modern surveyor to explore the building being surveyed and deal with any unforeseen dangers that come their way. Virtual Reality (VR) tools are going to evolve the intelligence work in the construction industry. Some intelligence in construction work tools may include documentation and workshop tools. Ones like these are great for taking notes and organizing workshop activities (Harte et al. 2012). The functions of intelligence in a construction project may also include the following:

1. Leading the team.
2. Problem-solving.
3. Controlling the management.
4. Make judgement decisions on a situation.
5. Ensure safety guidelines and rules are followed.
6. Monitor for and impede any type of emerging risks.

Exchange of Information

Information exchange is the traditional communication between vendors and/ or suppliers (Deeter-Schmelz and Kennedy 2004). Information exchange in the construction sector is an initiative under Measure 11 (Promotes integrated approaches and better coordination) of Hong Kong's Construction Industry Council's (CIC) Buildings Services Technology Roadmap. Measure 11 intends to set up electronic systems to capture design and site information electronically and then exchange the information with building owners and structural engineers to facilitate the more accurate and rapid design and commissioning (Wong et al. 2015). The exchange of information in the construction industry promotes an integrated approach and better coordination in buildings services technology.

CPSs can assist in both the intelligence collaboration and the exchange of information for the interoperability of BIM in construction project management practices (Linares et al. 2019).

Summary

Implementing the latest and most efficient technology impacts the builders or contractors time to complete the project. New building methods and materials also produce environmentally considerate construction projects. Such implementation is one way of showing that contractors embrace new technologies that have been proven at running more efficient building methods. Implementing the latest and most efficient technology in project management directly impacts the builder's time frame. New building methods and materials produce environmentally conscious construction projects. Such implementations are one way of showing that contractors are embracing new technology that has been proven at running more efficient building methods. The implementation of the CPSs technique is an effective way to reinforce the construction integrity and undertake condition monitoring in increments, to be able to react and point out deficiencies in a timely manner.

References

Abu Samra, S., M. Ahmed, A. Hammad and T. Zayed. 2018. Multiobjective framework for managing municipal integrated infrastructure. Journal of Construction Engineering and Management, 144(1), 4017091.

Adam, J. M., F. Parisi, J. Sagaseta, and X. Lu. 2018. Research and practice on progressive collapse and robustness of building structures in the 21st century. Engineering Structures, 173, 122–149.

Al Haadir, S. and K. Panuwatwanich. 2011. Critical success factors for safety program implementation among construction companies in Saudi Arabia. Procedia Engineering, 14(May 2014), 148–155. Retrieved from https://doi.org/10.1016/j.proeng.2011.07.017

Alaloul, W. S., A. S. I. Bin Ismail, S. Ammad and S. Saad. 2021. Health and Safety for Infrastructure Projects: PPE Adaptation and Barriers, 1–8. Retrieved from https://doi.org/10.1109/ieeeconf51154.2020.9319985

Alruqi, W. M. and M. R. Hallowell. 2019. Critical success factors for construction safety: Review and meta-analysis of safety leading indicators. Journal of Construction Engineering and Management, 145(3), 04019005. Retrieved from https://doi.org/10.1061/(asce)co.1943-7862.0001626

Ammad, S. 2020. Personal Protective Equipment In Construction, Accidents Involved in Construction Infrastructure Projects. (October). Retrieved from https://www.researchgate.net/profile/Mujahid_Ali21/publication/345081414_Personal_Protective_Equipment_In_Construction_Accidents_Involved_In_Construction_Infrastructure_Projects/links/5f9f82ac299bf1b53e59b84a/Personal-Protective-Equipment-In-Construction-

Ammad, S., W. S. Alaloul, S. Saad and A. H. Qureshi, N. Sheikh, M. Ali and Muhammad Altaf., 2020. Personal Protective Equipment in Construction, Accidents Involved in Construction Infrastructure Projects. Solid State Technology. 63.

Ammad, S., W. S. Alaloul, S. Saad and A. H. Qureshi. 2021a. Personal protective equipment (PPE) usage in construction projects: A scientometric approach. Journal of Building Engineering, 35(July 2020), 102086. Retrieved from https://doi.org/10.1016/j.jobe.2020.102086

Ammad, S., W. S. Alaloul, S. Saad and A. H. Qureshi. 2021b. Personal Protective Equipment (PPE) usage in construction projects: A systematic review and smart PLS approach. Ain Shams Engineering Journal, 12(4), 3495-3507. Retrieved from https://doi.org/https://doi.org/10.1016/j.asej.2021.04.001

Anderson, J. C., M. Rungtusanatham and R. G. Schroeder. 1994. A theory of quality management underlying the Deming management method. Academy of Management Review, 19(3), 472–509.

Artto, K., J. Kujala, P. Dietrich and M. Martinsuo. 2008. What is project strategy? International Journal of Project Management, 26(1), 4–12.

Berg, M. E. and J. T. Karlsen. 2007. Mental models in project management coaching. Engineering Management Journal, 19(3), 3–13.

Bergstroem, S. M., X. Chen, J. C. Gutiérrez-Marco and A. Dronov. 2009. The new chronostratigraphic classification of the Ordovician System and its relations to major regional series and stages and to δ13C chemostratigraphy. Lethaia, 42(1), 97–107.

Bissett, T. G. 2015. The development and use of digital spatial and relational databases: Analysis of Depression-era archaeological collections from the lower Tennessee Valley of Western Tennessee. Collections, 11(4), 305–324.

Brett, D. 1996. The construction of heritage. Cork University Press.

Chan, A. P. C., Y. Yang and A. Darko. 2018. Construction accidents in a large-scale public infrastructure project: Severity and prevention. Journal of Construction Engineering and Management, 144(10), 1–13. Retrieved from https://doi.org/10.1061/(ASCE)CO.1943-7862.0001545

Chen, Q. and R. Jin. 2013. Multilevel safety culture and climate survey for assessing new safety Program. Journal of Construction Engineering and Management, 139(7), 805–817. Retrieved from https://doi.org/10.1061/(ASCE)CO.1943-7862.0000659

Cheng, C. W., S. Leu, Sen, C.C. Lin and C. Fan. 2010. Characteristic analysis of occupational accidents at small construction enterprises. Safety Science, 48(6), 698–707. Retrieved from https://doi.org/10.1016/j.ssci.2010.02.001

Crotty, R. 2013. The Impact of Building Information Modelling: Transforming Construction. Routledge.

De, S., Y. Zhou, I. Larizgoitia Abad and Moessner. 2017. Cyber–physical–social frameworks for urban big data systems: A survey. Applied Sciences, 7(10), 1017.

Deeter-Schmelz, D. R. and K. N. Kennedy. 2004. Buyer-seller relationships and information sources in an e-commerce world. Journal of Business & Industrial Marketing. 19(3), 188–196. Retrieved from https://doi.org/https://doi.org/10.1108/08858620410531324

Drake, F.-D. 1988. Evaluating Cogeneration Options for a Campus Heating and Cooling Plant. Retrieved from http://digital.library.wisc.edu/1793/46700

Dwyer, L., R. Mellor, N. Mistilis and T. Mules. 2000. A framework for assessing "tangible" and "intangible" impacts of events and conventions. Event Management, 6(3), 175–189.

Gann, D. M. and A. J. Salter. 2000. Innovation in project-based, service-enhanced firms: The construction of complex products and systems. Research Policy, 29(7–8), 955–972.

Gil, N., I. D. Tommelein, R. L. Kirkendall and G. Ballard. 2001. Leveraging specialty-contractor knowledge in design-build organisations. Engineering, Construction and Architectural Management, 8(5/6), 355–367. Retrieved from https://doi.org/https://doi.org/10.1108/eb021196

Golden, L. 2012. The effects of working time on productivity and firm performance, research synthesis paper. International Labor Organisations (ILO) Conditions of Work and Employment Series (33).

Hager, G., C. Upton, R. Graycarek, V. Knowles, E. McNees and J. Perry. 2006. Information Systems can Help Prevent, but not Eliminate, Health Care Fraud and Abuse. Legislative Research Commission.

Halfawy, M. and T. Froese. 2005. Building integrated architecture/engineering/construction systems using smart objects: Methodology and implementation. Journal of Computing in Civil Engineering, 19(2), 172–181.

Harte, V., C. A. Watts and K. Wray. 2012. Using toolkits to achieve STEM enterprise learning outcomes. Education + training, 54(4), 259–277. Retrieved from https://doi.org/10.1108/00400911211236118

Heagney, J. 2016. Fundamentals of Project Management. Amacom.

Hedlund, G. 1994. A model of knowledge management and the N-form corporation. Strategic Management Journal, 15(S2), 73–90.

Hodell, C. 2013. SMEs from the ground up: A no-nonsense approach to trainer-expert collaboration (1st ed.). American Society for Training and Development. Retrieved from https://www.amazon.com/SMEs-Ground-No-Nonsense-Trainer-Expert-Collaboration/dp/1562868551

Jaafari, A. 2001. Management of risks, uncertainties and opportunities on projects: Time for a fundamental shift. International Journal of Project Management, 19(2), 89–101.

Jalaei, F., M. Zoghi and A. Khoshand. 2019. Life cycle environmental impact assessment to manage and optimize construction waste using Building Information Modeling (BIM). International Journal of Construction Management, 1–18.

Johnson, S. D., C. Suriya, S. W. Yoon, J. V. Berrett and J. La Fleur. 2002. Team development and group processes of virtual learning teams. Computers & Education, 39(4), 379–393.

Karakhan, A., Y. Xu, C. Nnaji and O. Alsaffar. 2019. Advances in Informatics and Computing in Civil and Construction Engineering. Springer International Publishing. Retrieved from https://doi.org/10.1007/978-3-030-00220-6

Kolarevic, B. and K. Klinger. 2013. Manufacturing Material Effects: Rethinking Design and Making in Architecture. Routledge.

Linares, D. A., C. Anumba and N. Roofigari-Esfahan. 2019. Overview of supporting technologies for cyber-physical systems implementation in the AEC industry. *In*: Computing in Civil Engineering 2019: Data, Sensing and Analytics (pp. 495–504). American Society of Civil Engineers Reston, VA.

Love, P. E. D., G. D. Holt, L. Y. Shen, H. Li and Z. Irani. 2002. Using systems dynamics to better understand change and rework in construction project management systems. International Journal of Project Management, 20(6), 425–436.

Manzoor, B., I. Othman and M. Manzoor. 2021. Evaluating the critical safety factors causing accidents in high-rise building projects. Ain Shams Engineering Journal, 12(3), 2485–2492. Retrieved from https://doi.org/https://doi.org/10.1016/j.asej.2020.11.025.

Maqbool, R., Y. Sudong, N. Manzoor and Y. Rashid. 2017. The impact of emotional intelligence, project managers' competencies, and transformational leadership on project success: An empirical perspective. Project Management Journal, 48(3), 58–75.

Marcelino-Sádaba, S., L. F. González-Jaen and A. Pérez-Ezcurdia. 2015. Using project management as a way to sustainability: From a comprehensive review to a framework definition. Journal of Cleaner Production, 99, 1–16.

Marcelino-Sádaba, S., A. Pérez-Ezcurdia, A. M. E. Lazcano and P. Villanueva. 2014. Project risk management methodology for small firms. International Journal of Project Management, 32(2), 327–340.

Naidoo, M. and A. Gasparatos. 2018. Corporate environmental sustainability in the retail sector: Drivers, strategies and performance measurement. Journal of Cleaner Production, 203, 125–142.

Nematchoua, M. K., J. A. Orosa, C. Buratti, E. Obonyo, D. Rim, P. Ricciardi and S. Reiter. 2020. Comparative analysis of bioclimatic zones, energy consumption, CO_2 emission and life cycle cost of residential and commercial buildings located in a tropical region: A case study of the big island of Madagascar. Energy, 202, 117754.

Ng, A. and M. Loosemore. 2007. Risk allocation in the private provision of public infrastructure. International Journal of Project Management, 25(1), 66–76.

Pandey, A. K., M. S. Hossain, V. V. Tyagi, N. Abd Rahim, A. Jeyraj, L. Selvaraj and A. Sari. 2018. Novel approaches and recent developments on potential applications of phase change materials in solar energy. Renewable and Sustainable Energy Reviews, 82, 281–323.

Park, M. W., N. Elsafty and Zhu. 2015. Hardhat-wearing detection for enhancing on-site safety of construction workers. Journal of Construction Engineering and Management, 141(9), 1–16. Retrieved from https://doi.org/10.1061/(ASCE)CO.1943-7862.0000974

Passian, A. and Imam. 2019. Nanosystems, Edge Computing, and the Next Generation Computing Systems. Sensors, 19(18), 4048.

Patel, D. A. and K. N. Jha. 2015. Neural network approach for safety climate prediction. Journal of Management in Engineering, 31(6), 1–11. Retrieved from https://doi.org/10.1061/(ASCE)ME.1943-5479.0000348

Paulus, P. 2000. Groups, teams, and creativity: The creative potential of idea-generating groups. Applied Psychology, 49(2), 237–262.

Pauwels, P., S. Zhang and Y. C. Lee. 2017. Semantic web technologies in AEC industry: A literature overview. Automation in Construction, 73, 145–165.

Pinto, J. K. and D. P. Slevin. 1987. Critical factors in successful project implementation. IEEE Transactions on Engineering Management, 1, 22–27.

Qureshi, A. H. and M. Altaf. 2020. Evaluating Safety Attributes in Infrastructure. 2020 Second International Sustainability and Resilience Conference: Technology and Innovation in Building Designs. Retrieved from https://doi.org/10.1109/IEEECONF51154.2020.9319936

Robichaud, L. B. and V. S. Anantatmula. 2011. Greening project management practices for sustainable construction. Journal of Management in Engineering, 27(1), 48–57.

Rojas, R. A. and M. A. R. Garcia. 2020. Implementation of Industrial Internet of Things and Cyber-Physical Systems in SMEs for Distributed and Service-Oriented Control. *In*: Industry 4.0 for SMEs (pp. 73–103). Palgrave Macmillan, Cham.

Salameh, T., M. E. H. Assad, M. Tawalbeh, C. Ghenai, A. Merabet and H. F. Öztop. 2020. Analysis of cooling load on commercial building in UAE climate using building integrated photovoltaic façade system. Solar Energy, 199, 617–629.

Schrapers, M. 2018. Applying Standards, Guidelines and Methods in Construction Project Management. Edinburgh Napier University.

Shewhart, W. A. and W. E. Deming. 1986. Statistical method from the viewpoint of quality control. Courier Corporation.

Shrivas, A. and H. K. Singla. 2020. Analysis of interaction among the factors affecting delay in construction projects using interpretive structural modelling approach. International Journal of Construction Management, 1–9.

Steiner, F. 2014. Frontiers in urban ecological design and planning research. Landscape and Urban Planning, 125, 304–311.

Tabassi, A. A. and A. H. A. Bakar. 2009. Training, motivation, and performance: The case of human resource management in construction projects in Mashhad, Iran. International Journal of Project Management, 27(5), 471–480.

Talebi, S., L. Koskela, M. Shelbourn and P. Tzortzopoulos. 2016. Critical review of tolerance management in construction. *In*: 24th Annual Conference of the International Group for Lean Construction (Vol. 63). Retrieved from http://eprints.hud.ac.uk/id/eprint/29142/

Thoben, K.-D., S. Wiesner and T. Wuest. 2017. "Industrie 4.0" and smart manufacturing – A review of research issues and application examples. International Journal of Automation Technology, 11(1), 4–16.

Toor, W. and S. Havlick. 2004. Transportation and Sustainable Campus Communities: Issues, Examples, Solutions. Island Press.

Wikström, S. 1996. Value creation by company-consumer interaction. Journal of Marketing Management, 12(5), 359–374.

Wong, A. K. D. and R. Zhang. 2013. Implementation of web-based construction project management system in China projects by Hong Kong developers. Construction Innovation.

Wong, J., J. Zhang and J. Lee. 2015. A vision of the future construction industry of Hong Kong. *In*: ISARC. Proceedings of the International Symposium on Automation and Robotics in Construction. Vol. 32, p. 1. IAARC Publications.

Zhou, Y., L. Y. Ding and J. Chen. 2013. Application of 4D visualization technology for safety management in metro construction. Automation in Construction, 34, 25–36. Retrieved from https://doi.org/10.1016/j.autcon.2012.10.011

Zorpas, A. 2010. Environmental management systems as sustainable tools in the way of life for the SMEs and VSMEs. Bioresource Technology, 101(6), 1544–1557.

Fundamentals of Cyber-Physical Systems

Abdul Hannan Qureshi, Wesam Salah Alaloul, and Khalid Mhmoud Alzubi

Introduction

In 2006, an American scientist Hellen Gil proposed cyber-physical systems (CPSs) as the main element and the technology of Industry Revolution 4.0 (IR4.0) (Lee 2006). Several concepts are associated with CPSs, which link physical reality with the virtual via integrating storage, computing, networking and designing the interactive environment, which leads to smart factories. This emerges from the concept of the Industrial Internet of Things (IIoT) and initiates the development of uniquely identifiable innovative products being monitored in real-time (Carvalho et al. 2018). CPSs are considered as integrating media for physical reality utilising computing infrastructures and communication networks forming automated distributed systems in IR4.0 (Wang et al. 2015). The working theme on which CPSs are designed is networking between devices and operations, making it superior to traditional embedded systems. It is intended to manage actuators and sensors as a control unit, exchanging and obtaining data from the physical world to cloud networks or other systems (Pivoto et al. 2021). Basically, CPSs can be defined as systems with the ability to receive and send data between devices through networking. These services and their information are obtained in real-time, irrespective of location but provided under internet support (Boyes et al. 2018). The whole operation demands reliability, stability, security, and efficiency. However, security is becoming the main agenda in IR4.0, and high-level security supports are recommended in the CPSs architectural layers during the information and data exchange processes (Alguliyev et al. 2018). The implementation of CPSs in the construction sector has benefited the built environment to improve safety, communication, and productivity for operations such as design changes, workforce training, safety management, progress monitoring, temporal conditions, and changes in site conditions.

The research community defines IR4.0 as a broad term, encompassing revolutionary theory towards IR4.0 evolving with the transformation to CPSs from embedded systems (Vogel-Heuser and Hess 2016). In simple words, CPSs is the group of technologies that interlinks the physical and virtual environments to construct a productive network environment permitting the interaction and communication of intelligent objects. Figure 2.1 illustrates the revolutionary path from Industry Revolution IR3.0 towards IR4.0. It can be seen that the IR4.0 journey begins with the evolving of embedded systems by networking towards CPSs, provided by IoT, along with data and services (Sawhney et al. 2020).

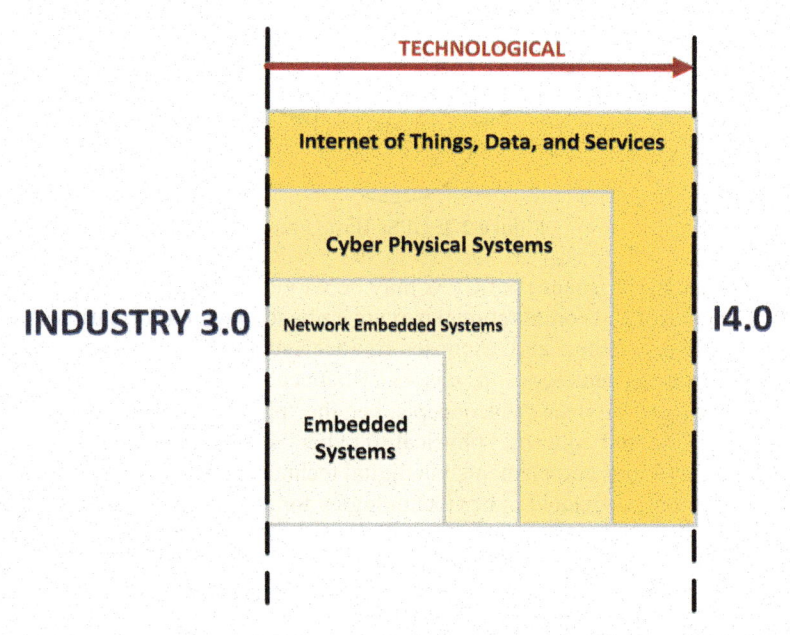

Figure 2.1: Evolution of Embedded Systems

A general concept of CPSs revolves around three Cs, i.e., computation, communication, and control, as shown in Figure 2.2. It shows the dynamics of the physical system are impeccably integrated with the computerised system, controlled and monitored by communication-enabled embedded systems.

Figure 2.2 illustrates the CPSs as a new system paradigm of integrated networked computational devices with the dynamics of physical processes. CPSs is not only a simple control system that provides connectivity between physical systems, networks, controls and computers but a real-life adaptive, predictive, networked, and intelligent system with minimal human interference (Tabuada et al. 2014).

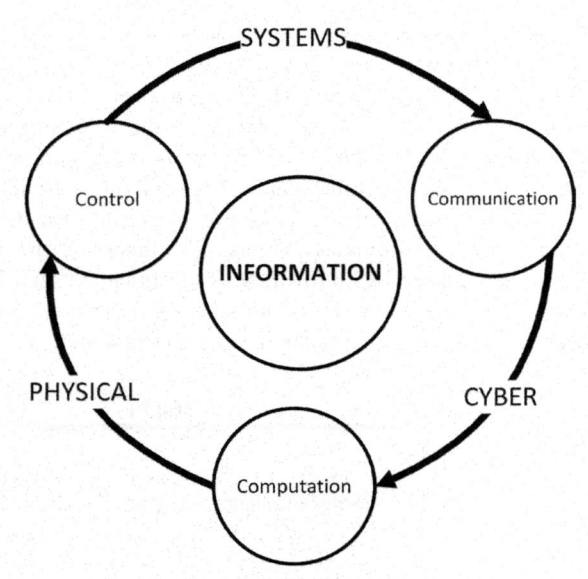

Figure 2.2: CPSs Basic Flow

The connectivity channel of CPSs may be wireless or wired communication media. The control and computational part are embedded with information. All the commands are distributed, and responses are received at CPSs, integrated into the physical system via actuators and sensors (Bhattacharjya et al. 2019). The CPSs working is bridged between two concepts, i.e., the "physical to cyber" and "cyber to physical". The first concept, "physical to cyber," covers detecting or tracking construction activities and elements via digital technologies. The data is collected and transferred to associated cyber technologies for processing. Whereas "cyber to physical" basically controls and manages the sensors' information to the system covering the actuation aspect. Actuation represents the transmission of pertinent information required for prompt decision making for an ongoing process (Bordel et al. 2017, Xia et al. 2011).

The conventional methods for integrating virtual and real worlds are passive, where CPSs provides active integration. The CPSs works on the bi-directional coordination approach, and for successful execution of the processes, the consistency between physical constructed activities and digital models are ensured (Anumba et al. 2010, Anumba et al. 2021).

CPSs Concept

In general, CPSs is not about combining cyber and physical environmental features but defining the intersection between them. CPSs is not just a combination network of wired or wireless sensors with computers, but CPSs integration is exemplified by specific properties, as discussed below (Zeadally and Jabeur 2016):

1. Provision of communication and cyber facilities in all available physical elements.
2. Reorganisation and reconfiguration of the system in reference to the dynamics of the available environment.
3. Huge scale networking.
4. The control loops provides high performance automated processes and computation.
5. The integrated cyber and physical elements advance the initial learning process to adaptation.
6. The dependable and certified operations to be considered as key elements.
7. CPSs is anticipated to provide auto-assembly, self-organised, and high-performance operations.

In other information and communication systems, CPSs are distinguished in the following properties:

1. Functionality/operability.
2. Performance metrics.
3. Dependability and security.
4. Cost-effectiveness.

In addition to the above-mentioned attributes, the overall dependability and security of the system are not constrained to adaptability, management and usability. Additional operational features are as follows:

1. CPSs will collect the input from the real environment, and via secured communication channels, the feedback will be sent.
2. CPSs will ensure a distributed controlling mechanism and a combined management approach.
3. CPSs will support the geographical coverage.
4. CPSs will fulfil the performance and communication requirements.
5. CPSs will lead to a system of systems (SoS), which is considered an imminent technology.

CPSs Characteristics

The CPSs characteristics help to identify or design the required system type. The following are the few characteristics as defined by the researchers for CPSs:

Technical Aspects

The CPSs framework integrates embedded and physical systems with Information Technology (IT) and communication systems. The technical devices managing CPSs workflow are particularly important, including incorporated devices supporting IT and data computing. The designed architecture of CPSs shapes the working capabilities. Therefore, in the designing phase, decisions are made considering their future workability. Such emphasis is placed by considering a system to attain synergies, optimisations and communication capabilities to off-load systems for cost-effective operations. The impact of CPSs on operations is associated with the design preferences on the capabilities and scale (Törngren et al. 2017).

Automation Aspect

The operational capabilities of CPSs vary based on the job description; based on this concept, the CPSs design caters to varying degrees of automation levels. In this aspect, autonomous vehicles have gained a lot of attention towards the attainment of automation capabilities under the standards developed by the Society for Automotive Engineers (Committee 2014). The central theme of designing CPSs is to be controlled independently without any human interference and making an intelligent decision. However, whole operational activities are triggered by human inputs and monitored under human supervision, including shared control. In shared controls, the human and machine interface systems are considered crucial and challenging. It is hard to clarify at times regarding operational controls and unintended decisions to be avoided. In other words, the level of automation can be related to the smartness and adaptability of CPSs (Song et al. 2016).

Cross-Cutting Aspect

Cross-cutting aspects cover system relevant legislation, standards, security, safety, and governance. These parameters refer to the limitations for organisational and operational responsibilities. The evolution in technological connectivity has enabled new applications to overcome related drawbacks and various conventional application domains. However, this revolution is creating new business opportunities but with new challenges and barriers towards effective implementation, such as providing data security while enhancing network connectivity.

Life-Cycle Integration

Cost, quality, and business concerns are the main factors contributing towards CPSs life-cycle integration. Researchers have referred to the life-cycle integration of CPSs as a spectrum. This spectrum has no integration to services, product, and data over life-cycle management to fully integrate operations and development. This also includes data collecting and upgrading capabilities from the operational system. The system will be considered beneficial by comparing the benefits with investment costs to ascertain the integration between functional devices and IT systems.

Technology Requirements of CPSs

Implementation of CPSs in the construction sector is challenging, as it demands a clear understanding of operations, characteristics, and requirements. The clarity in the aforementioned facets helps an organisation in making correct decisions, budgeting and scheduling linked to an effective execution plan. Researchers have reviewed and defined technology requirements for CPSs for three levels, which are device, platform, and system (Garcia and Roofigari-Esfahan 2020, Roofigari-esfahan 2020).

Requirements at the Device Level

At the device level, connectivity, data exchange, identifiers, and human interactions have been devised requirements for CPSs effective implementation.

Connectivity

In the CPSs network, all devices are required to be capable of connectivity to send and receive data between each other. Connectivity can be attained via a wired or wireless configured network system. The selection between wired or wireless devices is based on operational requirements, environmental constraints, and each has distant benefits. Wired devices are easy to install and considered economical in most operational layouts, which make their adoption more beneficial. It provides good latency, bandwidth, good quality of data transmission, and no specialised knowledge or training is required for its installation. Moreover, wired connectivity also provides power to the connected equipment, making wired networks more reliable and sustainable. However, complexity and specific site conditions sometimes make a wired network unsuitable. In such conditions, wireless connectivity systems are more suitable for operational networks. In recent times wireless systems are becoming more popular due to advancement in technologies. Companies are offering wireless devices with enhanced capabilities of being more secure, adaptable, scalable, and user-friendly. Also, various wireless platforms offer multiple devices connectivity and cloud platforms (Yue and He 2018). However, advanced training and knowledge are essential to set up a wireless operational system.

Data Exchange

Data exchange is an essential aspect of CPSs, as CPSs offers bi-directional data processing between connected physical devices and the virtual world. However, this is not always the case as sometimes sensors and actuators perform a one-way operation or single tasked elements, i.e., either perform sending function or receiving activity.

Identifiers

Defining the identifier is a necessary requirement of CPSs for all connected physical elements and devices. This helps in the establishing of an effective linkage between virtual replicas and physical devices. Identifiers help in the establishment of a valid identification scheme for the effective implementation of management practices. Basically, it is a unique, continuous, and technical ID or coding of the device for referencing and managing devices during operational activity. This helps the system to perform the whole activity without confusion and error.

Human Interaction

In the CPSs implementation operations, the human interference cannot be ignored. One of the reasons for this is due to the fact that a human's presence is considered to be represented digitally in the virtual side on the CPSs. Also, a few operational outcomes of a few CPSs elements are dependent on humans' feedback. In the architecture, engineering, and construction (AEC) industry, most tasks are done manually by humans (Manzoor et al. 2021), unlike in the manufacturing industry. Therefore, the requirements and constraints of the AEC industry vary from others. New technologies for CPSs in the AEC industry are designed to monitor, track, and predict human interactions with the environment and behaviour to improve the system (Cai et al. 2019).

Requirements at the Platform Level

In CPSs, platforms are the set of virtual or physical subsystems allowing the interaction among two realities of the system. Physical platforms consist of wireless sensor networks, whereas virtual platforms consist of cloud computing, building information modelling (BIM), or the internet. Selection and identification of the right platform facilitate the successful operation and flow of data. BIM integration, connectivity, interoperability, and cyber-security are the essential requirements of the applicable platform.

BIM Integration

The innovation of BIM has fueled the digital construction industry. Likewise, BIM integration with virtual applications, project design and post physical progress supports the CPSs. However, BIM integration with other applications or systems is critical to sustain the common central data environment at the platform level. The BIM integration fulfilling platform level requirements reflect the efficiency of the system for smooth transferring, updating and management of data. However, in the AEC industry, CPSs-BIM interoperability is considered challenging, but it enables smooth bi-directional information flow (Tang et al. 2019). Integration of BIM at the platform level is supported by various concepts and technologies, i.e., relational databases, document management systems, digital twins, cloud computing, 4D/5D, and mobile apps.

Connectivity

Other than at the device level, connectivity requirements are also considered at the platform level. At the platform level, the networking scheme for connectivity between the platform and devices must be refined. Moreover, systems are required to be compatible with other facets such as cost, interoperability, and reliability. Hybrid platforms, i.e., wireless and wired networking, are considered more popular and viable systems under various circumstances, especially in the construction sector.

Interoperability

It is hard to establish a unified platform integrating all the CPSs elements to be utilised properly in the construction sector. To overcome this limitation, multiple virtual and physical platforms are interconnected for successful receiving, translating and sharing of information or data. Few of these platforms are easily accessible; however, some do require proper procedures and guidelines to be followed for being utilised. One of the simple examples is the internet as a virtual platform, which is easily reachable. In contrast, software is hard to access and sometimes requires subscriptions to operate. Therefore, the provision of inter-platform interoperability is a rigorous exercise achieved through interactive databases, data transferring through open means, and application programming interface (API). However, these operations often compromise the data quality, loss of data and flow of data is slow. The interoperability between CPSs platforms is one of the barriers affecting the implementation process of CPSs operations in the AEC industry (Heiss et al. 2015).

Cyber Security

CPSs privacy and security have been highlighted as the significant future challenges and concerns for technological networks in all sectors, including AEC (Thomas et al. 2015). Even in automated systems, the transfer of knowledge between individuals and organisations have become a concern of an informational security breach. Researchers have highlighted controlling the security protocol of sensor networks and information security. Control security is related to the unauthorised controlling of the system or device. In contrast, informational security is linked with hacking or unauthorised access to data or information (Ashibani and Mahmoud 2017). System settings are also a vulnerable feature of CPSs networking, which can raise privacy concerns. Such concerns get aggravated for breach of information to personal data, violating the privacy, such as location data, images, etc. Hence, the system privacy should be transparent to the users and must be handled at the root of the problem (Chow 2017).

Requirements at the System Level

The requirements of the system-level define the operational capability and designed objectives to be achieved by the system. The system level is intended to support the needs of the device level and the platform level. The following are the essential requirements identified by researchers at the system level (Etxeberria-Agiriano et al. 2012).

Real-Time

The real-time response capability of CPSs is considered very effective and valuable in the AEC industry for multiple applications. This real-time capability is dependent on the system capacity, sensing devices, and limited to time or activity. The CPSs are designed to predict system behaviour under pertinent events (soft real-time) rather than projecting system behaviour at each particular instant even when not required (hard real-time). Soft real-time is preferred over hard real-time due to the requirements of enhanced information overload, resources, and resources capacity, which increase expenses.

Autonomy

An ideal CPSs is considered autonomous; however, in most cases, autonomy is hard to achieve; therefore, human feedback is required. In contrast, autonomy is more attainable in CPSs subsystems but not the whole system. Currently, autonomously processing raw information data perception is one of the main aspects that CPSs need to tackle. There is still a long way to attain a high level of automation in CPSs processes, and researchers are putting great efforts into it (Garcia and Roofigari-Esfahan 2020, Roofigari-esfahan, 2020).

Time Management

The CPSs operations and outputs are based on the physical occurrences of various activities at specific times and locations. Whilst operating through heterogeneous platforms and devices, the temporal aspect of the user data in the CPSs becomes essential. In the AEC industry, historical data analysis is considered an important tool to address issues and disputes (Hannan et al. 2017), such as related to financial, contractual, schedule, cost, technical, etc.

Reliability

The whole structure of the automated CPSs system is built on system reliability. Once the system is established, the organisation tends to rely on its outcomes and expect the system to work flawlessly to achieve the designed objectives. Poor performance or failure of CPSs elements reflects the collapse of the whole system. In case of system failure, identifying faulty components is tedious and time-consuming due to complex system networks. Therefore, CPSs malfunctions must be avoided, and performance indexes must be used to assess the system performance. Various approaches can be utilised to evaluate CPSs reliability, such as regulations, certifications, and validated standard operating procedures (SOP). Moreover, CPSs are designed to be more resilient and more self-reliant. Systems can be resilient by the provision of self-monitoring and self-repair. Self-reliant (self-reliance) can be achieved by designing the self-capable system to perform the desired operation even when the system elements or subsystems fail to operate properly. Moreover, the transparency of the systems also improve reliability, i.e., the status of the system must be shared with all stakeholders even when the system is faulty.

Integration

Effective integration at the system level performs an essential role in the success of the whole system, and operations are based on the interoperability of data between devices, subsystems, and platforms. Interoperability is still a challenge, and to overcome this, frameworks and architectures for data exchange have been created to establish protocols of data handling in the CPSs network. This includes the big-data framework (Han and Wang 2018), CPSs framework for AEC industry (Correa 2018), IoT and BIM integrated framework (Tang et al. 2019), CPSs decision-making knowledge management architecture (Fang et al. 2018), and many more.

Resource Optimisation

All the connected devices in the CPSs network have some constraints and defined capabilities such as energy consumption, storage options, processing power, and connectivity. Therefore, the CPSs devices and architecture must be designed considering their limitations for the optimum output.

Adaptability

The adaptability of CPSs is the decisive success factor in the AEC industry. The construction sector is a vast and versatile industry, and every construction site is unique due to various factors, such as project type, site location, changing project requirements, etc. The CPSs capacity to get configured under such varying environmental construction projects operated by multi-organisations makes it suitable for being adopted by industry stakeholders. The self-adaptability and self-adjustability to system requirements are considered as the ideal scenario for CPSs. Moreover, this is the area of interest now among the industry and research community to improve the self-adaptability of CPSs (Zhou et al. 2018). Other than that, the focus is also required on CPSs size variations, i.e., scalable CPSs, based on architecture and site requirements (Qiuchen Lu et al. 2019).

System Architecture

There are no defined standards on the design concept of CPSs architecture. Researchers have defined CPSs as integrating the dynamics of the real world with the virtual world via computing technologies (Ahmed et al. 2015, Zeadally and Jabeur 2016). In the early stages, the CPSs was divided into two simple tiers, which only covered the computation part and the physical part. The physical part was considered to be including sensors receiving collected data from the physical world. Later on, the computing part was evolved to self-decision making to process gathered data from the physical world after data analysis (Zeadally and Jabeur 2016). Subsequently, three-tier architecture was also proposed for CPSs, consisting of the environmental tier, service tier, and control tier. The environmental tier was considered to be composed of physical gadgets and end users' devices related to the physical environment. The service tier was designed for providing computing services and cloud computing. Whereas, the control tier was composed of sensors for receiving the required data and control decisions (Erickson and Cerpa 2012).

Most researchers redefined CPSs working based on three main elements, i.e., control and computation, and communication (3Cs). The control centres connect CPSs from the physical world via wired or wireless communication networks. The information or data are encoded in the control and computation part, which transmits the data to physical systems via actuators and sensors (Guo and Zeng 2019). Lately, the CPSs functional architecture has been defined based on bi-directional coordination approach and consists of four layers, which enables technologies to interact between physical and virtual models. The general workflow of CPSs is illustrated in Figure 2.3, and architectural layers are discussed below.

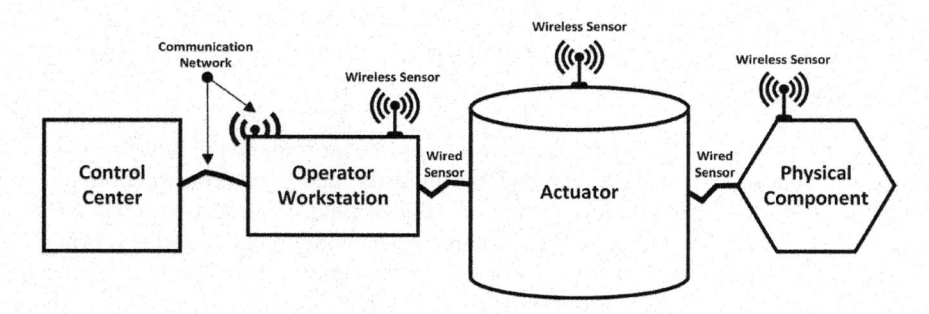

Figure 2.3: CPSs Workflow

Device and Sensing Layer

This layer consists of data detection systems and sensors. The layer performs the tracking of construction processes being completed during any phase of the project lifecycle.

Communication Layer

This layer collects information from the sensing layer for further data transmission and processing of information. The obtained raw data is converted into required formats to be read further by technologies. This layer also controls the communication networks (wired or wireless) and internet provision. It works as a connectivity mode between site staff and head office by enabling an information exchange between data capture systems and sensors.

Content and Application Layer

This layer performs the data storage purpose. The data (raw or processed) are stored in the database servers, local databases and also allows controlled data processing, depending upon the given CPSs application. The stored information may include resources details, cost and budgeting, scheduling, and other project management related information. This layer forms a bridge between the communication layer and the actuation layer.

Actuation Layer

The actuation layer enables the physical control of the real environment using actuators to retrieve information for better decision making. Virtual models play an essential role in this process under either a mixed reality environment or controlled user interface. The virtual models allow the user to visualise and inspect the effects of collected information on the system.

Evolution of CPSs Architectural Models

The implementation performance of IIoT and IR4.0 is dependent on the standardisation, security support, interoperability, and connectivity among devices (Chhetri et al. 2018, Nilsson and Sandin 2018, Weyer et al. 2015). To overcome the aforementioned constraints, a few CPSs design architectures have been standardised for references. The CPSs network may be cited as the platform IR4.0. This IR4.0 platform allows various companies to collaborate, such as the industrial internet consortium (IIC) with the senior executive council from industry to promote the technologies accelerating the industrial internet growth (Pivoto et al. 2021). In this section, the concept of various evolved CPSs architectural models will be explained for their operational designs.

5C Architectural Model

The architectural operational theme of 5C is based on automation, centred with data acquisition devices for industry-based models (J. Lee et al. 2015). The 5C architectural model provides good operational guidelines for CPSs ecosystems. However, it lacks some characteristics (Brettel et al. 2017), which includes a lack of horizontal flow of information such as machines and products considering the client feedback or input, and connectivity with distinct industries lacking internet of services (IoS). Table 2.1 illustrates the description and overview of five levels.

RAMI 4.0

RAMI 4.0 is considered as an architecture reference model for IR4.0, designed by Platform IR4.0 to define CPSs networking communicational structure and collective languages with its syntax, semantics, and vocabulary. This will help integrate IoT and related IR4.0 services with the outside world (Schweichhart

Table 2.1: Overview of 5C architectural levels

5C Level	Description
Configuration	The flow of knowledge from the physical to the virtual world, attaining self-adaptive and self-adjusting.
Cognition	Functions of prognostics and monitoring for maintenance optimisation and failure prediction.
Cybernetic	Generating virtual output based on received data and exchange of information among devices.
Data-to-information Conversion	The transition of data into information from monitoring devices and their application to the physical world.
Smart connection	Assimilation of the physical systems connected in CPSs network.

2016). Its architecture integrates IT components promoting the IR4.0 environment, which provides vertical integration between products and cloud, and horizontal integration among networks. Table 2.2 summarises the RAMI 4.0 model.

Table 2.2: RAMI 4.0 model

Architecture Layers	Description
Business	Group of the services to generate business links and processes and support business models under regulatory and legal boundaries.
Functional	Depiction of the logical functions of devices in the context of I4.0.
Information	Description of data and services being generated, used, modified or offered, during operation.
Communication	The regulated flow of data or information from events and services to the information layer and the integration layer from control commands and services. It concentrates on transmission procedures, connections and networks discovery.
Integration	Transition to the virtual environment from the physical world. It signifies the visible assets and their digital capacities, subsequently offering control through computers.
Asset	Interpretation of real things in the physical world may be human workers, hardware, documents, and components.

IIRA

The architectural theme of IIRA is open, which is being developed by the IIC following IIoT standards, focusing on the flow of smooth interoperability among the industry. This model is developed considering four viewpoints to classify and identify common concerns of IIoT architecture, which are being analysed and addressed. The results are recorded and related informational data in the particular viewpoints' associated views (Pivoto et al. 2021). Functional viewpoint, implementation viewpoint, usage viewpoint, and business viewpoint are the four defined viewpoints in IIRA, description shown in Table 2.3.

Table 2.3: IIRA viewpoints

Viewpoints	Description
Functional viewpoint	It concentrates on the functional elements, their interaction and interrelation with external components and with each other.
Implementation viewpoint	It highlights the technologies essential to execute the functional elements, their life-cycle processes, and their communication systems.
Usage viewpoint	It identifies the opportunities in the IIoT system to deliver the anticipated business objectives.
Business viewpoint	It classifies candidates along with their business objectives, values, and views in the IIoT network.

Summary

This chapter aims to develop a basic understanding of CPSs. CPSs is a significant element in IR4.0, and the concept of CPSs originated in 2006. In simple words, the CPSs is a system that sends and receives data between various connected devices. The main architectural design of CPSs revolves around 3Cs, i.e., computation, communication, and control. However, this concept has evolved to 5Cs, RAMI 4.0, and IIRA operational designs. This chapter covers the concept of CPSs, characteristics, technology requirements of CPSs, and evolution timeline of CPSs architecture. This information will be helpful for the readers to understand the base and working design of CPSs.

References

Ahmed, S. H., S. H. Bouk, D. Kim and M. Sarkar. 2015. Cyber-physical systems: Basics and fundamentals. Cyber-Physical System Design with Sensor Networking Technologies, 21.

Alguliyev, R., Y. Imamverdiyev and L. Sukhostat. 2018. Cyber-physical systems and their security issues. Computers in Industry, 100, 212–223.

Anumba, Chimay J., A. Akanmu and J. Messner. 2010. Towards a cyber-physical systems approach to construction. Construction Research Congress 2010: Innovation for Reshaping Construction Practice, 528–537.

Anumba, Chinemelu J., A. Akanmu, X. Yuan and C. Kan. 2021. Cyber-physical systems development for construction applications. Frontiers of Engineering Management, 8(1), 72–87. https://doi.org/10.1007/s42524-020-0130-4

Ashibani, Y. and Q. H. Mahmoud. 2017. Cyber physical systems security: Analysis, challenges and solutions. Computers & Security, 68, 81–97.

Bhattacharjya, A., X. Zhong, J. Wang and X. Li. 2019. Cyber-Physical Systems: Architecture, Security and Application. *In*: S. Guo & D. Zeng (Eds.), Springer. https://doi.org/10.1007/978-3-319-92564-6

Bordel, B., R. Alcarria, T. Robles and D. Martín. 2017. Cyber–physical systems: Extending pervasive sensing from control theory to the Internet of Things. Pervasive and Mobile Computing, 40, 156–184.

Boyes, H., B. Hallaq, J. Cunningham and T. Watson. 2018. The industrial Internet of Things (IIoT): An analysis framework. Computers in Industry, 101, 1–12.

Brettel, M., N. Friederichsen, M. Keller and M. Rosenberg. 2017. How virtualization, decentralization and network building change the manufacturing landscape: An industry 4.0 perspective. FormaMente, 12.

Cai, J., Y. Zhang and H. Cai. 2019. Integrating positional and attentional cues for construction working group identification: A long short-term memory based machine learning approach. *In*: Computing in Civil Engineering 2019: Data, Sensing, and Analytics (pp. 35–42). American Society of Civil Engineers Reston, VA.

Carvalho, N., O. Chaim, E. Cazarini and M. Gerolamo. 2018. Manufacturing in the fourth industrial revolution: A positive prospect in sustainable manufacturing. Procedia Manufacturing, 21, 671–678.

Chhetri, S. R., S. Faezi, N. Rashid and M.A. Al Faruque. 2018. Manufacturing supply chain and product lifecycle security in the era of industry 4.0. Journal of Hardware and Systems Security, 2(1), 51–68.

Chow, R. 2017. The last mile for IoT privacy. IEEE Security & Privacy, 15(6), 73–76.

Committee, S. A. E. O.-R. A. V. S. 2014. Taxonomy and definitions for terms related to on-road motor vehicle automated driving systems. SAE Standard J, 3016, 1–16.

Correa, F. R. 2018. Cyber-physical systems for construction industry. 2018 IEEE Industrial Cyber-Physical Systems (ICPS), 392–397. IEEE.

Erickson, V. L. and A. E. Cerpa. 2012. Thermovote: Participatory sensing for efficient building hvac conditioning. Proceedings of the Fourth ACM Workshop on Embedded Sensing Systems for Energy-Efficiency in Buildings, 9–16.

Etxeberria-Agiriano, I., I. Calvo, A. Noguero and E. Zulueta. 2012. Towards middleware-based cooperation topologies for the next generation of CPS. International Journal of Online Engineering (IJOE), 8(S4), 20–27.

Fang, Y., N. Roofigari-Esfahan and C. Anumba. 2018. A knowledge-based cyber-physical system (CPS) architecture for informed decision making in construction. Construction Research Congress 2018, 662–672. American Society of Civil Engineers.

Garcia, D. A. L. and N. Roofigari-Esfahan. 2020. Technology requirements for CPS implementation in construction. *In*: Cyber-Physical Systems in the Built Environment (pp. 15–30). Springer.

Guo, S. and D. Zeng. 2019. Cyber-Physical Systems: Architecture, Security and Application. Springer.

Han, Z. and Y. Wang. 2018. Research on a technical framework in smart construction based on big data. *In*: ICCREM 2018: Innovative Technology and Intelligent Construction (pp. 26–31). American Society of Civil Engineers Reston, VA.

Hannan, A., A. Ahmed, T. Ashraf and Q. Bai. 2017. Estimation of highway project cost using probabilistic technique. DEStech Transactions on Engineering and Technology Research, (ICTIM), 423–430. https://doi.org/10.12783/dtetr/ictim2016/5523

Heiss, M., A. Oertl, M. Sturm, P. Palensky, S. Vielguth and F. Nadler. 2015. Platforms for industrial cyber-physical systems integration: Contradicting requirements as drivers for innovation. 2015 Workshop on Modeling and Simulation of Cyber-Physical Energy Systems (MSCPES), 1–8. IEEE.

Lee, E. A. 2006. Cyber-physical systems – are computing foundations adequate. Position Paper for NSF Workshop on Cyber-Physical Systems: Research Motivation, Techniques and Roadmap, 2, 1–9. Citeseer.

Lee, J., B. Bagheri and H. A. Kao. 2015. A cyber-physical systems architecture for industry 4.0-based manufacturing systems. Manufacturing Letters, 3, 18–23.

Manzoor, B., I. Othman and J. C. Pomares. 2021. Digital Technologies in the Architecture, Engineering and Construction (AEC) Industry—A Bibliometric—Qualitative Literature Review of Research Activities. International Journal of Environmental Research and Public Health, 18(11), 6135. https://doi.org/10.3390/ijerph18116135

Nilsson, J. and F. Sandin. 2018. Semantic interoperability in industry 4.0: Survey of recent developments and outlook. 2018 IEEE 16th International Conference on Industrial Informatics (INDIN), 127–132. IEEE.

Pivoto, D. G. S., L. F. F. de Almeida, R. da Rosa Righi, J. J. P. C. Rodrigues, A. B. Lugli and A. M. Alberti. 2021. Cyber-physical systems architectures for industrial internet of things applications in Industry 4.0: A literature review. Journal of Manufacturing Systems, 58(PA), 176–192. https://doi.org/10.1016/j.jmsy.2020.11.017

Qiuchen Lu, V., A. K. Parlikad, P. Woodall, G. D. Ranasinghe and J. Heaton. 2019. Developing a dynamic digital twin at a building level: Using Cambridge campus as case study. International Conference on Smart Infrastructure and Construction 2019 (ICSIC) Driving Data-Informed Decision-Making, 67–75. ICE Publishing.

Roofigari-esfahan, N. 2020. Cyber-physical systems in the built environment. *In*: Chimay J. Anumba & N. Roofigari-Esfahan (Eds.), Cyber-Physical Systems in the Built Environment. https://doi.org/10.1007/978-3-030-41560-0

Sawhney, A., M. Riley and J. Irizarry. 2020. Construction 4.0: An Innovation Platform for the Built Environment. Routledge.

Schweichhart, K. 2016. Reference Architectural Model Industrie 4.0 (RAMI 4.0) – An Introduction. Publikationen Der Plattform Industrie, 4.

Song, H., D. B. Rawat, S. Jeschke and C. Brecher. 2016. Cyber-physical Systems: Foundations, Principles and Applications. Morgan Kaufmann.

Tabuada, P., S. Y. Caliskan, M. Rungger and R. Majumdar. 2014. Towards robustness for cyber-physical systems. IEEE Transactions on Automatic Control, 59(12), 3151–3163.

Tang, S., D. R. Shelden, C. M. Eastman, P. Pishdad-Bozorgi and X. Gao. 2019. A review of building information modeling (BIM) and the internet of things (IoT) devices integration: Present status and future trends. Automation in Construction, 101, 127–139.

Thomas, R. K., A. A. Cardenas and R. B. Bobba. 2015. First Workshop on Cyber-Physical Systems Security and PrivaCy (CPS-SPC) Challenges and Research Directions. Proceedings of the 22nd ACM SIGSAC Conference on Computer and Communications Security, 1705–1706.

Törngren, M., F. Asplund, S. Bensalem, J. McDermid, R. Passerone, H. Pfeifer, ... B. Schätz. 2017. Characterization, analysis, and recommendations for exploiting the opportunities of cyber-physical systems. *In*: Cyber-Physical Systems (pp. 3–14). Elsevier.

Vogel-Heuser, B. and D. Hess. 2016. Guest Editorial Industry 4.0 – Prerequisites and Visions. IEEE Transactions on Automation Science and Engineering. https://doi.org/10.1109/TASE.2016.2523639

Wang, L., M. Törngren and M. Onori. 2015. Current status and advancement of cyber-physical systems in manufacturing. Journal of Manufacturing Systems, 37, 517–527.

Weyer, S., M. Schmitt, M. Ohmer and D. Gorecky. 2015. Towards Industry 4.0 - Standardization as the crucial challenge for highly modular, multi-vendor production systems. Ifac-Papersonline, 48(3), 579–584.

Xia, F., A. Vinel, R. Gao, L. Wang and T. Qiu. 2011. Evaluating IEEE 802.15. 4 for cyber-physical systems. EURASIP Journal on Wireless Communications and Networking, 2011, 1–14.

Yue, Y.-G. and P. He. 2018. A comprehensive survey on the reliability of mobile wireless sensor networks: Taxonomy, challenges, and future directions. Information Fusion, 44, 188–204.

Zeadally, S. and N. Jabeur. 2016. Cyber-physical system design with sensor networking technologies. *In*: The Institution of Engineering and Technology. Vol. 53.

Zhou, Y., X. Gong, J. Li and B. Li. 2018. Verifying CPS for self-adaptability. 2018 IEEE/ACIS 17th International Conference on Computer and Information Science (ICIS), 166–172. IEEE.

Technology Requirements for Cyber Physical Systems Implementation in Construction

Khalid Mhmoud Alzubi, Wesam Salah Alaloul and Abdul Hannan Qureshi

Introduction

Cyber-Physical Systems (CPSs) are a set of incorporated physical processes, computation, and networking. The physical process is controlled and monitored using subsystems that are embedded by networked systems with feedback to change their conduct when needed (Asare et al. 2012). The subsystems work separately from each other with the capability to react with the exterior environment (Saqib et al. 2015, Wang et al. 2010). Various small devices accomplish the physical processes with computing, sensing, and communication (wired or wireless) abilities. These physical devices can be specified by physical information attributes or sensing equipment, such as Radio Frequency Identification (RFID) or infrared sensors, and can be connected to a networking system to deliver the collected data to the computational subsystem (Zhang et al. 2011). With the growing concentration on data processing capability, integration of information systems and data communications capability, and physical devices, the desire for integrating CPSs in various domains is also growing, resulting in closely gained attention from government agencies, industry, research, universities, and development labs (Lu et al. 2015). The development of CPSs is an essential milestone in advancing operations in many fields, including construction. This development is assisted by technological advancements that align with the CPSs objectives of intelligent interlinkage and automation among cyber and physical spaces. CPSs are supported by integrating several technologies that enable bi-directional interaction between cyber components and physical components to fulfil the automation. The application of CPSs in the construction industry requires the appropriate distribution of information and interchange between diverse stakeholders. This is due to the fact that the construction industry is highly fragmented, including several essential stakeholders (Motamedi and Hammad 2009).

Mainly the CPSs technology is divided into three main connected layers (Whiteman et al. 2018): the physical layer (perception layer), the information layer (application layer), and the network layer(transmission layer) as shown in Figure 3.1.

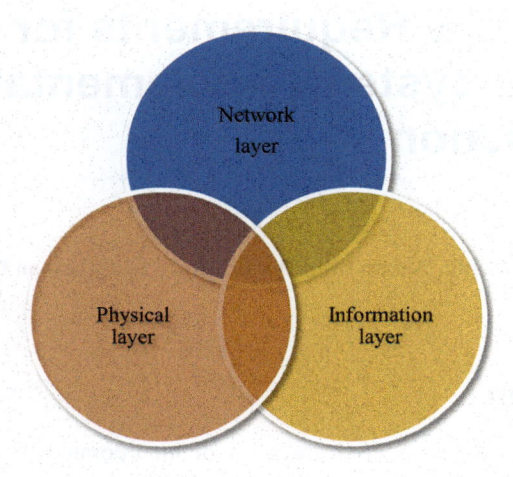

Figure 3.1: CPSs Layers

The Physical Layer

It is the first layer and it is called the recognition layer (Kumar and Patel 2014) or the sensors layer (Mahmoud et al. 2016). This layer has multiple terminal types of equipment such as actuators, sensors, Global Position Systems (GPSs), intelligent devices, cameras, laser scanners, RFID with readers and Two-Dimensional (2D) bar code labels (Lu et al. 2015, Zhang et al. 2011). Devices at the physical layer can gather real-time data necessary for a lot of purposes such as tracking and monitoring, interpreting the received data from the physical sphere, and implementing commands from the information layer. The physical layer comprises of numerous embedded systems, hardware such as sensors and actuators, and smart chips, which are taking responsibility for the gathering, transmission of information, and the execution of control signals as it is the base of the CPSs (Liu et al. 2017). The sensor samples sense the physical world, and the actuators indirectly or directly change the physical world (Whiteman et al. 2018). Sensors recognize and transfer information and data to cyberspace, and once the data is handled, the restored information is sent back to the physical sphere using actuators. All parts in a CPSs should have abilities for connectivity to be capable to receive and send data from and to the other parts in the CPS.

Sensors Layer

CPSs contain all types of information sensing devices, such as laser scanners, RFID, sensors, GPS, etc., that can form a network and are connected with the internet. The connection between the management and field equipment layers can easily be recognized through network protocols. Therefore, in the physical system, accurate and fast data acquisition becomes a significant factor in the processing of data from CPSs efficiently. The gathering of the perception data plays a significant role in CPSs; where high-precision sensing or low-precision sensor devices can be chosen according to particular application requirements (Whiteman et al. 2018). The subsystems of the sensor network contain several sink-nodes and sensor nodes that can sense some interesting information from the physical world. Perceived information is integrated into the gathering centre and after the necessary processing it is sent to the data centre to provide essential data that support the decision. Sensors monitor several aspects of the construction facilities, such as BIM and RFID tags for the management of facility components, real-time location sensing sensors for tracking the location and placement of key components, the temperature sensor for monitoring workspace temperature, and readers and RFID tags for identifying and sorting components' information. This layer can also provide the construction personnel access to control decisions depending on the type of sensor used.

Actuator Layer

This consists of a multitude of control nodes and actuator units. Control nodes receive the control command from the control centre and then send the command to specific actuator units for implementation. Specific physical attributes can be controlled and adjusted to modify the physical world(Liu et al. 2017).

Device Layer

The device layer contains the users' devices, such as mobile devices, through which the construction labours onsite can react with the system. This layer serves two objectives: it provides access to sensed data from the sensing layer and enables the entry of data through the user interface (Akanmu and Anumba 2015). Mobile devices are portable/small-sized computing devices with a display screen for accessing and embedding information needed to coordinate between the office and the job site. Mobile devices have long been found useful in the construction industry for progress management (El-Omari and Moselhi 2011), managing punch lists (Menzel et al. 2008), safety applications (Wang 2008), and maintenance (Kim et al. 2009). Examples of mobile devices include personal data assistant (PDA), tablet PCs and smartphones. Using these mobile devices, the construction labourers can send their concerns or inquiries about specific components to the design team and gain fast feedback, and access virtual models, and update changes in a short time. Construction personnel can also easily embed information to be written to RFID tags before erecting and installing construction building parts. Some mobile devices have embedded barcode scanners and RFID, which can be used to scan and read the embedded information.

Virtual Models

Virtual models work as a platform for embedding and visualizing the lifecycle information of the projects. Virtual models are capable of storing information that can be used over the lifecycle of a facility are called building information models. These models can be produced and navigated using software such as Autodesk Revit, Bentley architecture, and Navisworks. These models contain a virtual representation of physical components and can serve as a platform for visualizing and monitoring the construction activities' status. In the integration of CPSs, acquired information from wireless sensors is visualized in virtual models and occasionally stored in identical virtual components. Project stakeholders can inquire about the virtual components to access embedded information or to embed information. For example, designers can embed data and information (relating to design reviews or updates) into the virtual components, such that these are transmitted to the tags on the physical components and accessed on the construction job site and vice versa. The virtual models can also be a platform for remotely controlling the components of the physical world.

Connectivity Requirements

As a general requirement for CPSs, all the components are expected to communicate to support the CPSs' necessary operations. The capabilities of communication are essential for all CPSs components, which can be achieved through wireless or wired network configurations.

The Network Layer

Also known as the transport layer (Lu et al. 2015), it is responsible for the processing and interchanging of data and information between the physical and the information layer. Also, this is provided by a real-time information interchange and communication supported by the next-generation network. It is mainly supported by the internet (like local area networks, private networks, and communication networks) and other existing networks of data interaction and transmission. Also the data transport layer needs to have the ability to use intelligent management and process enormous amounts of information (Zhang et al. 2013).

The data transmission and interaction in this layer are achieved using communication networks, the internet, local area networks, or other existing networks through many technologies such as Fourth-Generation (4G), Bluetooth, Infrared, ZigBee, and Wi-Fi, depending upon the sensor devices (Khan et al. 2012). However, most of these interconnections are achieved by the internet for many causes, including cost-effectiveness and availability. This means that the used networks should support real-time operations. As this is important to process and manage a vast amount of data, the transmission layer with responsibility for reliable communication support can initially manage and process a massive amount of data and realize real-time transmission (Zhang et al. 2011).

In CPSs, communication, control, and computing technologies are tightly integrated, and nearly all CPSs are composed on the support of existing standards and communication networks. Beside the responsibility of information transmission, the network layer plays an important role in connecting the information layer and the physical layer, so it is regarded as an independent layer. It is also includes various communication devices and protocols of the network, like switches, hubs, and routers (Whiteman et al. 2018). All devices in a CPSs are required to have abilities for connectivity to be able to receive and send data among other CPSs components. It is expected that all the components of the system communicate in some manner as a general requirement for CPSs, to support the necessary operations of the CPSs. Connectivity can be achieved through wireless or wired network configurations.

Wired Network

This type of connectivity is widely used in several industries. The ease of setups for wired platforms and the simplicity of the wired devices makes it applicable for several applications. No specialized training and knowledge are required for wired network settings which usually involves a plug and connections of the wired components. Also, sometimes wired connectivity provides energy to devices, thus making wired systems more reliable and sustainable. The requirement of building infrastructure for wired networks makes the implementation CPSs complex and making use of this type of network limited in construction projects due to the constantly changing environments in such projects. If this system is in place, the network must be implemented at the beginning of the project and must be continuously adapted to accommodate the needs of the constantly changing construction site.

Wireless Network

Wireless networks have brought ease to diverse human activities and solved problems regarding productivity, business, communication, and mobility. Indeed, electromagnetic waves are the media now used to transmit information over the wireless network (Ahmadi et al. 2018). Based on the requirements of the system, it is essential to find the suitable available wireless standards. Therefore, flexibility in CPSs allows the designer to select the best combination of technologies for their systems. Different standards which can integrate various technologies are required to cover different areas of the communication scope because it is impossible to cover a single standard type of communications schemes and the need for CPSs and types of matching communication technology options. The following subsections provide brief details for the used wireless technologies.

Bluetooth Technology

Bluetooth is a low power consumption and short-range wireless communication system and providing connectivity for several electronic devices. Although it was grown by Ericson, it is standards were developed by the Bluetooth Special Interest Group (SIG) and running under their auspices; it has developed to provide faster speeds, far more capability than before, and greater flexibility. Bluetooth confirmed (IEEE 802.15.1) as the standard. Bluetooth technology has progressed significantly and has been expanded to provide not only the traditional short-range audio streaming but also applications like mesh connectivity for CPSs, machine-to-machine communications, and Internet of Things (IoT). Bluetooth Low Energy standard updated to close the energy efficiency break among Bluetooth and ZigBee for no streaming sensor-node-type applications (Burg et al. 2018).

ZigBee Technology

This is a wireless networking protocol with low power consumption, low data rate, and low cost, which was produced for automation control and sensor networks based on IEEE 802.15.4 standard. ZigBee specification provided by ZigBee Alliance. The ZigBee network can include a massive number of nodes up to sixty-five thousand and connect them in any industry using a single control network (Burg et al. 2018, Shi and Li 2017).

Wi-Fi (Wireless Fidelity)

It is a generic term that refers to the IEEE 802.11 wireless communication standard for Wireless Local Area Networks (WLANs) and works on a data link and the physical layer. The different variants are different standards within the overall series. By releasing updated variants, the overall technology has been able to keep pace with the ever-growing requirements for more data and higher speeds, etc. There are two types of WLAN network that can be formed using a Wi-Fi system, Ad-Hoc, and infrastructure networks. The infrastructure application is aimed at office areas or to provide a "hotspot". A backbone wired network to connect to a server is still required. The wireless network is split into several cells, each serviced by an Access Point (AP) or base station, which acts as a controller for the cell. The Ad-Hoc network is other type of networks that may be used. As Wi-Fi has developed, to accommodate the increasing speeds and performance by developing many new standards and variants, along with the current low power technologies like Low-Power Wireless Personal Area Networks (LoWPAN), Long-Range Wireless Area Networks (LoRaWAN), passive optical network, Bluetooth ZigBee, and 802.11 Wi-Fi standards are similarly making their way into the market with their own advantages in improved speed and wide range. Besides IEEE, Wi-Fi Alliance has a new standard for proximity applications (Burg et al. 2018, Shi and Li 2017).

Mobile Cellular Networks

Mobile cellular technologies are widely used, and have been accepted into everyday life, and are based upon the concept of frequency reuse by the application on a series of coverage cells. From growing nation to developed nation, mobile phone technology has been installed and used in all countries around the world. Each mobile phone generation (Third Generation (3G), fourth (4G), and Fifth Generation (5G)) had its own aims and was capable of providing various levels of functionality. Also, there may have been different standards within the different generations. Cellular telecommunications technology is based on using many base stations covering a cell or a small area. Each base station communicates with a reasonable number of users (Ahmadi et al. 2018, Xichun Li et al. 2009). Also, Mobile applications can be used for collecting construction data for monitoring construction sites. Mobile application uses in remotely monitoring temporary structures requires a complete integration of sensing, data transmission, alarm display and/or alerts, and decision making. This integration requires the development of sensory modules, a wireless network, and mobile devices, and this combination provides two-way data transmission between the sensory devices and actuators at the construction site and the system server in the site office (Moon 2017).

Passive Optical Network (PON)

PON is a system that brings optical fiber cabling and signals most of the way to the end-user. Depending on wherever the PON terminates. A PON consists of an Optical Line Termination (OLT) at the office of the communication company. Several optical network units simply describe the fact that optical transmission has no active electronic parts or power requirements once the signal is going through the network (Jianqing Liu et al. 2018).

Identifying the appropriate network will help guarantee the proper flow of information and proper functioning in the CPSs. The main requirements in selecting the appropriate network are latency, reliability, longevity, data rate, privacy, and cyber-security.

The Information Layer

Which is the most interactive layer. Its task is to process the received data and information from the data transmission layer and issue commands to be completed by the physical units, actuators and sensors (Peng et al. 2013). This layer works to make the correct decisions by implementing complex decision-making algorithms on the aggregated data (Saqib et al. 2015) and to take corrective actions by controlling the commands. In addition, this layer processes the received information from the perception layer and then determines the desired automated actions to be taken (Khan et al. 2012). At this layer data gathering from various resources and processing of vast data are performed by object control and management.

Also, cloud, middleware, computing, and data mining algorithms can be used in the management implementation of linked devices at the physical layer (Zhang et al. 2011). Also at this layer the monitoring of the system is performed, and its mission is to monitor the actions of physical processes and issue commands to modify the behaviour of physical devices to ensure the working environment works accurately and correctly. This layer also saves previous actions so that feedback can be given for ensuring future operational improvements. They create a smart environment and combine CPSs and industry professional applications which are the objective of this layer (Mahmoud et al. 2016).

Generally, the information layer is accountable for the processing of information, including the identification, calculation, pattern matching, and other processing of the collected information by the physical layer, the management and configuration of the system, the conservation of all kinds of information in the system, the making of orders and decisions based on perception, and the scheduling of resources and tasks (Whiteman et al. 2018). This layer consists of a data centre and a control centre.

Data Centre

Sensor networks transfers data to the data centre for storage by next-generation network systems. The data centre checks the integrity and authentication of received data and if they pass the inspection, it stores the data, otherwise it sends a message to the control centre which will then send control signals to the actuator, which would notify it to collect the data again by the sensor network nodes. Also, the data centre is responsible for the routine maintenance of the database and quick response to commands sent by the control centre, like a query. Also, to prevent the database from collapse, regular emergency treatments are needed.

Control Centre

The control centre is the most significant part of CPSs. It receives the query instructions sent by users and then sends query orders to the data centre after the authentication of its identity. It sorts the query results according to control strategies, if they meet the requirements, it is reports back to the user, otherwise finds out the location of the node-by-node positioning technology and sends control directives to actuators for corresponding processing. Control centre configuration policy can be adjusted dynamically according to users' requirements and needs. Conduct performance analysis and forecast analysis of CPSs behaviour through uncertainty processing technology and data mining technology. Detecting the failure of node and network through fault diagnosis technology and conduct corresponding processing, and through real-time control technology, it ensures the real-time control processing of CPSs.

Security and Privacy Control

Security challenges are increasing as the use of CPSs are increasing and they should be taken into consideration. Also, in the context of control security and information security, sensor networks security must be considered. The security of the Information involves securing information during data processing, data aggregation, and large-scale sharing in the network environment, especially open loosely coupled networks. Control security encompasses mitigating the control system from any attacks on system estimation and resolving any control issues in the network environment, and control algorithms (Cárdenas et al. 2011, Lu et al. 2013). Control security focuses on protecting the dynamics of control systems against cyber-attacks, while information security focuses on data protection (Lu et al. 2015).

Control security are the security risks that may happen when one system or device is controlled by an unauthorized person, a process also known as hacking. Information security is about unauthorized access to store and retrieve sensitive information and data that may be used in an improper way. Attacks on CPSs can lead to a great loss in many aspects of any industries, especially if these attacks were on the cyber layer, and construction industry is not exempted. Therefore, CPSs security is becoming more important and should be considered in the early stage of the design process (Ashibani and Mahmoud 2017). Privacy protection issues faced at this layer should have a lot of attention. Here in the information layer, the users' private information can be analyzed by attackers, and that can lead to the leakage of private data and privacy loss. Since this data might contain past and present locations that the users visited, some data protection techniques regarding data protection at this layer includes anonymous space, location camouflage, or space encryption. In addition, many applications in this layer apply to a users' social life, therefore, need to be protected (Jing et al. 2014).

General CPSs Requirements/Challenges

A lot of requirements and challenges are faced by the adoption of CPSs in any industry, including construction. The main requirements and challenges facing development, adoption, and innovation of CPSs are given in the following subsections (Gunes et al. 2014):

Dependability

Refers to the property of a system to implement desired functionalities through its operation without considerable degradation in its outcome and performance. This reflects the degree of trust set in the entire system. A highly dependable system has to deliver requested services as specified, operate properly without intrusion, and without fail during its operation. The words dependability and trustworthiness are often used interchangeably (Wan & Alagar 2011). Components of the cyber and physical system are inherently interdependent, and during the system operation the underlying components might be dynamically interconnected, which, in return, render the dependability analysis very difficult. A common language to express dependability related information across constitutive systems and underlying components have to be introduced in the design stage (Denker et al. 2012).

Maintainability

Refers to the property of a system to be fixed when a failure happens. A system that is repaired in a rapid and simple way with the minimum costs of supporting resources and free from causing further faults through the maintenance process called a highly maintainable system.

Availability

Available system refers for the system to be ready for access even when faults happen. A highly available system should insulate the malfunctioning part from itself and keep operating without it. Malicious cyber-attacks prevent the availability of system services significantly.

Safety

Refers to the ability of a system to not cause any harm, risk, or hazard inside or outside of the system during its operation. A highly safe system has to comply to a great extent with general and application-specific safety regulations and deploy safety assurance mechanisms if some problem occurs.

Reliability

Reliability refers to the degree of correctness which a system provides to perform its function. A highly reliable system makes sure that it does things right every time. So, the certification of system abilities about how to do things correctly does not mean that they are done correctly.

Component-based CPSs are expected to operate reliably in uncertain and dynamic environments. For construction safety applications involving postures or equipment, a slight deviation or change from the planned performance may result in fatalities (Yuan et al. 2016). Potential errors, uncertainties in knowledge, characteristics, and outcomes in the processes of construction should be quantified during the design of component based CPSs.

Robustness

This refers to the capability of a system to keep withstanding any failures and to keep its stable configuration. A highly robust system should keep operating even when any failures occurs without a change in the fundamentals of its original configuration and prevent those failures from stopping or hindering its operation. Also, the presence of disturbances possibly arising from actuator inaccuracies, sensor noises, potential hardware errors, faulty communication channels, or software bugs may affect the overall robustness of CPSs.

Predictability

Refers to the degree of expecting of a system's functionality and behaviour either quantitatively or qualitatively. A highly predictable system should guarantee the specified outcome of the system's functionality and behaviour to a great extent and meeting all system requirements every time it operates. The dynamic nature and uncertainties of construction projects make it difficult to predict project outcomes and this makes construction projects a candidate for CPSs. Predictable activities of construction projects will need to assure the outcomes of the system's behaviour and functionality whenever operational while also meeting all requirements of the system.

Accuracy

Accuracy refers to the degree of closeness of a system's observed and measured outcome to its calculated and actual one. The outcomes of the highly accurate system should be as close as possible to the actual outcome.

Compositionality

Refers to the property of how well a system can be understood completely by checking every portion of it. A system that provides great insight about the whole from the derived behaviours of its constituent components and parts of its highly compositional system. It is very challenging to achieve high compositionality in the CPSs design especially due to the messy behaviour of constituent physical subsystems.

Sustainability

This means having the ability of being long-lasting without compromising the system requirements while renewing the system's resources and using them efficiently. A system that is a long-lasting system which has dynamic tuning and self-healing capabilities under evolving circumstances is recognized as a highly sustainable system.

Adaptability

Adaptability refers to the ability of a system to create variations in its state to survive in response to different circumstances in the environment by adjusting its own configuration. A highly adaptable system should be quickly adaptable to evolving circumstances and needs.

Component-based CPSs should have the ability to respond and sense the changes, abnormalities and uncertainties that typically happen through the lifecycle of construction buildings projects and infrastructure systems. In construction, variations in site conditions and unexpected circumstances like equipment failure, weather conditions, and human factors relating to performance and delays trigger changes. Construction projects need to be monitored to quickly detect and respond to these deviations which is very important for ensuring that the project meets budget and schedule.

Resilience

Resilience refers to the capability of a system to maintain operations and delivery of services in an acceptable quality even when the system is exposed to any outer or inner difficulties like malfunctioning components, sudden defects, and a rising workload that does not exceed its ability limit.

Reconfigurability

This refers to the property of a system to change its configurations in case of failure or upon inner or outer requests. A system that is able to fine-tune itself dynamically, is self-configurable, and can coordinate the operation of its components at finer granularities which are recognized as a highly reconfigurability system.

Efficiency

Efficiency refers to the number of costs, time, and energy resources the system needs to deliver specified functionalities. A system that operates properly under the optimum amount of system resources is defined as a highly efficient system.

Integrity

This refers to the property of a system to protect itself or information within it from unauthorized modification or unauthorized manipulation to maintain the correctness of the information. A high integrity system should provide extensive authorization check mechanisms. CPSs need to be developed with greater assurance by providing integrity check mechanisms on several occasions like identifying false data injection, distinguishing malicious behaviours from the ambient noise, data integrity of network packets, and compromised actuator and sensor components. Properties of the processes of the physical and cyber should be well-understood and thus can be used to define desired integrity assurance (Mo and Sinopoli 2012).

Confidentiality

This refers to the property of allowing only the authorized parties to access sensitive information generated within the system. The confidentiality of data circulation needs to be retained to a reasonable degree by employing the most secure methods of protection from unauthorized disclosure, access, or tampering, because the confidentiality of data transmitted through attacked sensor nodes can be compromised, and that can cause critical data to be eavesdropped upon, data flow in the network to be directed over compromised sensors, or fake node identities to be generated in the network. also, this can lead to the injection of false data into the network over those fake nodes. (Loukas et al. 2013).

Interoperability

This refers to the capability of the components and systems to exchange and use data and information to provide specified services. A highly interoperable system should accept or provide services conducive to effective interoperation and communication between system components.

Composability

Refers to the property of different components to be combined within a system and their inter-relationships. A highly composable system should satisfy specific system requirement by allowing the recombination of the system components repeatedly. Composability should be tested in several levels such as device composability, service composability, system composability, and code compossibility. Certainly, the need for well-defined composition methodologies that follow composition properties from the bottom up makes system composability more challenging.

Heterogeneity

This refers to the property of a system to incorporate a set of various types of interconnected and interacting components forming a complex whole. CPSs are inherently heterogeneous because of computational elements, constituent physical dynamics, control logic, and diverse communication technologies deployment.

Scalability

This refers to the capability of a system to remain functioning fully even in the case of increased workload or change in its size and the chance to take full advantage of it. The raise in the throughput of the system should be proportional to the raise in resources of the system. A highly scalable system should scatter and gather mechanisms for effective communication and workload balancing protocols to enhance the performance.

Educational and Legal Challenges

The experienced and skilled workforces, professionals, educational trainers, and knowledgeable experts, with a deep understanding of CPSs are expected to remain as a major challenge in front of the development, innovation, and adoption of CPSs due to the short supply at least over the next decade. This is mainly due to the fact that the field of CPSs requires the integration of knowledge from multiple engineering areas like computing engineering, computer science, mechanical, civil, electrical, or systems engineering, with a good balance between practice and theory. Education in this field is challenging due to the breadth and depth of knowledge required for the development and innovation of CPSs. The implementation of the CPSs in various sectors requested different regulations and legislation concerning the safety and security of systems and users, privacy of data, and liability testing and certification of CPSs. Moreover, considering that

CPSs may span over different states, countries, or even continents, new legal terms and standards may be needed to specifically label the requirements and needs of CPSs (Törngren et al. 2015).

Real-Time Requirements

The processing of CPSs data must meet the requirements of real-time to ensure appropriate results are given within a restricted time. Most CPSs are established to support real-time applications, like real-time monitoring, real-time observation, real-time forecasting, and real-time control, to implement the substantial control and intervention on physical equipment and environments by means of network control and to keep updated on a physical devices' current situation. The approach for a real-time application can be based on the capacity of the system, the demands of the sensed elements, or event and time constraints.

Building components are subjected to a several processes from the planning phase to the operations and maintenance phase of the constructed facility. The real-time ability of component based CPSs means that information or instructions required to engage with the components needs to timely transmitted. Real-time data or information about the handling, context, and condition of the components is critical for identifying and resolving issues or risks as soon as possible. Supply chain, installation, and resource status are critical for decision making and control of construction activities during the construction phase. However, CPSs in the construction industry can maximum the advantages of the use of a less stringent system of behaviour by prioritizing predictable behaviours under relevant events rather than predicting behaviours at every specific moment even when the system is idle. In other words, rather than recording every time period of the system, the dependability of a CPSs in the construction industry can be enough if the behaviour of the system is consistent under substantial events or time frames. Reasons to prefer soft real-time over hard real-time include the additional expenditure on resources, an overload of information, and increased capacities of the resource.

Researchers have explored the advantages and benefits of real-time monitoring for supply chain management (Irizarry et al. 2013), progress monitoring (Azimi et al. 2011, Ranaweera et al. 2013), site layout management (Akanmu et al. 2016), safety management (Cheng and Teizer 2013, Giretti et al. 2008), and inventory management (Kasim et al. 2012). Likewise, access to real-time conditions of installed components such as heating, ventilation and air-conditioning systems can improve early detecting of the potential failure of equipment, thereby improving the efficiency and comfort of building occupants (Djuric & Novakovic 2009, Liang and Du 2007).

Human Interaction

Some components of the CPSs are prone to interacting with humans, and the human actors are considered a substantial ingredient of the CPSs that requires it to be represented digitally in the cyber part of a CPSs. Therefore, when designing CPSs platforms and selecting the system devices, humans must take into consideration as a part of the design. As such, the ability of human interaction is a requirement for the CPSs components that have to interact with humans. This plays a significant role in less automated industries such as construction where many activities are conducted manually by workers, compared to manufacturing which can be more automated than construction. Several research and experimental projects have been performed in the construction domain to consider humans as a part in the system (Marks and Teizer 2012, C. Zhang et al. 2017). In considering humans as a component of a system, capturing human attributes is particularly challenging due to the complex nature of the human like psychological, physiological, and behavioural behaviours (Stankovic 2014).

The construction industry is a labor-intensive sector. So, human participants should be considered as a significant component in the applicable component-based CPSs. Component-based CPSs must be integrated with the behaviours of the worker in construction environments (Munir et al. 2013). This is significant for the needed communicating information and in assisting the decision-making processes of construction labours (Munir et al. 2013). Human involvement assists in collecting data on physical phenomena such as body temperature or heart rate, or nonphysical events such as social media posts or a human's contact list. Such types of data collection enable the system to further identify patterns of activities, human's physiological or psychological states, and external conditions. Human involvement assists in collecting records on physical phenomena which includes the heart rates and temperature of bodies, or nonphysical events like contact lists or social media posts. Such forms of data collection also allow the systems to further become aware of activities patterns, psychological or physiological states of human, and outside conditions. Also, to have a reliable, adaptive system, and robust system there is a need for a feedback process. The feedback process observes the monitored environment or phenomena and if further actions are required it provides more input to the system. Also, it is noteworthy that the system may face challenges or changes in its lifecycle that might prevent it from performing in the best way. User feedback can enhance the system and can direct it toward the desired outcomes. For this aim, the system can learn from human preferences, observation, and decisions in addition to the self-adopting process (Z. Liu et al. 2011).

Cost

Cost is always a key consideration when deciding to apply new technologies to different scales of a construction project (West and Blackburn 2017). The scope and purpose of the project are essential in providing an adequate cost estimate for the application of CPSs. The cost of applying CPSs technology can vary depending on the level of sophistication, efforts and time utilized in developing the CPSs. The level of knowledge required to develop the CPSs can affect the cost, and therefore, designing the CPSs for reuse can significantly reduce cost.

Status of Technologies Implementation in the Construction Industry

Several researchers have investigated the integration of the physical construction and virtual models using different acquisition data technologies such as photographs, laser scanners, and RFID tags in recent years. Some of these integration efforts and their limitations are briefly discussed here. Bosche et al. (2008) developed an approach that involves integrating 3D CAD models and 3D laser scanned data for tracking project progress automatically. By using the laser scanning, the approach enables an automated recognition of 3D CAD model objects. The major drawback of the use of the laser scan and digital photographs is that a number of images needs to be taken to fully capture the construction activities, and further processing of the images is required, thus hindering access to real-time information.

Several researchers have utilized RFID tags for integrating the physical construction and virtual models: Chin et al. (2005a) examined the use of RFID tags and 4D CAD for monitoring progress in supply chain management. RFID tags were placed on structural parts such as curtain walls and structural steel to observe their status from the ordering stage through the delivery, receipt, and the erection stage. The sensed status was captured in a 3D model to indicate the status of progress. The disadvantage of this approach by (Chin et al. 2005a, Hu, 2008) is that access to progress information or installation status is dependent on when the construction personnel embedded information into the tags. Hu,(2008) developed an integrated model of 4D CAD and RFID for tracking the status for components of construction. Construction components like equipment, pipes, beams, and steel columns are tagged with RFID passive tags, and an RFID reader is used to track their status from the fabrication or manufacturing plant to where they are installed the construction site. (Motamedi et al. 2009) investigated the use of BIM and RFID tags for lifecycle management of facility components. The authors proposed permanently attaching RFID tags to facility components where the memory of the tags is populated with BIM information. There have also been attempts by the industry to integrating field BIM and precast concrete installation using RFID tags; the status of precast concrete pieces were tracked from the fabrication yard to installation using tags (Sawyer 2008). The pieces are identified using RFID reader communication with a Tablet personnel computer with Vela Systems Materials Tracking software installed.

The above mentioned research projects have demonstrated the capability to integrate the physical construction and virtual models for better modelling of the proposed facility, observing and tracking components on the construction site, and progress monitoring. However, these integration approaches do not provide the opportunity for providing feedback or control of construction activities; specifically, there are still few or no mechanisms for ensuring bi-directional coordination between the physical construction and the virtual models. For example, when a key component or sub-assembly is changed or constructed in the physical environment, there is no means of automatically updating the virtual model to reflect this change. Conversely, if the design or erection sequence of a set of steel members is altered in the virtual model, there is no real-time communication of this change to the construction personnel on-site. Also, there is a lost opportunity to use embedded instrumentation and sensors to control the construction process and constructed facility.

Summary

The growth of CPSs is a fundamental milestone in advancing operations in many industries, including construction. There are three main layers in the CPSs technology: the physical layer, the information layer, and the network layer. As a general requirement for CPSs, it is expected that all the system components have the ability to communicate in some manner to support the necessary functions of the CPSs. As it is the foundation of the CPSs, the physical layer comprises of many embedded systems, hardware such as sensors and actuators, smart chips, etc., taking charge of the collection and the transmission of information and the execution of control signals. Sensors perceive and transfer data to cyberspace, and once the data is processed, the retrieved information is sent back to the physical world through actuators. The network layer plays an important role in connecting the physical layer and the information layer and it is responsible for the transmission of information. The information layer is responsible for the processing of information. Several researchers have investigated the integration of virtual models and physical construction using different data acquisition technologies such as photographs, laser scanners and RFID tags. Despite the benefits of applying CPSs in construction, a lot of requirements/challenges faced in the adoption of CPSs in any industry, including construction which should be taken into consideration. Also, the cost of the endeavor is always a key consideration when deciding to apply new technologies to the different scales of a construction project. The cost of applying CPSs technology can vary depending on the level of sophistication, efforts and time utilized.

References

Ahmadi, A., M. Moradi, C. Cherifi, V. Cheutet and Y. Ouzrout Wireless. 2018. Wireless Connectivity of CPS for Smart Manufacturing: A Survey. Vol. 8. https://hal.archives-ouvertes.fr/hal-01952355

Akanmu, A. and C. J. Anumba. 2015. Cyber-physical systems integration of building information models and the physical construction. Engineering, Construction and Architectural Management, 22(5), 516–535. https://doi.org/10.1108/ECAM-07-2014-0097

Akanmu, A., O. Olatunji, P. E. D. Love, D. Nguyen and J. Matthews. 2016. Auto-generated site layout: An integrated approach to real-time sensing of temporary facilities in infrastructure projects. Structure and Infrastructure Engineering, 12(10), 1243–1255. https://doi.org/10.1080/15732479.2015.1110601

Anumba, C. J., A. Akanmu and J. Messner. 2010. Towards a cyber-physical systems approach to construction. Construction Research Congress 2010: Innovation for Reshaping Construction Practice. Proceedings of the 2010 Construction Research Congress, 528–537. https://doi.org/10.1061/41109(373)53

Anumba, C. and N. Roofigari-Esfahan. 2020. Cyber-Physical Systems in the Built Environment. https://link.springer.com/content/pdf/10.1007/978-3-030-41560-0.pdf

Asare, P., D. Broman, E. A. Lee, M. Torngren and S. S. Sunder. 2012. Cyber-Physical Systems – A Concept Map. Online. https://ptolemy.berkeley.edu/projects/cps/

Azimi, R., S. Lee, S. M. Abourizk and A. Alvanchi. 2011. A framework for an automated and integrated project monitoring and control system for steel fabrication projects. Automation in Construction, 20(1), 88–97. https://doi.org/10.1016/j.autcon.2010.07.001

Bosche, F., C. T. Haas and P. Murray. 2008. Performance of automated project progress tracking with 3D data fusion. *In*: pureapps2.hw.ac.uk. https://pureapps2.hw.ac.uk/ws/files/785787/CSCE_2008_CO_449_Final.pdf

Burg, A., A. Chattopadhyay and K. Y. Lam. 2018. Wireless communication and security issues for cyber-physical systems and the internet-of-things. Proceedings of the IEEE, 106(1), 38–60. https://doi.org/10.1109/JPROC.2017.2780172

Cárdenas, A. A., S. Amin, Z. S. Lin, Y. L. Huang, C. Y. Huang and S. Sastry. 2011. Attacks against process control systems: Risk assessment, detection, and response. Proceedings of the 6th International Symposium on Information, Computer and Communications Security, ASIACCS 2011, 355–366. https://doi.org/10.1145/1966913.1966959

Cheng, T., M. Venugopal, J. Teizer and P. A. Vela. 2011. Performance evaluation of ultra wideband technology for construction resource location tracking in harsh environments. Automation in Construction, 20(8), 1173–1184. https://doi.org/10.1016/j.autcon.2011.05.001

Cheng, Tao and J. Teizer. 2013. Real-time resource location data collection and visualization technology for construction safety and activity monitoring applications. Automation in Construction, 34, 3–15. https://doi.org/10.1016/j.autcon.2012.10.017

Djuric, N. and V. Novakovic. 2009. Review of possibilities and necessities for building lifetime commissioning. *In*: Renewable and Sustainable Energy Reviews (Vol. 13, Issue 2, pp. 486–492). Pergamon. https://doi.org/10.1016/j.rser.2007.11.007

Duan, Q., E. Al-Shaer, M. Islam and H. Jafarian. 2018. CONCEAL: A strategy composition for resilient cyber deception-framework, metrics and deployment. 2018 IEEE Conference on Communications and Network Security, CNS 2018. https://doi.org/10.1109/CNS.2018.8433196

El-Omari, S. and O. Moselhi. 2011. Integrating automated data acquisition technologies for progress reporting of construction projects. Automation in Construction, 20(6), 699–705. https://doi.org/10.1016/j.autcon.2010.12.001

Golparvar-Fard, M., S. Savarese and F. Peña-Mora. 2009. Interactive visual construction progress monitoring with D4A - 4D augmented reality - Models. Building a Sustainable Future - Proceedings of the 2009 Construction Research Congress, 41–50. https://doi.org/10.1061/41020(339)5

Gunes, V., S. Peter, T. Givargis and F. Vahid. 2014. A survey on concepts, applications, and challenges in cyber-physical systems. KSII Transactions on Internet and Information Systems, 8(12), 4242–4268. https://doi.org/10.3837/tiis.2014.12.001

Hu, W. 2008. Integration of radio-frequency Identification and 4D CAD in construction management. Tsinghua Science and Technology, 13(SUPPL. 1), 151–157. https://doi.org/10.1016/S1007-0214(08)70142-1

Hutchins, M. J., R. Bhinge, M. K. Micali, S. L. Robinson, J. W. Sutherland and D. Dornfeld. 2015. Framework for identifying cybersecurity risks in manufacturing. Procedia Manufacturing, 1, 47–63. https://doi.org/10.1016/j.promfg.2015.09.060

Irizarry, J., E. P. Karan and F. Jalaei. 2013. Integrating BIM and GIS to improve the visual monitoring of construction supply chain management. Automation in Construction, 31, 241–254. https://doi.org/10.1016/j.autcon.2012.12.005

Jing, Q., A. V. Vasilakos, J. Wan, J. Lu and D. Qiu. 2014. Security of the Internet of Things: Perspectives and challenges. Wireless Networks, 20(8), 2481–2501. https://doi.org/10.1007/s11276-014-0761-7

Kasim, N., S. Liwan, A. Shamsuddin and R. Zainal. 2012/n.d. Improving On-Site Materials Tracking for Inventory Management in Construction Projects. Academia. Edu. Retrieved June 21, 2021, from https://www.academia.edu/download/30957027/MGT091.pdf

Khan, R., S. U. Khan, R. Zaheer and S. Khan. 2012. Future internet: The internet of things architecture, possible applications and key challenges. Proceedings - 10th International Conference on Frontiers of Information Technology, FIT 2012, 257–260. https://doi.org/10.1109/FIT.2012.53

Kim, C., H. Kim and Y. Ju. 2009. Bridge construction progress monitoring using image analysis. 2009 26th International Symposium on Automation and Robotics in Construction, ISARC 2009, 101–104. https://doi.org/10.22260/isarc2009/0023

Kumar, J. S. and D. R. Patel. 2014. A survey on internet of things: Security and privacy issues. International Journal of Computer Applications, 90(11). https://course.ccs.neu.edu/cs7680su18/resources/pxc3894454.pdf

Lee, G., J. Cho, S. Ham, T. Lee, G. Lee, S. H. Yun and H. J. Yang. 2012. A BIM- and sensor-based tower crane navigation system for blind lifts. Automation in Construction, 26, 1–10. https://doi.org/10.1016/j.autcon.2012.05.002

Li, Xichun, A. Gani, R. Salleh and O. Zakaria. 2009. The future of mobile wireless communication networks. Proceedings of the 2009 International Conference on Communication Software and Networks, ICCSN 2009, 554–557. https://doi.org/10.1109/ICCSN.2009.105

Liu, Jie, D. Wang, C. Zhang, Z. Tang, Z. Jiang, J. Liu and Y. Xiang. 2017. Reliability assessment of cyber physical distribution system. Energy Procedia, 142, 2021–2026. https://doi.org/10.1016/j.egypro.2017.12.405

Liu, Y., Y. Peng, B. Wang, S. Yao and Z. Liu. 2017. Review on cyber-physical systems. IEEE/CAA Journal of Automatica Sinica, 4(1), 27–40. https://doi.org/10.1109/JAS.2017.7510349

Loukas, G., D. Gan and T. Vuong. 2013. A review of cyber threats and defence approaches in emergency management. Future Internet, 5(2), 205–236. MDPI AG. https://doi.org/10.3390/fi5020205

Lu, T., J. Lin, L. L. Zhao, Y. Li and Y. Peng. 2015. A security architecture in cyber-physical systems: Security theories, analysis, simulation and application fields. International Journal of Security and Its Applications, 9(7), 1–16. https://doi.org/10.14257/ijsia.2015.9.7.01

Lu, T., B. Xu, X. Guo, L. Zhao and F. Xie. 2013. A New Multilevel Framework for Cyber-Physical System Security. terraswarm.org. http://www.terraswarm.org/pubs/136/lu_newmultiframe_edge.pdf

Mahmoud, R., T. Yousuf, F. Aloul and I. Zualkernan. 2016. Internet of things (IoT) security: Current status, challenges and prospective measures. 2015 10th International Conference for Internet Technology and Secured Transactions, ICITST 2015, 336–341. https://doi.org/10.1109/ICITST.2015.7412116

Marks, E. and J. Teizer. 2012. Proximity sensing and warning technology for heavy construction equipment operation. Construction Research Congress 2012: Construction Challenges in a Flat World, Proceedings of the 2012 Construction Research Congress, 981–990. https://doi.org/10.1061/9780784412329.099

Menzel, K., Z. Cong and L. Allan. 2008. Potentials for Radio Frequency Identification in AEC/FM. Tsinghua Science and Technology, 13(Suppl. 1), 329–335. https://doi.org/10.1016/S1007-0214(08)70170-6

Mo, Y. and B. Sinopoli. 2012. Integrity attacks on cyber-physical systems. HiCoNS'12 – Proceedings of the 1st ACM International Conference on High Confidence Networked Systems, 47–54. https://doi.org/10.1145/2185505.2185514

Moon, S. 2017. Application of mobile devices in remotely monitoring temporary structures during concrete placement. Procedia Engineering, 196, 128–134. https://doi.org/10.1016/j.proeng.2017.07.182

Motamedi, A. and A. Hammad. 2009. Lifecycle management of facilities components using radio frequency identification and building information model. Journal of Information Technology in Construction (ITcon), 14(18), 238-262. http://www.itcon.org/2009/18

Munir, S., J. A. Stankovic, C. J. M. Liang and S. Lin. 2013. Cyber physical system challenges for human-in-the-loop control. 8th International Workshop on Feedback Computing (Feedback Computing 13).

Ranaweera, K., J. Ruwanpura and S. Fernando. 2013. Automated real-time monitoring system to measure shift production of tunnel construction projects. Journal of Computing in Civil Engineering, 27(1), 68–77. https://doi.org/10.1061/(asce)cp.1943-5487.0000199

Saqib, A., R. W. Anwar, O. K. Hussain, M. Ahmad, M. A. Ngadi, M. M. Mohamad, Z. Malki, C. Noraini, B. A. Jnr and R. N. H. Nor. 2015. undefined. (n.d.). Cyber security for cyber physcial systems: A trust-based approach. J. Theor. Appl. Inf. Technol., 71(2), 144-152.

Sawyer. 2008. Modeling Supply Chains. https://trid.trb.org/view/859177

Shi, G. and K. Li. 2017. Signal Interference in WiFi and ZigBee Networks. Springer International Publishing. https://doi.org/10.1007/978-3-319-47806-7

Stankovic, J. A. 2014. Research directions for the internet of things. IEEE Internet of Things Journal, 1(1), 3–9. https://doi.org/10.1109/JIOT.2014.2312291

Teizer, J., T. Cheng and Y. Fang. 2013. Location tracking and data visualization technology to advance construction ironworkers' education and training in safety and productivity. Automation in Construction, 35, 53–68. https://doi.org/10.1016/j.autcon.2013.03.004

Törngren, M., R. Passerone, S. Bensalem, A. Sangiovanni-Vincentelli, J. McDermid and B. Schätz. (2015). Education and training challenges in the era of cyber-physical systems: Beyond traditional engineering. 2015 Workshop on Embedded and Cyber-Physical Systems Education, WESE 2015 – Proceedings. https://doi.org/10.1145/2832920.2832928

Wan, K. and V. Alagar. 2011. Dependable context-sensitive services in cyber physical systems. Proc. 10th IEEE Int. Conf. on Trust, Security and Privacy in Computing and

Communications, TrustCom 2011, 8th IEEE Int. Conf. on Embedded Software and Systems, ICESS 2011, 6th Int. Conf. on FCST 2011, 687–694. https://doi.org/10.1109/TrustCom.2011.88

Wang, E. K., Y. Ye, X. Xu, S. M. Yiu, L. C. K. Hui and K. P. Chow. 2010. Security issues and challenges for cyber physical system. Proceedings – 2010 IEEE/ACM International Conference on Green Computing and Communications, GreenCom 2010, 2010 IEEE/ACM International Conference on Cyber, Physical and Social Computing, CPSCom 2010, 733–738. https://doi.org/10.1109/GreenCom-CPSCom.2010.36

Wang, J. and S. Razavi. 2019. TECHNOLOGY Peer-Reviewed for Safe Construction Sites. onepetro.org. https://onepetro.org/journal-paper/ASSE-19-02-41

Wang, L. C. 2008. Enhancing construction quality inspection and management using RFID technology. Automation in Construction, 17(4), 467–479. https://doi.org/10.1016/j.autcon.2007.08.005

West, T. D. and M. Blackburn. 2017. Is Digital Thread/Digital Twin Affordable? A Systemic Assessment of the Cost of DoD's Latest Manhattan Project. Procedia Computer Science, 114, 47–56. https://doi.org/10.1016/j.procs.2017.09.003

Whiteman, M. L., P. L. Fernández-Cabán, B. M. Phillips, F. J. Masters, J. A. Bridge and J. R. Davis. 2018. Multi-objective optimal design of a building envelope and structural system using cyber-physical modeling in a wind tunnel. Frontiers in Built Environment, 4, 13. https://doi.org/10.3389/fbuil.2018.00013

Yuan, X., C. J. Anumba and M. K. Parfitt. 2016. Cyber-physical systems for temporary structure monitoring. Automation in Construction, 66, 1–14. https://doi.org/10.1016/j.autcon.2016.02.005

Zhang, B., X-X. Ma and Z. G. Qin. 2011. Security Architecture on the Trusting Internet of Things. Journal of Electronic Science and Technology, 9(4), 364. https://doi.org/10.3969/j.issn.1674-862X.2011.04.014

Zhang, C., P. Tang, N. Cooke, V. Buchanan, A. Yilmaz, S. W. St. Germain, R. L. Boring, S. Akca-Hobbins and A. Gupta. 2017. Human-centered automation for resilient nuclear power plant outage control. Automation in Construction, 82, 179–192. https://doi.org/10.1016/j.autcon.2017.05.001

Zhang, L., Q. Wang and B. Tian. 2013. Security threats and measures for the cyber-physical systems. Journal of China Universities of Posts and Telecommunications, 20(Suppl. 1), 25–29. https://doi.org/10.1016/S1005-8885(13)60254-X

Zhou, Z., Y. M. Goh and Q. Li. 2015. Overview and analysis of safety management studies in the construction industry. Safety Science, 72, 337–350. Elsevier B.V. https://doi.org/10.1016/j.ssci.2014.10.006

Internet of Things (IoT) for Construction Cyber-Physical Systems

Abdul Hannan Qureshi, Wesam Salah Alaloul and Khalid Mhmoud Alzubi

Introduction

Internet of Things (IoT) has emerged as a new advanced concept under Information Technology (IT), which in turn has gained significant importance in academia, industry, and government sectors. IoT has widely been utilised in many domains, which includes logistics, healthcare, and production. In 1999, Kelvin Ashton introduced an innovative concept related to the internet termed 'Internet of Things' (IoT) (Ashton 2009). The main concept has been devised from Radio Frequency Identification (RFID) systems, implying an integrated wireless-based communication network of various computing devices and sensors to uniquely detect objects to transmit information without or with limited human involvement over the internet (Wang et al. 2015). The basic theme of IoT revolves around connecting various things/devices, which can perform specific tasks using the internet as a platform (Al-Qaseemi et al. 2016). The IoT platform utilises internet connectivity to support all the connected devices in order to communicate via sending and receiving data, for performing certain activities forming a connected network (Gamil et al. 2020; Gubbi et al. 2013). In the IoT platform, all devices and things are connected to be utilised by anyone or controlled users, depending on a systems' configurations, established via wired or wireless built-in networks. This assembly provides an accessible linkage to all the stakeholders, easing the control and monitoring process using the internet. This whole IoT platform executes operations under four layers, i.e., physical layer, network layer, perception layer, and application layer. Each layer supports IoT operations and certain aspect of the process. The physical layer comprises hardware, which may include smart devices and other appliances. The network layer covers the communication network and elements related to network coverage. The perception layer carries the technologies, including communication devices and sensors used for data transferring and receiving. The application layer implies general themes or practices, consisting of intelligent homes, smart transport and smart cities (Kumar et al. 2016).

The introduction of IoT in the construction sector has benefited many processes linked with quality, controlling, monitoring, and reducing project costs as well as project time. Moreover, due to the accessibility to real-time data statistics, project stakeholders are able to employ in-time, and effective decision making (Dave et al. 2016, Ning and Xu 2010). This also helps in the efficient monitoring of the project and improves emergency response towards crisis management (Zhao et al. 2013). The IoT has been applied extensively in various domains linked with commercial, consumers, and infrastructure-related projects (Li and Zheng 2010, Perera et al. 2015). Although, the implementation of IoT in the construction sector has faced various hurdles due to the rigid attitude of the sector towards the adoption of new technologies, as construction projects they are complex in nature and have high risks (Alaloul et al. 2020). However, irrespective of such obstacles, IoT technologies are progressing well in the construction sector. They are being adopted in various processes linked with controlling and monitoring several project types such as offshore facilities, onshore facilities, tunneling projects, railway projects and bridges (Zhong et al. 2017). Other than that, IoT networks are also adopted to detect risks, real-time safety warnings, and observe building performance during disasters (Ding et al. 2013). A few of the highlighted applications of IoT by the researchers are as follows:

1. Indication of preventive maintenance related to site machinery, when broken via embedded sensors and systems.
2. Reducing base cost by providing a precise forecast via big data and intelligent systems.
3. Active monitoring of the projects with the help of digital data-acquisition and detection technologies.
4. IoT is helping towards improving construction management strategies by providing advanced communication networks, which helps in better cost and time management.
5. IoT is proving itself to be the best option for effective human resource management by tracking labours and related activities.
6. Project safety has been improved as hazardous places can be detected early to provide better site safety for labour.

Researchers have defined IoT as sharing similar characteristics to Cyber-Physical Systems (CPSs) (Bordel et al. 2017). In this context, IoT exemplifies the idea of various unique interacting components cooperating with their surroundings to achieve some specific goal (Atzori et al. 2010). The aforementioned IoT definition is similar to CPSs in a few aspects, i.e., connected devices to perform common goals. Technically, IoT and CPSs are different concepts consisting of an interconnected group of technologies; however, both are related in various other aspects. Researchers have defined IoT and CPSs as closely related and parallel concepts (Koubâa and Andersson 2009). This scenario has distributed the research community into four groups, and four theories circulate in this respect. The first theory defines IoT and CPSs as independent systems and concepts with different realities. Some researchers also believed that both IoT and CPSs are associated with the same scenario but exemplify a different theme. They associate IoT with a horizontal view for technologies and hardware devices for communication, creating worldwide connectivity. Whereas CPSs is associated with a vertical approach consisting of interlinked networked physical devices providing data services, control policies, and computational models (Chen et al. 2012). The second theory proposes that CPSs and IoT belong to a similar reality. Researchers supporting this concept vary in opinion; few researchers consider both terms as interchangeable as being synonyms. However, one group takes IoT as an extended concept of RFID technologies. Whereas others take CPSs and IoT as the something but also believe that CPSs is being supported by American institutes and IoT by Chinese and European scientists (Chen 2010). The third theory defines CPSs, IoT and other related terminologies as "buzzwords" for implying a future connected world. Whereas the fourth theory relates CPSs with IoT, considering CPSs as a specific scenario or new pattern of IoT (Wan et al. 2013).

The IoT is considered one of the pillars of Industry 4.0 (I4.0), and the IoT concept has also been extended as the Industrial Internet of Things (IIoT) (Campeanu 2018). The IIoT theme has been developed by considering the industrial scenarios, mostly manufacturing industries, and it contributes by providing the network of technologies between industrial devices (Akhtari et al. 2019, Assawaarayakul et al. 2019, Occhiuzzi et al. 2019). IIoT network comprises multiple industrial actuators, robots, and sensors, which are interlinked with communication devices. This whole assembly allows the system to analyse and monitor the operations, to change, collect, and deliver the information and data in an efficient way, without any difficulty. IIoT provides horizontal integration and vertical integration through the network chain, which allows the users to attain the full I4.0 theme. Horizontal integration in the systems is attained by integrating the real and virtual world across the complete value chain to provide end-to-end engineering and by supporting the business strategies of the company. Whereas vertical integration is linked with networking manufacturing systems. IIoT under I4.0 generates a convergent network of Information Technologies-Operational Technologies (IT-OT) in the industrial environment. OT and IT domains are converged by interlinking communication and computing processes, data storage, and central controls. OT are not part of integrated networks, but they are considered to be software and hardware systems that control the floor operations. However, OT elements can transmit data/information with central servers, other equipment and machines via IT network with IT-OT converging network systems. This evolution of IIoT is proving to be beneficial for industrial processes in terms of efficient decision-making, controlling operational durations, cost of resources, better performance, product services, and the emergence of new business models to expand businesses. Regardless of the innovative advantages of the IIoT theme in the industry, it is a complicated procedure requiring complex architectural network designs, finances and one of the major issues is linked with the data interoperability between systems, networks and technologies (Pivoto et al. 2021).

Key Enabling Technologies in IoT and CPSs

The significant purpose of IoT is to expedite the network connectivity among various technologies smartly. In support of this, various technologies are being utilised in improving the system's performance in the physical and virtual world. To support IoT bionics, related technologies encompasses advanced communication and perception capabilities (Lin and Cheung 2020). Moreover, various advanced sensor-based technologies have been introduced recently, with capabilities to detect movement, temperature, and light. These sensors on attaching to various equipment or devices make them capable of comprehending and communicate with the physical environment. In addition, smart connectivity between communication technologies and networks allows Big Data (BD) to be automatically collected and analysed, which enables the exchange of data, smart judgements, and reaction responses by the system (Sawhney et al. 2020). IoT and CPSs applications are supported by BD, cloud technologies, Wireless Sensor Network (WSN), and various technologies play an important part role in their progression (Wang and Wang 2018). In this respect, a brief discussion has been provided for RFID, BD, cloud technologies, WSN, and Building Information Modelling (BIM).

RFID

RFID is the detection-based technology capable of providing distinctive identification to objects by scan able attached tags. Among IoT based technologies, RFID is the earliest one (Ashton 2009, Lin and Cheung 2020). IoT operational themes work over the internet, enabling the communication among wireless data technologies and RFID generating an IoT network capable of automatically identifying objects and smart data sharing (Sarma et al. 2000). The RFID identification process utilises electromagnetic fields, which detects the RFID tags being attached to various objects as each tag stores unique electronic information (Zhu and Hou 2020). A simple RFID working assembly consists of three main elements, i.e., a coil or antenna, a transponder (RFID tag), and a decoding transceiver, as shown in Figure 4.1.

RFID operates by transmitting electromagnetic signals to the tags via antenna, which are generated by the transceiver. The tags get activated on receiving signals and share the unique ID to get recognized individually. The detection range of

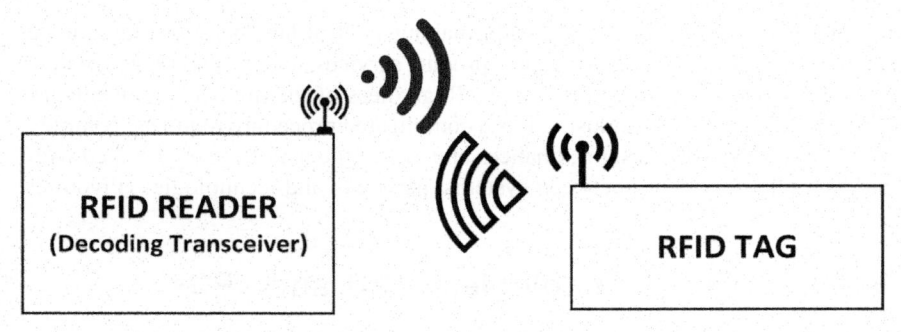

Figure 4.1: RFID Main Components

RFID varies based on designed radio frequency and power output. One of the benefits of RFID is to simultaneously detect the number of tags and process the information to the central system. However, RFID's overall operation is time-consuming, as each tag is supposed to be attached to each object to be detected (Pour Rahimian et al. 2020). Moreover, the presence of liquids and metals sometimes may disrupt the signals and output (Jaselskis and El-Misalami 2003, Xie et al. 2011).

The RFID tags are divided into two types, and each type has distinctive data storage capability. The first type is called Read-Only (RO) tags, and the second type is called Read/Write (RW) tags. RO tags lack data storage capability; they are identified by a pre-written unique ID. On the other hand, RW tags have storage capability.

RFID systems are also distributed based on frequency bands, i.e., ultra-high frequency (UHF) systems, high frequency (HF) systems, and low frequency (LF) systems (Fernández-Caramés et al. 2017). Operational specifications for frequency bands are summarised in Table 4.1.

Table 4.1: RFID frequency bands specifications

RFID Systems	Operational Frequency	Range	Remarks
LF RFID	125 kHz	10 cm	Utilised for industrial automation and identification
HF RFID	13.56 kHz	1 m	Utilised for payments and ticking
UHF RFID	860–960 MHz and 2.45 GHz	10 m	Inventory management and logistics

RFID tags are also categorised as "Passive" and "Active". One of the main differences between active and passive tags is that active tags have built-in batteries for enhanced reading range. Whereas passive tags develop electric power to get activated via an electromagnetic field generated by RFID readers (Dobrykh et al. 2021, Domdouzis et al. 2007, Karuppuswami and Reddy 2020). The electronic product codes of the RFID generate distinct IDs for objects they are attached too. This also complies with the detection requirement of IoT systems via BD. RFID technologies are being adopted in various IoT applications, including smart construction, monitoring activities, logistics, supply chain management, etc., and this technology is still evolving.

Big Data (BD)

BD defines the analytical based on large data collections. Improvements in network-based system memory and computing performance have enabled BD analytics to collect and analyse unprecedented amounts of information or data (Bhattacharya and Gupta 2021, Sam 2021). The unavailability of cloud computing may cause an intensive and huge amount of data to become ineffective; thus, a BD effective operation is very dependent on efficient cloud computing services. Cloud computing enables the users to process insignificant BD to be converted into significant data effectively and efficiently. The evolutionary development of industrialisation and IT has increased the requirement for value-added data services. Industrial computer-aided design, enterprise resource planning, industrial automation control systems, barcodes, RFID, sensors, and other related technologies are progressively rich in the heterogeneous and huge industrial data volume, which is difficult to process. To counter this issue, approaches of adding the value of data and cleaning data have been designed for integrating and extracting such data. Moreover, various Artificial Intelligence (AI)-based algorithms are applied to analyse and extract useful information. This makes BD applications providing a new paradigm towards achieving smart industrial processes and data-based services. It also allows for a processing data exchange, including the interaction of information or data among mega industrial resources. IoT and CPSs enable the management to collect a huge amount of data (BD) from physical systems for analysing. BD is pertinent to IT and non-technical systems. However, BD applications in the context of CPSs has made them more interesting due to the implications of the physical world in terms of cost, technical risks, and skills (Abdali et al. 2021, Montoya-Múnera et al. n.d.).

Cloud Computing

Nowadays, the concepts of generation of BD volumes and real-time data analyses has become popular, and new methods are required to manage such explosive growth. Such needs have emerged with cloud computing concepts being employed to manage the demands related to volume and speed calculations. Cloud computing is defined as a "large-scale distributed computing paradigm that is driven by economies of scale, in which a pool of abstracted, virtualised, dynamically scalable, managed computing power, storage, platforms, and services are delivered on-demand to external customers over the internet" (Foster et al. 2008). Also, cloud computing is referred to as a new business paradigm, which defines a computed model for supplement, consumption, and delivery for IT services over the internet (Pathaka and Palb 2015). There are three main general service models of cloud computing, i.e., Infrastructure as a Service (IaaS), Platform as a Service (PaaS), and Software as a Service (SaaS), which suggest an operational systems network in the cloud platform, required hardware resources, databases and executable environment to programme, and provide working opportunities to developers for creating, testing, deploying and executing the applications (Ren et al. 2017). The emergence of cloud computing has changed the thinking approach of IT, service providers and users. It proposes applications and business models in the forms of services to provide applications, software, platform, and infrastructure (Mell and Grance 2011). The success of cloud computing technology has inspired the industry towards the improvement of various systems related processes. Cloud computing operations implies integrated CPSs, which deliver on-demand physical and digital services by utilising optimum resources (L. Wang et al. 2014a, 2014b). Cloud computing works on creating a pool of shared resources and allowing the users to utilise them, which may be in the form of facilities, software, etc. Cloud computing may be considered as the deployment of software applications in the cyber cloud; other than virtual machines and data storage, the integrated physical cloud resources allows it to collect, adapt, and provide on-demand services over IoT based network systems (Crutcher et al. 2021, Wang et al. 2021).

Wireless Sensor Network (WSN)

The area of wireless networking and communication is gaining a lot of attention among the research community, and significant research progress has been observed in the domains of WSN (Wang and Wang 2018). WSN is considered as a major application among IoT technologies, which creates the capabilities of interaction and perception among connected devices. The main designed objective of WSN is the delivery of data collected via sensors. WSN is composed of several sensor nodes, which work in parallel to obtain information from its surroundings. Sensors communicate via wireless interfaces forming a network for data gathering and act as a base of data transfer and processing. These sensors are designed to gather information via measuring and sensing data from the surroundings, which is then transmitted to the desired user following a communication protocol based on smart decision processing. Resources availabilities impede the development and application of a comprehensive volume of data collection by making designs more complex. WSN integration with various domains empowers CPSs as a major force that controls and manages information from the physical world beyond the virtual world. ZigBee, Bluetooth, and Wi-Fi are considered common wireless network applications (Sawhney et al. 2020). WSN node comprises four main modules, i.e., power unit, transceiver unit, processing unit, and sensing unit. The power unit is responsible for the provision of operational power to the sensor node. The purpose of the transceiver unit is to transmit information to the user via radio signals. The processing unit consists of a processor and storage elements. The data is withdrawn by the processor from the storage and transfers the data to the neighbouring nodes by interpreting wireless signal packets. Whereas the sensing unit concludes two parts, the Analog-to-Digital Converters (ADC), and a sensor. The sensor accumulates information from the surrounding in the form of the analogue signal, which is later converted into a digital signal by the ADC for processing (Jassim et al. 2021, Lin and Cheung 2020). The IoT systems normally track individually operational and moving objects. Therefore, knowledge about the consumption of optimum power becomes important for WSN design. Moreover, data transmission effectiveness is related to the operational design of IoT systems; network configuration and distance between nodes affect the data transmission efficiency. The transmission distance directly impacts the power consumption of the overall network system. In case the user is far away from the sensor node, nodes based on a multiple-hop relay is established forming a network routing protocol of WSN applications and transmission distance can be increased.

Three roles are related to WSN architecture, i.e., router, coordinator, and end device. The whole assembly works so that the coordinator is accountable for data collection, coordinating, network launching, and acting as a host. The main objective of the router is to enhance WSN detection distance and coverage, which is accomplished by transferring radio signals to nearby nodes. The end device is composed of several sensors, which measures the environmental conditions and returns the collected data (Farahani 2011). Although various parameters affect the WSN performance, a few of the critical aspects to be considered in WSN systems are as follows:1) power consumption, 2) transmission channel, 3) operational environment, 4) network topology, 5) sensor hardware limitations, 6) hardware price, 7) network scalability, and 8) network fault tolerance. Among semiconductors, networks, and sensors, the WSN applications will support a more complicated IoT by becoming more diversified and deeper systems. Furthermore, WSN integrated with cloud computing and BD impacts the applications and IoT operations to infinity.

Building Information Modelling (BIM)

BIM is defined as "a digital representation of physical and functional characteristics of a facility" (NIBS 2019) and also as "a shared digital representation of physical and functional characteristics of any built object (including buildings, bridges, roads, etc.), which forms a reliable basis for decisions" (ISO 2016). BIM is recognised as a revolutionary technology of informatisation and digitalisation in the construction sector capable of integrating information into digital 3D models. BIM incorporates spatial information, construction materials, assets, databases, and models. Moreover, BIM is capable of providing energy analysis, cost estimation, progress management, and simulations. Other than the operations, and maintenance (O&M) phase, the execution phase, designing phase, and planning phase, BIM also analyses the entire project life cycle, which makes it popular in Architecture, Engineering and Construction (AEC) industry (Cerovsek 2011, Eastman et al. 2011, Sacks et al. 2018). BIM can manage labour activities, operating facilities, and various processes during the operational phase in real-time. The evolution in IoT systems and technologies has improved sensors application in developing an infrastructure able to communicate and assess the environment, highlighting the importance of BIM in the O&M stage as potential technology (Haines 2016). IoT based integrated devices share the status and locational data for objects, which can be linked with BIM models for displaying real-time and spatial relations concurrently. IoT applications are integrated with BIM based framework to analyse the management of O&M significantly. Also, BIM integrated IoT models provide support to CPSs based operations to manage their construction projects. The gathered vast amount of information creates a BD environment, providing ample information for improvement via analysing. The BIM integrated IoT environment establishes the virtual representation of project, in which information related to assets, facilities, people, and project status is provided by IoT applications. Whereas BIM establishes a framework to spatially demonstrate and systematically integrate the IoT based information. BIM combined with IoT systems establishes and an active project model with CPSs application to achieve optimal management and operations, enhancing the theme of smart construction.

Internet of Things and Services (IoTS)

The theme of IoT has been evolved to a new concept termed as "Internet of Things and Services" (IoTS). IoTS is defined as a platform supporting daily used heterogeneous smart devices and their increasing numbering under one umbrella (Hernández and Reiff-Marganiec 2014). Researchers have also defined IoTS as a combination of various technologies collectively supporting each other and not as an independent technology (Windelband et al. 2010). To understand IOTS, it is useful to understand IoT and the "Internet of Services" (IoS) as different concepts based on different operational themes. IoT is defined as the "linkage of physical objects (things) with a virtual representation on the internet or a similar structure to the internet. The automatic identification by means of RFID technology is a possible expression of the IoT; through the sensor and actuator technology the functionality can be extended by detection of status and execution of actions" (Kagermann et al. 2013). Whereas IoS is "part of the internet, which provides services and functionalities as granular, web-based software components. Service providers under IoS makes such facilities available on the internet and offers them based on actual demand. Companies can orchestrate individual software components to complex but still flexible solutions (based on service-oriented architectures)" (Bartodziej 2017). The operational theme of IoS supports the technical systems and end-users for requesting partner companies to provide business functions. In the IoS, the major part is performed as negotiation, reusability, or random combination (Glotzbach 2009).

In simple, IoTS is the supporting platform, enabling the interconnection and integration of various industrial sectors. IoTS offers innovative business opportunities by producing localised and identifiable random objects, irrespective of the interconnected things' locations (Botthof and Bovenschulte 2011). The IoTS results are considered as long-term but not entirely predictable. However, even considering the short-term prospects, many industry stakeholders and academicians are fascinated by IoTS, due to its profitable prospects (Bartodziej 2017, Fortino et al. 2014).

Application of IoT in Construction Sector

The introduction of IoT applications in the construction sector processes may prove advantageous for collecting site status, monitoring workers and equipment, and risk mitigation in case of emergency. Thus, IoT as a part of a construction project improves the management effectiveness and efficiency of processes by providing safety and a better site environment. The following are a few IoT based applications being adopted in the construction sector, as discussed below.

Safety Management

IoT technologies are progressively being adopted for safety management processes due to long-lasting operational capabilities. Construction site monitoring against expected risk factors, including loud noises, vibration, smog, and fire, is performed via installing several WSN devices in different locations. Such arrangements could prevent severe disaster. In case of any incident, the site working staff can be alerted and evacuated due to timely activation of safety devices, thus automatically eliminating the hazards. Likewise, by embedding RFID and sensors into personnel wearing gear such as a vest, helmets, etc., the location and identity of an employee or working staff can be determined. On detecting unusual situation, the IoT connected devices will alert and immediately generate auto-request for assistance. The IoT based safety management monitoring system enables the administration to get the live site status and immediate response to any occurred incident or risk factor in real-time. In the domain IoT based safety management systems, researchers are performing and evaluating various site safety models. Valero et al. (2017) offered a novel data processing framework and scheme by adopting WSN, which delivers understandable and instinctive motion-related data for site working staff considering the bricklaying activity. The designed framework was integrated with the wireless devices, such as Inertial Measurement Unit (IMU), with body area network, and assessment of working postures of body (defined under International Organization for Standardization (ISO)) were processed via robust state machine-based approach. Likewise, the study performed by Ding et al.(2013) developed an early warning safety system, which was capable of precluding site accidents and improving the safety monitoring processes for underground constructed projects in real-time, by adopted IoT technologies. This designed system was tested, verified and validated on the construction site of the project named as the Yangtze Riverbed Metro Tunnel project in China, shown in Figure 4.2.

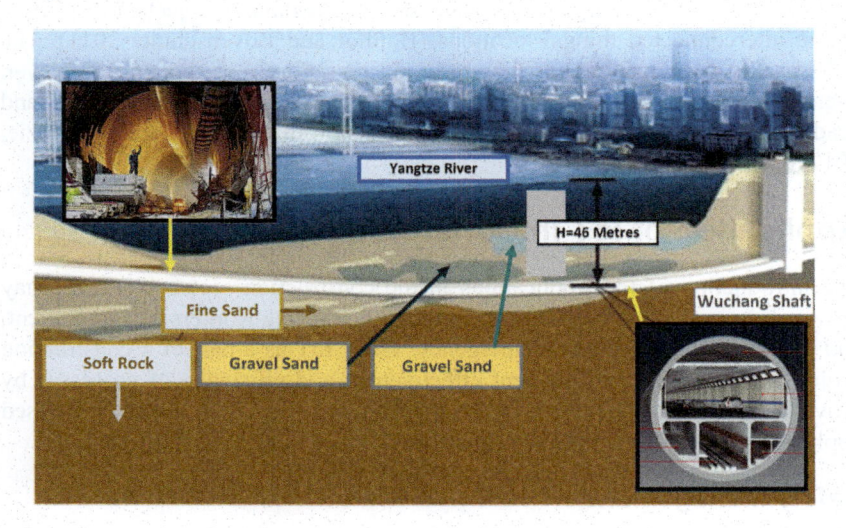

Figure 4.2: Yangtze Riverbed Metro Tunnel

Structural Health Monitoring (SHM)

The structural health of a facility is important for the safety of occupants and surroundings; the ageing of structures and materials may cause disasters and crash incidents. Therefore, the SHM for facility becomes a significant concern in structural maintenance and operations. Adopting IoT based WSN systems, various environmental and physical structural behaviours and conditions that can be inspected in real-time, such as wind speed, temperature, compressive and tensile stresses, deformation, and vibrations. Such aforementioned information can be collected via wireless network systems for data analyses. This data also assists in evaluating structural damages due to natural disasters (earthquakes, etc.) and estimating the health of a structure for its service life. This reduces the structural maintenance cost and improves overall safety. Many researchers have applied IoT based applications for SHM of building structures. Hasni et al. (2018) proposed a novel methodology for detecting damage in steel frames via adopting a hybrid network of acceleration sensors and piezoelectric strain. This numerical based study was verified on a steel-based frame with bolted connections. The apparatus was introduced to cyclic loading and damage was made by loosening the bolts and creating cracks. For acceleration and strain sensors, bimorph PZT cantilever plates and Circular Lead Zirconate Titanate (PZT) piezoelectric transducers were utilised. Using the finite element (FE) model, the acceleration and strain time histories were recorded. The obtained results indicated that strain-based accelerometers and sensors are more vulnerable to bolt loosening and cracks. Bae et al. (2013) evaluated the performance of WSN for bridge structure considering the obstructed environment. Liu et al. (2018) proposed an innovative hybrid methodology for performing global sensitivity analysis and analysing input-output relationships for structurally related safety risk factors, minimising the cognitive uncertainty in tunneling structures. The study adopted a stochastic and deterministic finite element (FE) model for analysing association between output and input factors with a high level of accuracy. The FE model simulated data helped in the construction of a meta-model, based on the "Particle Swarm Optimization- Least Square Support Vector Machine (PSO-LSSVM)" model.

Surveying, Mapping, and Security

The use of unmanned aerial vehicles (UAVs) is becoming popular, and a few of the main reasons are advanced flight control software and its affordable price. Likewise, the use of UAVs on construction sites is also increasing especially for monitoring, with real-time data collection via images or videos, of various operations for improving management practices. UAV types vary depending on models' specifications, such as multi-rotor aircraft or rotor (helicopter), and either fixed-wing (aircraft), equipped with a Global Positioning System (GPS) and high-resolution camera. UAVs can be operated by smartphones and provide great precision for measurements. Nowadays, UAV technology is relatively mature, and in the construction sector, they are mostly utilised for the following (Lin and Cheung 2020, Sawhney et al. 2020):

1. Construction progress monitoring, inspection and remote area monitoring. With the help of captured images or videos, the work progress is inspected for deficiencies and compared against as-planned progress.
2. For performing rescue operations and investigation of areas affected due to natural disasters, information can be gathered, and rescue operations can be performed efficiently without the involvement of any humans.
3. UAV technology can also be utilised for performing the measurements of vast areas efficiently. However, such UAVs require high specifications or high-resolution camera. Moreover, such information for calculating volume by generating spatial models for topographical mapping. Moreover, UAV technology can also be integrated with BIM for attainment of the aforementioned mapping.
4. One of the major aspects of using UAV technology is safety management. Field or site surveys are performed for identifying unsafe conditions, monitoring personnel activities and providing timely warnings. In case of accidents, the site location can be determined in less time for rescue actions, thus improving overall construction site safety management processes.

Supply Chain and Facilities Management

Implementing of the Fourth Industrial Revolution (IR4.0) practices in the construction projects is proving effective in terms of project costs and project timelines, which are more like a lean construction approach executing construction processes at the lowest cost and highest value. In following the lean construction approach, the implementation of effective supply chain management (SCM) is an important aspect. Conventional SCM practices are mostly manual, making the overall process less efficient, less effective, and real-time assets management is hard to maintain. However, IoT-based SCM models utilise digital technologies, such as RFID and sensors, which helps to identify stock quantity and status. RFID via scanning of RFID tags enables quick collection of information and data for materials and elements.

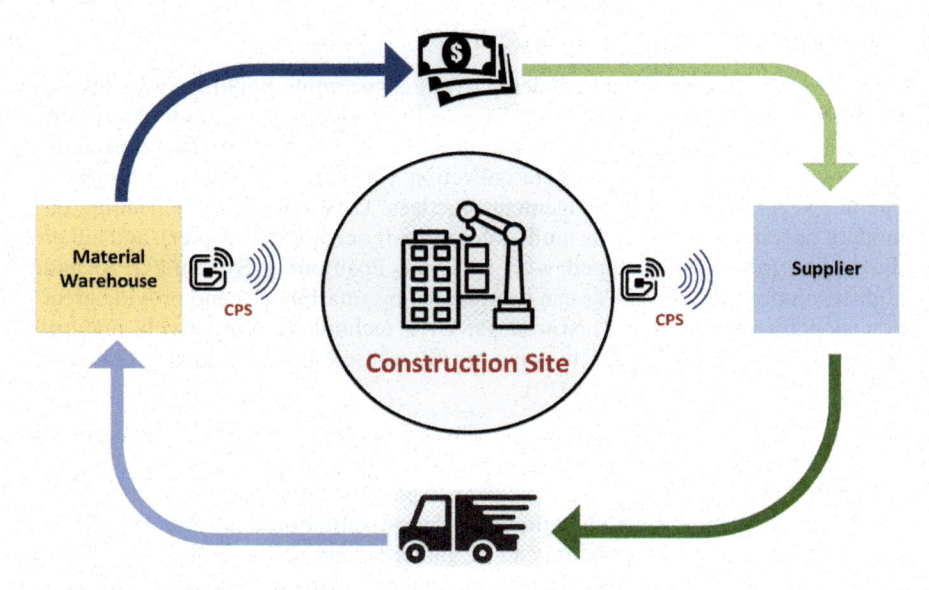

Figure 4.3: Basic Supply Chain Management Model

Moreover, SCM IoT-based systems automatically perform stock calculations, and in case of low stock, systems generate a request to purchase particular items. Sensors also play an important role by monitoring the operational conditions of machinery or equipment, inform for timely maintenance, and regulate aberrant situations. Therefore, selecting the right technology is very important for the effectiveness and efficiency of site operations (Alaloul et al. 2021). Researchers have performed various studies using IoT-based technologies proving the effectiveness of systems in SCM and lean construction processes. Ko et al. (2016) designed a cloud computing-based automated, cost-effective tracking and materials management system integrated with RFID. Xu et al. (2018) designed a cloud computed-based IoT network system to assign IoT technologies flexibly and economically. Figure 4.3 shown a basic supply chain management model for a construction site.

Summary

This chapter highlights the role of IoT in the implementation of successful IR4.0 system along with CPSs devices in the construction sector. Generally, IoT is defined as the connectivity of various things/ devices, which can perform specific tasks using the internet. However, the IoT acts like an essence for the IR4.0 network. This chapter also covers key enabling technologies in IoT and CPSs, which discusses RFID, cloud computing, WSN, BD, and BIM as few of the leading technologies benefitting from the IoT theme. The concept of IoTS has also been shared to give readers a broader picture of IoT evolution in the industry. Moreover, some of the IoT based applications in the construction sector have also been discussed, highlighting the supreme advantages gained under the IR4.0 umbrella, such as SCM, surveying and security, safety management, and SHM.

References

Abdali, T.-A. N., R. Hassan, A. H. M. Aman and Q. N. Nguyen. 2021. Fog Computing Advancement: Concept, Architecture, Applications, Advantages, and Open Issues. IEEE Access.

Akhtari, S., F. Pickhardt, D. Pau, A. Di Pietro and G. Tomarchio. 2019. Intelligent embedded load detection at the edge on Industry 4.0 Powertrains Applications. 2019 IEEE 5th International Forum on Research and Technology for Society and Industry (RTSI), 427–430. IEEE.

Al-Qaseemi, S. A., H. A. Almulhim, M. F. Almulhim and S. R. Chaudhry. 2016. IoT architecture challenges and issues: Lack of standardization. 2016 Future Technologies Conference (FTC), 731–738. IEEE.

Alaloul, W. S., M. S. Liew, N. A. W. A. Zawawi and I. B. Kennedy. 2020. Industrial Revolution 4.0 in the construction industry: Challenges and opportunities for stakeholders. Ain Shams Engineering Journal, 11(1), 225–230. https://doi.org/10.1016/j.asej.2019.08.010

Alaloul, W. S., A. H. Qureshi, M. A. Musarat and S. Saad. 2021. Evolution of close-range detection and data acquisition technologies towards automation in construction progress monitoring. Journal of Building Engineering, 43, 102877. https://doi.org/10.1016/j.jobe.2021.102877

Ashton, K. 2009. That 'internet of things' thing. RFID Journal, 22(7), 97–114.

Assawaarayakul, C., W. Srisawat, S. D. N. Ayuthaya and S. Wattanasirichaigoon. 2019. Integrate digital twin to exist production system for industry 4.0. 2019 4th Technology Innovation Management and Engineering Science International Conference (TIMES-ICON), 1–5. IEEE.

Atzori, L., A. Iera and G. Morabito. 2010. The internet of things: A survey. Computer Networks, 54(15), 2787–2805.

Bae, S.-C., W.-S. Jang and S. Woo. 2013. Prediction of WSN placement for bridge health monitoring based on material characteristics. Automation in Construction, 35, 18–27.

Bartodziej, C. J. 2017. The Concept Industry 4.0. Springer Fachmedien Wiesbaden GmbH. https://doi.org/10.1007/978-3-658-16502-4

Bhattacharya, I. and S. Gupta. 2021. A novel partitioning algorithm to process large-scale data. *In*: Proceedings of Research and Applications in Artificial Intelligence (pp. 163–171). Springer.

Bordel, B., R. Alcarria, T. Robles and D. Martín. 2017. Cyber–physical systems: Extending pervasive sensing from control theory to the Internet of Things. Pervasive and Mobile Computing, 40, 156–184. https://doi.org/10.1016/j.pmcj.2017.06.011

Botthof, A. and M. Bovenschulte. 2011. Die Autonomik als integratives Technologieparadigma. Working Paper des Instituts für Innovation und Technik in der VDI/VDE-IT …

Campeanu, G. 2018. A mapping study on microservice architectures of Internet of Things and cloud computing solutions. 2018 7th Mediterranean Conference on Embedded Computing (MECO), 1–4. IEEE.

Cerovsek, T. 2011. A review and outlook for a 'Building Information Model' (BIM): A multi-standpoint framework for technological development. Advanced Engineering Informatics, 25(2), 224–244.

Chen, D., G. Chang, D. Sun, J. Jia and X. Wang. 2012. Modeling access control for cyber-physical systems using reputation. Computers & Electrical Engineering, 38(5), 1088–1101.

Chen, G. 2010. Internet of things towards ubiquitous and mobile computing. Microsoft Research Asia Faculty Summit, Shanghai.

Crutcher, P. D., N. K. Singh and P. Tiegs. 2021. Cloud Computing. *In*: Essential Computer Science (pp. 195–224). Springer.

Dave, B., S. Kubler, K. Främling and L. Koskela. 2016. Opportunities for enhanced lean construction management using Internet of Things standards. Automation in Construction, 61, 86–97.

Ding, L. Y., C. Zhou, Q. X. Deng, H. B. Luo, X. W. Ye, Y. Q. Ni and P. Guo. 2013. Real-time safety early warning system for cross passage construction in Yangtze Riverbed Metro Tunnel based on the internet of things. Automation in Construction, 36, 25–37.

Dobrykh, D., I. Yusupov, A. Mikhailovskaya, S. Krasikov, D. Shakirova, A. Bogdanov,, … P. Ginzburg. 2021. High-permittivity ceramic tags miniaturization for long-range RFID Applications. 2021 15th European Conference on Antennas and Propagation (EuCAP), 1–4. IEEE.

Domdouzis, K., B. Kumar and C. Anumba. 2007. Radio-Frequency Identification (RFID) applications: A brief introduction. Advanced Engineering Informatics, 21(4), 350–355.

Eastman, C. M., C. Eastman, P. Teicholz, R. Sacks and K. Liston. 2011. BIM handbook: A guide to building information modeling for owners, managers, designers, engineers and contractors. John Wiley & Sons.

Farahani, S. 2011. ZigBee Wireless Networks and Transceivers. Newnes.

Fernández-Caramés, T. M., P. Fraga-Lamas, M. Suárez-Albela and L. Castedo. 2017. Reverse engineering and security evaluation of commercial tags for RFID-based IoT applications. Sensors, 17(1), 28.

Fortino, G., A. Rovella, W. Russo and C. Savaglio. 2014. On the classification of cyberphysical smart objects in the internet of things. UBICITEC, 86–94.

Foster, I., Y. Zhao, I. Raicu and S. Lu. 2008. Cloud computing and grid computing 360-degree compared. 2008 Grid Computing Environments Workshop, 1–10. IEEE.

Gamil, Y. A., M. Abdullah, I. Abd Rahman and M. M. Asad. 2020. Internet of things in construction industry revolution 4.0. Journal of Engineering, Design and Technology, 18(5), 1091–1102. https://doi.org/10.1108/JEDT-06-2019-0164

Glotzbach, U. 2009. Intelligente Objekte-klein, vernetzt, sensitiv: Eine neue Technologie verändert die Gesellschaft und fordert zur Gestaltung heraus. Springer.

Gubbi, J., R. Buyya, S. Marusic and M. Palaniswami. 2013. Internet of Things (IoT): A vision, architectural elements, and future directions. Future Generation Computer Systems, 29(7), 1645–1660.

Haines, B. 2016. Does BIM have a role in the Internet of things? Retrieved November 1, 2016.

Hasni, H., P. Jiao, A. H. Alavi, N. Lajnef and S. F. Masri. 2018. Structural health monitoring of steel frames using a network of self-powered strain and acceleration sensors: A numerical study. Automation in Construction, 85, 344–357.

Hernández, M. E. P. and S. Reiff-Marganiec. 2014. Classifying smart objects using capabilities. 2014 International Conference on Smart Computing, 309–316. IEEE.

ISO. 2016. ISO – Standards. Retrieved June 18, 2021, from https://www.iso.org/standards. html

Jaselskis, E. J. and T. El-Misalami. 2003. Implementing radio frequency identification in the construction process. Journal of Construction Engineering and Management. https://doi.org/10.1061/(ASCE)0733-9364(2003)129:6(680)

Jassim, H. F., M. A. Tawfeeq and S. M. Mahmoud. 2021. Overlapped hierarchical clusters routing protocol for improving quality of service. Telkomnika, 19(3), 705–715.

Kagermann, H., W. Wahlster and J. Helbig. 2013. Umsetzungsempfehlungen für das Zukunftsprojekt Industrie 4.0 [Implementation recommendations for the future project Industry 4.0]. Frankfurt/Main: Acatech.

Karuppuswami, S. and C. J. Reddy. 2020. RFID in packaging surveillance: Impact of simulation tools in design, coverage planning and placement of "Smart" readers along the supply chain. 2020 Antenna Measurement Techniques Association Symposium (AMTA), 1–6. IEEE.

Ko, H. S., M. Azambuja and H. F. Lee. 2016. Cloud-based materials tracking system prototype integrated with radio frequency identification tagging technology. Automation in Construction, 63, 144–154.

Koubâa, A. and B. Andersson. 2009. A vision of cyber-physical Internet. 8th International Workshop on Real-Time Networks.

Kumar, S. A., T. Vealey and H. Srivastava. 2016. Security in internet of things: Challenges, solutions and future directions. 2016 49th Hawaii International Conference on System Sciences (HICSS), 5772–5781. IEEE.

Li, L. and Y. Zheng. 2010. The application of the internet of things in education. Modern Educational Technology, 20(2), 8–10.

Lin, Y.-C. and W.-F. Cheung. 2020. Internet of Things (IoT) and internet enabled physical devices for Construction 4.0. In: Construction 4.0 (pp. 350–369). Routledge.

Liu, W., X. Wu, L. Zhang, Y. Wang and J. Teng. 2018. Sensitivity analysis of structural health risk in operational tunnels. Automation in Construction, 94, 135–153.

Mell, P. and T. Grance. 2011. The NIST Final Version of NIST Cloud Computing Definition Published. NIST Spec. Publ, 145, 7.

Montoya-Múnera, E., J. Aguilar, J. A. Monsalve-Pulido, C. Salazar, D. Varela-Tabares, M. Jiménez-Narváez and E. Montoya-Jaramillo. (n.d.). Toward the application of artificial intelligence in academic content: An autonomous recommendation system. Education 4.0: A View from Different Digital Proposals, 12.

NIBS. 2019. About the National BIM Standard-United States® | National BIM Standard – United States. Retrieved June 18, 2021, from https://www.nationalbimstandard.org/ about

Ning, H.-S. and Q. Y. Xu. 2010. Research on global internet of things' developments and it's construction in China [J]. Acta Electronica Sinica, 11, 2590–2600.

Occhiuzzi, C., S. Amendola, S. Nappi, N. D'Uva and G. Marrocco. 2019. RFID technology for industry 4.0: Architectures and challenges. 2019 IEEE International Conference on RFID Technology and Applications (RFID-TA), 181–186. IEEE.

Pathaka, P. and P. R. Palb. 2015. Cloud computing–issues research and implementations. International Journal of Advance Research in Computer Science & Management.

Perera, C., C. H. Liu and S. Jayawardena. 2015. The emerging internet of things marketplace from an industrial perspective: A survey. IEEE Transactions on Emerging Topics in Computing, 3(4), 585–598.

Pivoto, D. G. S., L. F. F. de Almeida, R. da Rosa Righi, J. J. P. C. Rodrigues, A. B. Lugli and A. M. Alberti . 2021. Cyber-physical systems architectures for industrial internet of things applications in Industry 4.0: A literature review. Journal of Manufacturing Systems, 58(PA), 176–192. https://doi.org/10.1016/j.jmsy.2020.11.017

Pour Rahimian, F., S. Seyedzadeh, S. Oliver, S. Rodriguez and N. Dawood. 2020. On-demand monitoring of construction projects through a game-like hybrid application of BIM and machine learning. Automation in Construction, 110(October 2019), 103012. https://doi.org/10.1016/j.autcon.2019.103012

Ren, L., L. Zhang, L. Wang, F. Tao and X. Chai. 2017. Cloud manufacturing: Key characteristics and applications. International Journal of Computer Integrated Manufacturing, 30(6), 501–515.

Sacks, R., C. Eastman, G. Lee and P. Teicholz. 2018. BIM Handbook: A Guide to Building Information Modeling for Owners, Designers, Engineers, Contractors, and Facility Managers. John Wiley & Sons.

Sam, M. K. 2021. Machine Learning Regression in Traffic Management Control Systems. Springer.

Sarma, S., D. L. Brock and K. Ashton. 2000. The Networked Physical World. Auto-ID Center White Paper MIT-AUTOID-WH-001.

Sawhney, A., M. Riley and J. Irizarry. 2020. Construction 4.0: An Innovation Platform for the Built Environment. Routledge.

Valero, E., A. Sivanathan, F. Bosché and M. Abdel-Wahab. 2017. Analysis of construction trade worker body motions using a wearable and wireless motion sensor network. Automation in Construction, 83, 48–55.

Wan, J., M. Chen, F. Xia, L. Di and K. Zhou. 2013. From machine-to-machine communications towards cyber-physical systems. Computer Science and Information Systems, 10(3), 1105–1128.

Wang, J., C. Xu, J. Zhang and R. Zhong. 2021. Big data analytics for intelligent manufacturing systems: A review. Journal of Manufacturing Systems. (In Press)

Wang, L., A. Mohammed and M. Onori. 2014a. Remote robotic assembly guided by 3D models linking to a real robot. CIRP Annals, 63(1), 1–4.

Wang, L., X. V. Wang, L. Gao and J. Váncza. 2014b. A cloud-based approach for WEEE remanufacturing. CIRP Annals, 63(1), 409–412.

Wang, L., M. Törngren and M. Onori. 2015. Current status and advancement of cyber-physical systems in manufacturing. Journal of Manufacturing Systems, 37, 517–527.

Wang, L. and X. V. Wang. 2018. Latest Advancement in CPS and IoT Applications. *In*: Cloud-Based Cyber-Physical Systems in Manufacturing (pp. 33–61). https://doi.org/10.1007/978-3-319-67693-7_2

Windelband, L., C. Fenzl, F. Hunecker, T. Riehle, G. Spöttl, H. Städtler and K.-D. Thoben. 2010. Qualifikationsanforderungen durch das Internet der Dinge in der Logistik. Abschlussbericht. Bremen.

Xie, H., W. Shi and R. R. A. Issa. 2011. Using RFID and real-time virtual reality simulation for optimization in steel construction. Electronic Journal of Information Technology in Construction, 16, 291–308.

Xu, G., M. Li, C.-H. Chen and Y. Wei. 2018. Cloud asset-enabled integrated IoT platform for lean prefabricated construction. Automation in Construction, 93, 123–134.

Zhao, J., X. Zheng, R. Dong and G. Shao. 2013. The planning, construction, and management toward sustainable cities in China needs the Environmental Internet of Things. International Journal of Sustainable Development & World Ecology, 20(3), 195–198.

Zhong, R. Y., Y. Peng, F. Xue, J. Fang, W. Zou, H. Luo and G. Q. Huang. 2017. Prefabricated construction enabled by the Internet-of-Things. Automation in Construction, 76, 59–70.

Zhu, H. and M. Hou. 2020. Research on the Application of RFID in Equipment Management in Universities. *In*: Recent Trends in Intelligent Computing, Communication and Devices (pp. 591–595). Springer.

Cyber-Physical Systems and Digital Twins (DT) in Construction Projects

Abdul Hannan Qureshi, Wesam Salah Alaloul and Khalid Mhmoud Alzubi

Introduction

The emergence of Industry Revolution 4.0 (IR4.0) and its integration with Information and Communication Technologies (ICT) with the manufacturing industry initiated a new era of automation. A high level of operational capabilities was achieved, including decision-making, predicting, understanding, monitoring, and adapting (Kusiak 2018, Thoben et al. 2017, Yao et al. 2019). All these aforementioned capabilities require system's working on knowledge-centric networks such as Cyber-Physical Systems (CPSs), the Industrial Internet of Things (IIoT), and the Internet of Things (IoT) (Cheng et al. 2018, Lu and Cecil 2016). The CPSs blend the virtual world with the physical world and operate on an information based knowledge-centric environment (Lee et al. 2015, Monostori et al. 2016). The physical world components are referred to as manufacturing enablers, such as robots, actuators, computing devices, sensors, machines, tools, etc., all required to execute real-world activities under IoT based infrastructure. The virtual world output dependents on the computational entities (decision-making systems, algorithms, data analytics, etc.) are linked with cloud computing storage platforms for big data, historical data, information, etc. In this concept of IR4.0, the relation of CPSs and Digital Twins (DT) has gained researchers attention. DT is defined as "a computable virtual abstraction of a segment of the real world" (Ghosh et al. 2020, Glaessgen and Stargel 2012). Under the IR4.0 theme, DT is the processing and digitisation of any targeted object. Moreover, this phenomenon is adopted in the manufacturing sector for enablers and operational activities (Ghosh et al. 2019).

The origin of the DT concept was originated from the aerospace field (Shafto et al. 2012), which later was extended to manufacturing industrial processes

(Tchana et al. 2019, Zhang et al. 2019), and currently, it has attained attention in the area of the built environment (Deng et al. 2021). Considering the IR4.0 environment, DT is classified into three types, i.e., phenomenon twin, process twin and, object twin. The phenomenon twin is the simulated abstraction of the computable manufacturing process, such as chatter vibration, surface roughness, work-piece deformation, cutting temperature, tool wear, etc. On the other hand, process twin is the simulated abstraction of a computable production plan or process such as bill of materials, planning purchase order, etc. However, object twin is the simulated abstraction of the computable facility for topological and geometrical structures of a product such as an assembly line and/or machine tool, etc. These aforementioned three types populate the CPSs for the knowledge-centric network to attain the IR4.0 related requirements. This process resulted in an evolving theme of DTs in the construction sector, and the purpose is to generate the DTs for the specific construction processes. Following this, there should be another system, termed as "digital twin adaptation system" which integrates DTs into related manufacturing processes. Thus, this initiates a flow of information, via sensor signals, between manufacturing enablers (such as, systems, devices, and activities linked with manufacturing process) and related processes with data retrieving from cloud based storage capability (such as, historic data) which are aligned to the DT construction and CPSs supported framework (Boschert and Rosen 2016, Tao et al. 2018).

The literature reveals that the information and knowledge received from cloud storage (learning data), related to manufacturing processes, manufacturing enablers (such as data describing manufacturing systems, equipment, devices, and activities), and data received from the manufacturing environment in the form of sensor signals defines the type of DT adopted. There are various themes found in the literature for implementing DT. The most adopted are semantic modelling, virtual engineering factory, virtual engineering process, set of experience knowledge structure-based virtual engineering object, decisional DNA approach, modular approach, data-driven approach, and machine learning algorithms. However, the design architecture of DT and the construction process lags critical and detailed explanations required for systems engineering (Ghosh et al. 2020).

Cyber-Physical Systems (CPSs) are realised through DT for optimisation, prediction, analysation, simulation, modelling, and visualisation (Pan and Zhang 2021). DT comprises three elements, i.e., virtual entity, physical entity, and formation of the practical loop via the data connection (Min et al. 2019). In DT, the dynamic mapping is performed in two ways. In a first way, the virtual model is simulated and optimised, with the help of learning data collected from various sources, to predict the behaviour of the related process, making it adaptable to changing environment. In the other way, inspection data is collected from the real world for analyses performed in the virtual world (Qi and Tao 2018). Moreover, for the provision of smart construction processes, researchers have included data mining, IoT, and Building Information Modelling (BIM) technologies in DT (Boje et al. 2020). Based on the working concept of BIM, digital modelling in

BIM can be taken as a start point of DT, which is enriched by the collected data of the IoT web-based integrated systems. DT synchronises and constantly exchanges information from as-designed and as-built models by making them accessible. Various Artificial Intelligence (AI) and data mining techniques are adopted to apply DT technology in processes such as the monitoring of structural health, value chain management, optimising construction scheduling and logistics, early probable problems detection, automated construction progress monitoring, and many more. The evolution in the industrialisation theme has inclined researchers towards advancement in DT related processes. Moreover, researchers are focusing on the practical implementation of DT linked with IoT based services under a cloud computing environment integrated with diverse sub-services at the city level, such as people, transportation infrastructure, utilities, and building (Lu et al. 2020). Virtual Reality (VR) technology is capable of paring with human-centered DT for modelling, monitoring, and predicting one's intellectual behaviour. In the future, this achievement will likely become the central element of infrastructure operating based on smart communication and information technologies in smart cities (Du et al. 2020).

The Digital Twin (DT) Paradigm

The need to manage and track assets towards technical innovation for the lifecycle has forced many knowledge domains into the analyses related to DT and prospects. Most of the knowledge areas which are being studied adopting BIM, as DT modelling requires enhanced detailing and accuracy, ranging from small estates to nationwide DT (Bolton et al. 2018). The concept of DT was incorporated in a university course on 'Product Lifecycle Management' in 2003 (Grieves 2014). Later, this concept evolved with the development of new technologies in related fields and recently, smart cities have been linked with this concept. Various studies relate DT as cyber-physical integration. However, with DT as no model abstraction can portray things with identical fidelity. The idea of 'System of Systems' (SoS) deals with sustainability and scalability of systems aimed at a more efficient and informed exchange of data associated with DT. Figure 5.1 shows the concept components of DT, i.e., physical components, virtual models, and connecting data (Shahinmoghadam and Motamedi 2019).

The key feature of DT is the ability to digitally replicate the original object. The ideal case scenario of DT is the maximum accuracy of the simulated reality (Batty 2018). Although this precise Virtual Reality (VR) appears to be achievable on smaller scales for mass production, the requirements differ where the infrastructures, buildings, or local districts are specified. The degree and corresponding degrees of accuracy of VR varies depending on the use and scope of simulation applications. Subsequently, the framework that adopts a DT must be compliant with these requirements. The feedback in sensor-data-based simulations depends on the sensor quality, accuracy, precision, etc. This potentially affects the required sensitivity for each job in comparison to on-site sensing. If the DT

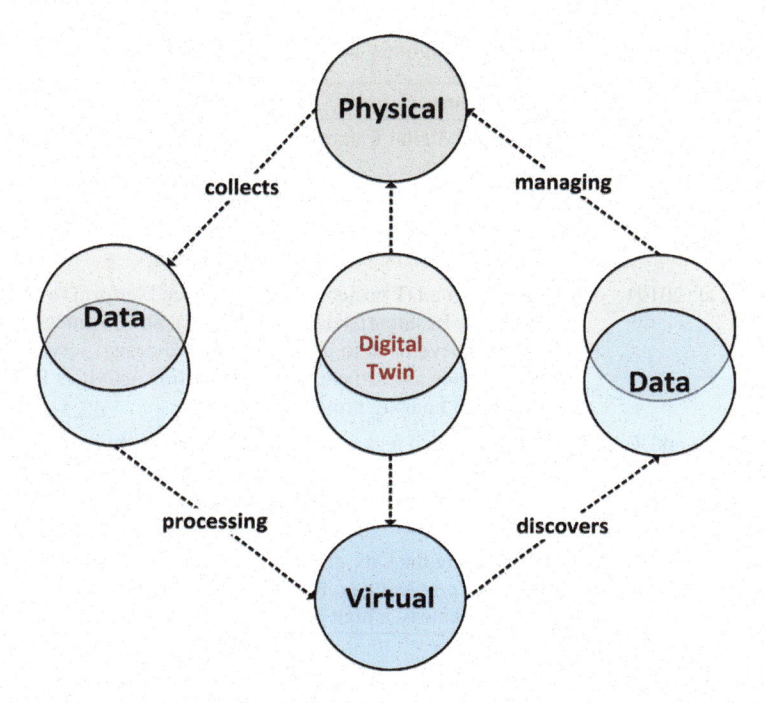

Figure 5.1: DT Conceptual Model

is to incorporate all physical twins in-depth, this establishes an optimisation challenge in terms of the efficient application of the asset in accordance with multiple objectives. The optimisation, estimation, and simulation abilities of a DT are co-dependent and work together to overcome this challenge. The decision-making process raises the issue related to the optimisation mechanism, which is dependent on the simulated prediction ("What will happen?") (Díaz et al. 2017). The operational costs and output of the Physical Twins are tending to be reduced by a universal optimisation driver. In the manufacturing sector, the smart distribution of resources ensures process optimisation (Tao et al. 2019). The design and construction process of buildings and infrastructure have a massive impact on operational expenditures over the lifecycle, thus dividing the built environment from manufacturing industries. However, in the construction sector, the optimisation targets do not always align with those in practice, and this establishes a rift across the lifecycle.

DT Conceptual Framework

Literature supports various DT conceptual prototypes or frameworks proposed by researchers in the domain of the built environment. A summary of few recent studies is illustrated in Table 5.1.

Table 5.1: Literature summary for ideal DT frameworks

Reference	Description
Qiuchen Lu et al. (2019)	UK-based digital framework was proposed on infrastructure.
Lu et al. (2020)	A systematic architecture was proposed for the West Cambridge Campus considering the dynamic of DT integrated with heterogeneous data sources.
Alonso et al.(2019)	Worked on a DT project named "Service Platform to Host and Share Residential data" (SPHERE), an ICT integrated platform developed to provide improved design services, performance assessment, and construction activities for residential housing projects.
Mohammadi and Taylor (2019)	Recommended a game based theoretical methodology designed to analyse city-scale DT. The proposed framework was developed to assimilate technology, infrastructure, and human in decision-making processes.
Schrotter and Hürzeler (2020)	Considering the City of Zurich, a DT framework was depicted, proposing numerous potential measures to evolve the DT theme to a high level.

A study performed by Deng et al. (2021) defied ladder taxonomy levels to categories and classified studies performed for BIM in the domain of the built environment. Level 1 is given to simple BIM-related studies, reviewing general BIM capabilities, i.e., a simple DT model. Level 2 is assigned to BIM supported simulations, considering the real-world applications of DT such as building energy performance evaluations, 4D construction processes, etc. Level 3 covered BIM integrated with sensors, i.e., IoT integrated technologies for real-time built environment management to monitor the precise status of ongoing activities. Level 4 described BIM integrated with AI, with higher-level applications and covering emerging research areas. Up to level 1–4, the built environment is empowered with smart feedback control based on advanced AI techniques, enabling the system to take automatic responses depending on control strategies and optimised results. Level 5 is given to ideal DT concepts in the built environment, a framework providing real-time monitoring, forecasting, and generating an automated feedback system to control the adjustment of building parameters based on the requirement. Level 5 ideal DT is termed as "next-generation DTs" (NGDTs). The expected capabilities of NGDTs for the built environment are recommended as real-time visualisation, predictive models with real-time decision making, and automated optimised system response and management approaches. Figure 5.2 illustrates the summary of aforementioned ladder taxonomy levels.

Deng et al. (2021) described varying requirements of NGDTs capabilities to support different building scales, i.e., building scale, community scale, and city scale. A summary of expected capabilities of NGDTs to support the aforementioned scales has been shared in Table 5.2.

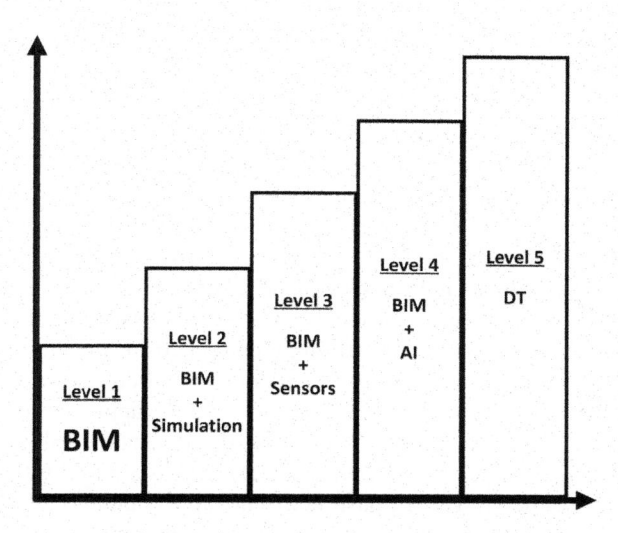

Figure 5.2: BIM-Ladder Taxonomy Levels

Table 5.2: NGDTs and building scales

Building Scales	Description
Single building scale	Real-time data collection.
	Real-time occupant's comfort prediction (such as building energy performance, thermal comfort prediction, indoor thermal flow prediction).
	Minimum participation of humans in decision making.
	BIM integrated systems with capabilities such as simulations and predictions, visualisation on the cloud, prediction models on the cloud, collection of indoor sensing data and visualisation on the cloud, outcomes feedback to support building control system.
Community scale	Effective and efficient mode of communication between various buildings.
	Effective systems for real-time data sharing and management for whole community.
	Provision of the wide variety of data source interfaces such as renewable energy systems.
City scale	Tracking the mobility of individuals.
	Adoption of smart cities theme.

Role of BIM and DT

The development of BIM has enhanced the knowledge about the built environment exchanged and stored between the project team. Digital technologies, IoT, and AI (machine learning, data analytics, etc.) influences all the fields towards advancements. Whilst the BIM concept was established to enhance the design and execution processes; it also affected the related research areas at infrastructure and buildings around the construction sector (Boje et al. 2020). In the perspective of BIM, the 4D modelling method suggests a graphical interpretation of a distinct time dimension that certifies that the BIM method can now be interpreted, portrayed and assessed in a quick way in all aspects (operation, safety concerns, graphic models, expenses, etc.). The modelling evaluation of nD BIM indicates that each level is a further element of BIM dimensions (Ghaffarian Hoseini et al. 2017). However, it was also believed that 4D is the final dimension of BIM since it is the final variable that can be assessed and taken into account in a time-space continuum. However, many professionals and researchers tend to accept the fifth dimension (5D), which involves determining project cost estimates (Vigneault et al. 2020). Nevertheless, some studies based on 5D BIM do not treat 4D BIM as the point of departure but instead limit the cost estimate approach to 3D models. Moreover, researchers have defined BIM sixth dimension (6D) for facility management, and BIM seventh dimension (7D) for sustainability (Charef et al. 2018). Current studies have demonstrated innovative domains of applications such as lean construction, health and safety, site surveillance, environmental aspects, which offer fresh approaches of examining and employing BIM nD model specifics.

Today, the introduction of BIM models has become essential in order to achieve more efficient and more collaborative practices, also seen as granting practitioners market benefit. DT and BIM improved procedures can be implemented for several construction sector activities, a few of which are considered below offered by IoT, along with data and services (Sawhney et al. 2020).

Safety Management

BIM can be implemented to plan site safety since the safety risks vary in space and time by combining numerous construction sequences and identifying potential hazards on the construction site.

Site Monitoring

BIM is often employed to track the progress on the site and effectively incorporated with numerous monitoring technologies to identify the collected data accurately and associate current digital models.

Construction Logistics

BIM can be implemented for devising a virtual system for the site layout in terms of the positioning of resources, equipment, and zones. The conception of such a system will help the planners to forecast impending concerns.

Cost Estimation and Scheduling

BIM can also be implemented for project planning (4D BIM model) and cost estimation (5D BIM model). Moreover, BIM is adept at controlling and monitoring the whole project lifecycle.

Quality Control

As part of the nD modelling procedure, quality control strategies are visualised around BIM, where the 3D information (product) is ascribed to quality checks, which are associated to a planned process.

Clash Detection

BIM 4D models can help identify clashes between activities and offer the chance to explore schedule conflicts, resources, cost dispute analysis, and site conflict analysis.

Summary

The concept of DT is progressing in the field of the civil construction industry, especially after the adoption of IR4.0. However, in the domain of the built environment, DT is still a relatively young area and lacks maturity. Researchers are working on the development theories of DTs by exploring their various capabilities under the construction environment; however, in this view, very few studies can be found. This chapter covers the concept of DT in the construction sector and DT various frameworks defined by researchers. Moreover, the role of BIM has been discussed with regards to DT technology for its effective operation capabilities under a built environment.

References

Alonso, R., M. Borras, R. H. E. M. Koppelaar, A. Lodigiani, E. Loscos and E. Yöntem. 2019. SPHERE: BIM digital twin platform. Multidisciplinary Digital Publishing Institute Proceedings, 20(1), 9.

Batty, M. 2018. Digital twins. Environment and Planning B: Urban Analytics and City Science. https://doi.org/10.1177/2399808318796416

Boje, C., A. Guerriero, S. Kubicki and Y. Rezgui. 2020. Towards a semantic construction digital twin: Directions for future research. Automation in Construction, 114, 103179.

Bolton, A., M. Enzer and J. Schooling. 2018. The Gemini Principles. University of Cambridge, UK 2018. https://doi.org/10.17863/CAM.32260

Boschert, S. and R. Rosen. 2016. Digital twin—The simulation aspect. *In*: Mechatronic Futures (pp. 59–74). Springer.

Charef, R., H. Alaka and S. Emmitt. 2018. Beyond the third dimension of BIM: A systematic review of literature and assessment of professional views. Journal of Building Engineering, 19, 242–257. https://doi.org/10.1016/j.jobe.2018.04.028

Cheng, Y., Y. Zhang, P. Ji, W. Xu, Z. Zhou and F. Tao. 2018. Cyber-physical integration for moving digital factories forward towards smart manufacturing: A survey. The International Journal of Advanced Manufacturing Technology, 97(1), 1209–1221.

Deng, M., C. C. Menassa and V. R. Kamat. 2021. From BIM to digital twins: A systematic review of the evolution of intelligent building representations in the AEC-FM industry. Journal of Information Technology in Construction, 26(November 2020), 58–83. https://doi.org/10.36680/j.itcon.2021.005

Díaz, H., L. F. Alarcón, C. Mourgues and S. García. 2017. Multidisciplinary Design Optimization through process integration in the AEC industry: Strategies and challenges. Automation in Construction. https://doi.org/10.1016/j.autcon.2016.09.007

Du, J., Q. Zhu, Y. Shi, Q. Wang, Y. Lin and D. Zhao. 2020. Cognition digital twins for personalized information systems of smart cities: Proof of concept. Journal of Management in Engineering, 36(2), 4019052.

GhaffarianHoseini, A., T. Zhang, O. Nwadigo, A. GhaffarianHoseini, N. Naismith, J. Tookey and K. Raahemifar. 2017. Application of nD BIM Integrated Knowledge-based Building Management System (BIM-IKBMS) for inspecting post-construction energy efficiency. Renewable and Sustainable Energy Reviews. https://doi.org/10.1016/j.rser.2016.12.061

Ghosh, A. K., S. U. AMM and A. Kubo. 2019. Hidden Markov model-based digital twin construction for futuristic manufacturing systems. Artificial Intelligence for Engineering Design, Analysis and Manufacturing: AI EDAM, 33(3), 317–331.

Ghosh, A. K., A. S. Ullah, A. Kubo, T. Akamatsu and D. M. D'Addona. 2020. Machining phenomenon twin construction for industry 4.0: A case of surface roughness. Journal of Manufacturing and Materials Processing, 4(1), 11. https://doi.org/10.3390/jmmp4010011

Glaessgen, E. and D. Stargel. 2012. The digital twin paradigm for future NASA and US Air Force vehicles. 53rd AIAA/ASME/ASCE/AHS/ASC Structures, Structural Dynamics and Materials Conference 20th AIAA/ASME/AHS Adaptive Structures Conference 14th AIAA, 1818.

Grieves, M. 2014. Digital Twin: Manufacturing Excellence through Virtual Factory Replication. *In*: A Whitepaper. https://doi.org/10.5281/zenodo.1493930

Kusiak, A. 2018. Smart manufacturing. International Journal of Production Research, 56(1–2), 508–517.

Lee, J., B. Bagheri and H-.A. Kao. 2015. A cyber-physical systems architecture for industry 4.0-based manufacturing systems. Manufacturing Letters, 3, 18–23.

Lu, Q., A. K. Parlikad, P. Woodall, G. Don Ranasinghe, X. Xie, Z. Liang and J. Schooling. 2020. Developing a digital twin at building and city levels: Case study of West Cambridge campus. Journal of Management in Engineering, 36(3), 5020004.

Lu, Y. and J. Cecil. 2016. An Internet of Things (IoT)-based collaborative framework for advanced manufacturing. The International Journal of Advanced Manufacturing Technology, 84(5–8), 1141–1152.

Min, Q., Y. Lu, Z. Liu, C. Su and B. Wang. 2019. Machine learning based digital twin framework for production optimization in petrochemical industry. International Journal of Information Management, 49, 502–519.

Mohammadi, N. and J. Taylor. 2019. Devising a game theoretic approach to enable smart city digital twin analytics. Proceedings of the 52nd Hawaii International Conference on System Sciences, 1995-2002. Retrieved from https://hdl.handle.net/10125/59639

Monostori, L., B. Kádár, T. Bauernhansl, S. Kondoh, S. Kumara, G. Reinhart and K. Ueda. 2016. Cyber-physical systems in manufacturing. CIRP Annals, 65(2), 621–641.

Pan, Y. and L. Zhang. 2021. Roles of artificial intelligence in construction engineering and management: A critical review and future trends. Automation in Construction, 122(December 2020), 103517. https://doi.org/10.1016/j.autcon.2020.103517

Qi, Q. and F. Tao. 2018. Digital twin and big data towards smart manufacturing and industry 4.0: 360 degree comparison. IEEE Access, 6, 3585–3593.

Qiuchen Lu, V., A. K. Parlikad, P. Woodall, G. D. Ranasinghe and J. Heaton. 2019. Developing a dynamic digital twin at a building level: Using Cambridge campus as case study. International Conference on Smart Infrastructure and Construction 2019 (ICSIC) Driving Data-Informed Decision-Making, 67–75. ICE Publishing.

Sawhney, A., M. Riley and J. Irizarry. 2020. Construction 4.0: An Innovation Platform for the Built Environment. Routledge.

Schrotter, G. and C. Hürzeler. 2020. The digital twin of the city of Zurich for urban planning. PFG – Journal of Photogrammetry, Remote Sensing and Geoinformation Science, 1–14.

Shafto, M., M. Conroy, R. Doyle, E. Glaessgen, C. Kemp, J. LeMoigne and L. Wang. 2012. Modeling, Simulation, Information Technology & Processing Roadmap. National Aeronautics and Space Administration.

Shahinmoghadam, M. and A. Motamedi. 2019. Review of BIM-centered IoT deployment: State of the art, opportunities and challenges. Proceedings of the 36th International Symposium on Automation and Robotics in Construction, ISARC 2019, (ISARC), 1268–1275. https://doi.org/10.22260/ISARC2019/0170

Tao, F., J. Cheng, Q. Qi, M. Zhang, H. Zhang and F. Sui. 2018. Digital twin-driven product design, manufacturing and service with big data. The International Journal of Advanced Manufacturing Technology, 94(9), 3563–3576.

Tao, F., H. Zhang, A. Liu and A. Y. C. Nee. 2019. Digital Twin in industry: State-of-the-art. IEEE Transactions on Industrial Informatics. https://doi.org/10.1109/TII.2018.2873186

Tchana, Y., G. Ducellier and S. Remy. 2019. Designing a unique digital twin for linear infrastructures lifecycle management. Procedia CIRP, 84, 545–549.

Thoben, K.-D., S. Wiesner and T. Wuest. 2017. "Industrie 4.0" and smart manufacturing – A review of research issues and application examples. International Journal of Automation Technology, 11(1), 4–16.

Vigneault, M. A., C. Boton, H. Y. Chong and B. Cooper-Cooke. 2020. An innovative framework of 5D BIM solutions for construction cost management: A systematic review. Archives of Computational Methods in Engineering. https://doi.org/10.1007/s11831-019-09341-z

Yao, X., J. Zhou, Y. Lin, Y. Li, H. Yu and Y. Liu. 2019. Smart manufacturing based on cyber-physical systems and beyond. Journal of Intelligent Manufacturing, 30(8), 2805–2817.

Zhang, H., L. Ma, J. Sun, H. Lin and M. Thürer. 2019. Digital twin in services and industrial product service systems: Review and analysis. Procedia CIRP, 83, 57–60.

Modelling and Simulation of Construction Cyber-Physical Systems

Syed Saad, Wesam Salah Alaloul, Kumeel Rasheed and Syed Ammad

Introduction

Cyber-Physical Systems (CPSs) in the building and construction sector is a system of interconnected physical entities such as people, sensors, materials, actuators, and the co-configured environment to monitor, and sense data, and control physical devices or processes. Intelligent building systems have evolved in complexity from simple lighting or heating to highly interconnected smart grid networks, robotics, heating, ventilation, air conditioning (HVAC) systems (heating ventilation and air conditioning), closed-circuit television (CCTV) cameras, etc. The next step is towards the greater integration of human beings (Labeodan et al. 2015). The human element will be integrated via new technologies. This includes Augmented Reality (AR) headsets for visualisation purposes, body-mounted sensor nodes for sensing health data and wearable computers with advanced natural language understanding software. With conversational interfacing with digital assistants; and remote human assistance at work. This is through telepresence technology where remote expert workers provide onsite services remotely using an AR headset. Awareness is growing that to achieve a competitive advantage, organisations need to design their buildings and infrastructures and anticipate current needs, as well as future demands on those buildings by their occupants. Living within this space provides us with convenience, but there are certain negative effects. To address these challenges, it is important to understand how changes in the architecture of a space can affect behaviour, leading to optimising sustainability objectives such as reducing energy use or increasing productivity. These changes include designing around factors like cognitive load level (the ease at which people process information), spatial memory type (the ability of an individual's brain processing systems) either short-term working memory or long-term semantic memory when remembering directions.

CPSs are hybrids of computation and physical processes. Embedded computers and networks normally track and manage the physical process with a feedback system (Lee 2008), which affects the computations of physical processes and vice versa. As a result, designing such systems necessitates an understanding of the interplay of computers, software, networks, and physical processes. When researching CPSs, some core problems that are uncommon in so-called general-purpose computing arise. For example, in general-purpose applications, the time it takes to complete a task is a performance issue rather than a correctness issue. It is not wrong to take longer to complete a job. It is simply less convenient, and therefore less desirable. The time it takes to complete a task in CPSs can be crucial to the system's proper operation. Furthermore, several things happen at the same time in CPSs, unlike in the software processes, which are profoundly rooted in sequential steps, physical processes are composed of several things happening simultaneously. Many parallel processes combine to form physical processes. The key tasks of embedded systems are to measure and monitor the dynamics of these processes by orchestrating acts that affect the processes. As a result, concurrency is built into CPSs (Lee 2007). Many of the technical difficulties in developing and analysing the embedded software derives from the need to link an inherently sequential semantics to an inherently concurrent physical environment. This chapter aims to highlight progress on an incredibly difficult and complex issue, the design of CPSs that has been made but has mostly yet to be accepted by the community at large.

Wireless CPSs Modelling

The environment control, real-time health and safety, and material transportation are all examples of where CPSs are being used in the construction industry. These systems have recently emerged as a promising method for monitoring, controlling, coordinating, and integrating the activities of physical and engineered systems through a computing and communication centre. However, integrating typically heterogeneous hardware and software facilities into the same CPSs infrastructure is currently driving intensive research and development efforts, resulting in divergent viewpoints on what constitutes a CPSs.

Concept of WSN, MANET, and M2M in CPSs

In the fast-growing fields of wireless networking, significant progress has been made over the last few decades and endorsed and adopted by the construction industry (Shi et al. 2016). Mobile Ad Hoc Networks (MANETs), Machine-to-Machine (M2M), and cellular sensor networks are all examples of CPSs connections wireless sensor networks (WSNs). Significant development has been made in the fields of M2M and WSN technology (Khanna and Kaur 2019). MANET is a self-configuring network made up of mobile devices that can travel freely and autonomously in either way. Devices that are widely used as routers to forward traffic that is incidental to their own application must have the ability to connect with other devices using interconnected protocols. The major advancements in wireless networking and embedded computing technology have helped MANET in particular (Macker and Corson 2004). WSNs have arisen as a special kind of MANET by allowing smoother communications between a network and its surrounding environment using micro-sensing MEMS (micro-electro-mechanical systems) technologies. WSNs, for example, also use spatially dispersed sensing instruments that monitor physical or environmental environments. Sensors also collaborate to accomplish targets that are beyond their individual capacities due to their limited energy and processing capabilities. With the addition of mobility to WSNs, significant resources for observing, gathering, and reporting related data on activities and areas of value have opened up. M2M is a catch-all term for any technology that allows networked machines to share data and execute activities without the need for human intervention (Graham and Marvin 2001). The described instruments must be of the common form or at least sharing a similar working capacity. Radio Frequency Identification (RFID), sensors, Wi-Fi, WiMAX, or cellular networking connections are the key components of an M2M system. They also have a computing software component for interpreting data and making decisions hosted on a remote server. M2M applications, like WSNs, have unique characteristics such as the ability to accommodate a large number of nodes, smooth domain integration, decentralised function, and self-organisation. Besides that, while M2M methods and developments are used in realistic autonomous systems, their potential for cognitive processing information, such as data fusion, distributed real-time management, and artificial neural networks, is often overlooked. Communication poses a priority for M2M technology due to the heterogeneity of devices and their mobility habits, and the massive volume of data generated. The CPSs paradigm has gained prominence as a positive path for improving object-to-object, human-to-object, and human-to-human experiences in both the virtual and physical worlds (Kiel et al. 2020). The setup of CPSs is very complex, with a near combination and synchronisation between computational and physical components. The actuator and networks of the wireless sensor are generally considered to be the originator of CPSs. Usually, CPSs use smart-enforcing sensors and actuators at various levels, including physical encounters, distributed real-time monitoring, cross-domain optimisation and data routing and security. While there are parallels in MANET, WSN, M2M, and CPSs in certain networking ways, several significant variations exist. MANET usually aims to expand infrastructure network coverage or to facilitate ad hoc communications. A WSN is designed primarily for the transportation of sensor data. In general, M2M networks are constructed to be equipment or function-specific in view of the lack of a homogeneous linked computer networks. Moreover, these technologies continue to concentrate on allowing the connectivity of machines between devices through several communication protocols. CPSs comprises of several sensor networks and the internet and several sensor data dimensions and seeks to create knowledge around these fields.

Models of Computation

Models of Computation (MoC) define the process used to carry out computations (Jantsch and Sander 2005). Making a clear boundary between computations performed in components and communication is now normal practise. Modules can be reused in a variety of ways, and device components can be plug-and-play owing to the separation. Many computations will be performed only after the completion of other computations.

Dependence graphs are often used to depict the dependence. Relation distinctions, nodded structures, access to resources, time and periodic organization are all project graphs that feature extensions of dependency for data sets. At a more granular stage, it can be helpful to differentiate amongst scheduling restrictions and coordination between computations. Edges may also represent contact, but additional details, such as the timing of communication and the quantity of information shared, will be required with each of the edges. Hierarchical graph nodes are extremely useful for avoiding periodic shifts in granularity. Nodes, for example, can represent complicated operations at a higher hierarchical level, basic components at a lower level, and independent arithmetic logic units, although on a smaller scale. Computations can seek exclusive access to a resource, such as an input/output system or a communication region in memory. During the scheduling process, information about necessary exclusive access should be considered. The graphs may provide information about exclusive access to services. Arrival dates, timelines, intervals, and completion time are all possible for tasks. This data might be beneficial to add in the graphs so that they can be displayed graphically as many calculations, especially in signal curves, which are periodic.

Computational Arrangement in Models

Computational arrangement in models can be classified into five categories, i.e. finite state machines (FSMs), von-Neumann model, discrete event model, differential equations model, data flow model and continuous-time model.

First Model Arrangement

The first arrangement is FSMs. The concept of a finite set of states, inputs, outputs, and transitions between states underpins this model (Walkinshaw et al. 2016). CFSM comprises many of these machines that are needed to communicate with one another.

Second Model Arrangement

The second arrangement is the von-Neumann model. This model is based on the execution of primitive computation sequences in sequential order (Burks et al. 1982).

Third Model Arrangement

The third arrangement is the discrete-event model. There are events in this model that have a fully ordered time stamp that indicates when the event happens. A global event queue, sorted by time, is common in discrete event simulators (Wolfe et al. 2016). This is the order in which entries from this queue are processed. The downside is that this model is based on a global concept of event queues, which makes mapping the semantic model to parallel deployments challenging.

Fourth Model Arrangement

The fourth arrangement is the differential equations model. Analogue circuits and physical structures can be modelled using differential equations. As a result, they can be used to model cyber-physical systems (Fritzson 2014).

Fifth Model Arrangement

The fifth arrangement is based on the Data Flow. The availability of data activates the potential execution of operations in the data flow model (Pop and Cohen 2013).

Sixth Model Arrangement

The sixth arrangement is the Continuous-Time Model (Brooks et al. 2008). A hybrid framework may be used to model a CPS, in which State machines, data-flow models, synchronous/reactive models, and/or DE models are used to describe physical processes. On the other hand, state machines, data-flow models, synchronous/reactive models, and/or DE models are used to characterise computations. Continuous-time simulations employ solvers that numerically estimate the solutions to differential equations but are often complex to develop.

Software Development Methodologies for CPSs

One of the key aspects to developing software for CPSs is creating high-level abstractions that ensure the modularity and testability of software design. For a single device or process, it is not enough to know what you want it to do; you also need to know how each component in that device interacts with one another. The methods in system development makes sure that the testing of software designs can be done error free and reliably using a software development process. There are two approaches which are considered important in software development, i.e., SDL and cleanroom software engineering. These approaches process paradigms that eliminates flaws before they become major problems. To verify software fitness for use, the methodology blends mathematical-based approaches of software specification, design, and correctness verification with statistical, usage-based testing.

Systems Development Methodologies

It is used by engineers who create their own tools or architecture, have little time and large teams. It is difficult to define "general" software engineering principles because these vary depending on the domain and type of application being created.

The most general principle is to follow the data because an application starts from data and ends with data. For example, a quantity estimation application starts with the stakeholder's information (the input) and displays estimated consumption projections (the output). In CPSs, there are also distributed applications where some components are on one side of the room while others are on the other side of the world. To create high-level abstractions that ensure modularity and testability in software design for CPSs, one can use Software Development Methodologies such as SDL or Cleanroom Software Engineering. The steps involved in these methodologies include:

1. Requirements analysis.
2. Designing components.
3. Coding for each component.
4. Testing each component by running it through typical scenarios or simulations with which it will be used by humans or by machines.

SDL Approach

The SDL is an approach to software development that emerged in the 1990s and has been applied to problems of all sizes, from embedded systems, internet applications through enterprise systems (AlBreiki and Mahmoud 2014). The basic idea behind SDL is that there are seven aspects that must be controlled for a successful software project: quality requirements management (QRM), security requirements management (SRM), performance requirements management (PeRM), reliability requirements management (RRM), maintainability requirements management (MRM), testability requirements management (TRM and portability requirements management (PoRM). This methodology is designed for any kind of system where safety or security concerns exist, such as medical devices or public transportation infrastructure. In that case, you need to create simulations that attempt the impossible and see what happens. One way to create these simulations is by using formal methods like model checking. Formal methods provide the ability to create mathematical descriptions of a system and then use computers to explore the properties of the system. This methodology can also provide increased security if someone's password is revealed, or an employee leaks their private information.

Cleanroom Software Engineering Approach

It was designed for industries with safety-critical systems where strict regulatory requirements exist. In this approach, you can only apply your software after it has been reviewed and approved by a team that does not know how your software will work (Prowell et al. 1999). The idea behind this approach is that if you don't know what's inside the black box (your piece of code), you cannot hurt it while testing it. CPSs have many similarities with traditional computing architectures, but they also introduce new challenges such as security, reliability and safety issues because these systems contain physical components that require design considerations like resilience against wear or ageing, which are not required in general-purpose computing systems.

Software's and Languages for CPSs Development

The language and software are what can make the CPSs different from others. There are a variety of languages to choose from for coding, e.g., C, C++, Java, Python, and LabVIEW. The choice of software will depend on the type of device you want to control or analyse in your project. Developing a CPSs is a time-consuming process it requires the use of high-level languages and software to implement the system. Some popular software for the development of a CPSs are listed below:

Differential Equations Model

One of the most challenging and intriguing aspects of this project is to combine the equations from different fields to create a realistic model. The differential equations are used to mathematically model the relationship between a system's state and its evolution over time. The most common of these models is the linear ordinary differential equation (ODE). The differential equations model for CPSs modelling can be developed following the Modelica, Simulink, and VHDL-AMS approach.

Modelica Approach

Modelica is used for engineering, analysis, design, and education. Modelica provides the features of object-oriented modelling languages such as C++ or Java but has been specialised to provide building construction models that can be analysed and predicted by simulations based on ODEs. Modelica can represent many nonlinear physical systems with a level of abstraction that is much higher than traditional programming languages (Figueiredo et al. 2021). For example, Modelica represents the dynamics of springs using an equation that only needs to contain two parameters – natural frequency and damping coefficient – while traditional modelling languages typically require six values (such as coordinates and forces) to represent a spring's motion. Modelica includes entities for components such as motors, electric circuits, switches, or servo controls majorly used in construction machines; these entities are divided into domains like electrical power electronics or mechanical systems. The standard library includes predefined entities for common devices in these domains, e.g., resistors in electric circuits or cams in mechanical systems. A domain may contain parameterised functions to describe other elements not part of the standard library, e.g., custom

Table 6.1: Software for development of CPSs

Software	Advantages	Disadvantages	Reference
MATLAB	High-level data processing, plotting commands, built-in support for graphics and sound, advanced algorithms, numerical linear algebra and eigenvalue problems.	It takes longer to execute than compiled languages, more expensive than other compilers, MATLAB compiler SDK not supported.	(Günther et al. 2000)
Simulink	Integrated set of tools for designing state-space models, generating and optimising code, documenting designs.	It is not possible to directly include real-world models. semiconductors with a lot of power, Simulink tools do not work with Simscape blocks	(Su et al. 2002)
SCADA lab	Graphical environment to design, analyse and simulate digital circuits, integrated set of tools for designing and analysing analogue circuits.	IP performance over head, Web assisted SCADA hosts users to remotely monitor, web browser security concerns	(Ralston et al. 2007)
NI lab view	Graphical environment to design, analyse and simulate control systems, parallel processing as part of language, Lowered obstacle to access for FPGA based programming.	Database communication, modern GUI development, code version portability	(Maksarov and Efimov 2018)
QUCS	Cross platform and released for Linux, Windows and Mac OS, file format is XML-based and comes with documentation, transform S parameters to Y and Z parameters.	Small number of library components, slower modeller.	(Brinson andKuznetsov 2016)
Circuit lab	Saves multiple designs, simulate the designs, easy to share designs	Poor accuracy, no interactive simulation mode, cannot import/ export to other design tools.	(Wu et al. 2017)
VISSIM	Allow models to be more extensively shared, creates target specific code for on-chip devices	Slower COM performance	(Yatskiv and Savrasovs 2021)

(Contd.)

Table 6.1: (*Contd.*)

Software	Advantages	Disadvantages	Reference
Arduino	integrated set of tools for assembling printed circuit boards, graphical environment to design, analyse, and simulate electronic circuits	Data is difficult to understand, long time is needed for testing a simulation model.	(Wheat 2011)
Lab view	Tools for designing test benches and implementing controller code, offers graphical user interface, built-in Math and signal processing functions, open connectivity with other tools such as Multisim, Excel, Mathcad, Mathematica	Familiarize its built-in functions, debugging is complex, single sourced software.	(Bitter et al. 2017)
Ptolemy II	Graphical environment to design and analyse, tools for designing models.	Slower than C++ implementation, 3 seconds to start up.	(Ptolemaeus 2014)

motors with specific performance parameters. They can be described using generic functions from another domain like electric circuits. Which use voltage-current relationships defined there without involving any calculus derivations specific to this application field, such as flux linkage equations from construction methods. Models created with it are compiled into executable code for simulation purposes, they also serve as executable results where appropriate, often based on finite-element analysis (FEA) algorithms applied via FEMLAB running on desktop computers (PCs). FEA tools offers a free FEA software package that compiles Modelica models into executables compatible with Windows platforms running Windows SP4 or newer versions operating system under either a 32-bit processor architecture or 64-bit processor architecture requirements respectively via x86 CPU architecture. In contrast to general-purpose FEA software packages like ANSYS Field Simulation & Electromagnetics products. Which only allows restricted usage after purchasing licenses from the company owning this product suite license model. The distribution method adopted by both free FIELDSOFT & FREEFEM open-source programs. Which makes it possible for students educators alike without any investment expenses involved in acquiring these general-purpose FEA toolsets, thus enabling them to "create", "simulate", and "analyse" 3D structures composed from arbitrary meshes made up of triangular faces interconnected via nodes.

Simulink Approach

Simulink is a multi-domain dynamical system modelling/simulation and analysis graphical programming environment based on MATLAB (Reyneri et al. 2000). Its main interface is a diagrammatic graphical block and a personalised collection of block libraries. It is strongly integrated with the rest of the MATLAB environment and can drive or script MATLAB. In multi-domain simulation and model-based architecture, Simulink is commonly used in automatic control and digital signal processing. Simulink is based on MATLAB and therefore has many features. It also offers a large library of pre-configured blocks for modelling specific types of systems and can be combined in a block diagram to form complex systems. Models can be simulated by running them step-by-step, or they can be run in parallel with multiple threads, where each thread represents an individual event occurring at the same time. All models contain variables such as numbers or strings representing the state of the system being modelled and changed during execution (e.g., due to user input). There are many types of Simulink variables, including scalars (single number), vectors (columns or rows), matrices (2D arrays), signals, images, strings and Boolean values. Variables have a type of information associated with them so that they know how to behave when interacting with other blocks; there are different ways to declare variable types in Simulink depending on how precise you want your model's behaviour to be. The Simulink modelling environment is divided into two main components: the MATLAB Editor and the Simulink Editor. The MATLAB Editor provides a text editor to create, save, load, and edit M-files (the executable files containing Simulink models). The interpreter will run the M-file if it contains a main function or can be used as an operator in other functions; otherwise, it must be converted to an executable model with "slm filename.slx" before being run. After opening the desired M-file in the MATLAB Editor, one can edit it with syntax highlighting and auto-completion features and execute lines of code within it. One can also create new files by selecting File > New from within the editor or by typing "edit filename" on any command-line prompt in MATLAB. The second component of Simulink is called "Simulink Editor". It contains all the blocks which are arranged hierarchically under tabs representing categories such as "Control", "Signal Processing", etc., allowing quick access to common blocks for modelling certain types of systems. Blocks are arranged from basic building blocks like constants and arithmetic operators to more complex objects. Like finite state machines or PID controllers, many different block libraries exist for modelling specific domains such as control systems engineering or image processing algorithms, among others. To create a model one selects needed blocks from these libraries according to what type of system they want to model (e.g., noise cancellation) then arranges them on their desired layout using drag-and-drop functionality on graphical interfaces resembling flowcharts without requiring any programming knowledge beyond specifying where each block should go and its input/output connections with other blocks in its local area; all connections between blocks are set automatically when they are dropped together so that there is no need for manually specifying connections between signals going into various sections of a system (e.g., different algorithms) depending on where each section should reside relative to other sections within the same model's hierarchical structure, this greatly simplifies how models behave while running because connecting each signal output coming out of one section directly back into an input connection coming into another section would cause undefined behavior during execution if changes were made after configuring some connections but not others; since inputs always connect back to outputs automatically when dropping them next to each other, this problem never arises because mathematically everything comes out equal due timing wise regardless how many steps you simulate forward/backward during execution.

VHDL-AMS

VHDL-AMS is a hardware description language derivative VHDL (IEEE standard 1076-1993). It includes the extensions of analogue and mixed signals (AMS), which describes the behaviour of analogue and mixed signals. In order to allow designers of analogue and mixed-signal systems and integrated circuits to build and use modules encapsulating high-level behavioural descriptions as well as structural descriptions of systems and elements, the VHDL-AMS standard was developed (Li et al. 2021). VHDL-AMS is an industry-standard mixed-signal modelling language. It offers continuous and event-driven simulation semantics as well as analogue, digital and analogue/digital mixed circuitry. It is near to ideal for verifying highly complex integrated analogue, mixed signals, and frequencies. The VHDL-AMS language is specified in IEEE standard 1815-2002 and is used in many popular analogue circuit simulation packages. The following list provides some of the main differences between VHDL and VHDL-AMS:

1. Unlike a pure hardware description language, such as Verilog or System Verilog, VHDL-AMS provides design engineers with a complete set of features for modelling behavioural and structural descriptions.
2. It includes high-level behavioural descriptions and structural descriptions of analogue and mixed-signal systems, which enables designers to create modules that encapsulate behaviour so that it can be reused without modification in other applications.
3. Analog and mixed-signal extensions are included, which enable modelling for very complex systems, including models for noise (interference), coupling (cross talk), nonlinearities (inherent limitations), transient response, etc.
4. Multipliers with saturation support provide the necessary engineering realism required to accurately model propagation delays due to loading effects such as capacitance mismatch.
5. Mixing of discrete and continuous models is included to enable the modelling of both digital and analogue components.
6. Support for data conversion between analogue, mixed-signal, and digital domains is included, which efficiently enables the verification of designs.
7. Communication protocols are defined for the transmission of information between functional modules.
8. The language provides support for behavioural modelling (e.g., Boolean equations).

9. Modules can be nested to facilitate hierarchical design using synthesisable designs with a hierarchy that mimics that used in the printed circuit board design process.
10. The language is extensible to accommodate future changes such as new functions, new types, etc., via the addition of user-defined nonstandard functions and packages which would not require any modifications to previously created code or modules to work correctly.
11. VHDL-AMS provides two types of diagrams: structural and behavioural diagrams (state machine) and a subset diagram capability called S&S Diagrams (Structural & State Machine).
12. Enhanced features include conditional expressions based on simulation time/ event-driven behaviour, asynchronous event handling, complex numbers & algebraic expressions, hierarchical pin connectivity diagrams with gate-level schematics downloadable into HDL editors like Xilinx ISE etc., advanced timing constructs including automatic signal sequencing & gated logic events, and event correlation.
13. There is a standard for behavioural modelling that is extensible, unlike Verilog or System Verilog, which uses procedural description.
14. The syntax includes features that are not included in other analogue circuit simulation languages such as hierarchical modules, built-in gate-level schematics editor and gated logic events.
15. Support for both digital and analogue components is included.
16. The syntax includes the ability to mix discrete and continuous models, which enables the modelling of both digital and analogue components.
17. VHDL-AMS can be automatically translated into Xilinx ISE, Synopsys Design Compiler (formerly Advanced Digital Design System or ADDS), Cadence Extraction tools or any other popular HDL design tool that supports VHDL-AMS.

Communicating Finite State Machines (CFSMs)

CFSMs are a software abstraction of finite state machines which can be used in modelling CPSs. A CFSM can express the behaviour of a computer system by defining its states and the conditions that must be satisfied for transitions between those states. The CFSM model has been shown to describe physical system behaviour well and is often considered as a mathematical model for computer-based control of physical processes. CFSMs are usually expressed using equations or tableau representations. State Chart and SDL are some approaches that are used in CPSs.

State Chart

State Charts or State Diagrams are used to provide an abstract representation of a system's actions. This action is examined and described by a sequence of events that may occur in one or more states. There are several different types of state diagrams, each with its own semantics. Each diagram normally depicts a single class of objects and tracks the various states of those objects as they move through the scheme. One of the earliest examples of a state diagram was introduced by Charles Babbage in 1871. Babbage was interested in designing an automatic loom for use by handloom weavers, and to this end, he proposed a system of wires and sliders, which cams would control. Each wire or slider had a different function; to control the machine, one had to identify the location of each part at any given time. To do this with minimal effort, Babbage developed an "analytical expression" (now called a state diagram) that showed all possible states at once rather than individually as they were changed from one event to another. A state diagram may be used to model computer hardware or software systems such as microprocessors, digital logic circuits or applications programs, respectively. State diagrams are also used in modelling biological processes such as gene expression levels under various conditions. State diagrams are typically not suitable for modelling mechanical objects like automobiles because these objects have a finite sets of states but can change between these states very quickly while retaining their physical integrity at every instant during the transition process, this kind of behaviour is best modelled using other tools like Petri nets and flowcharts instead (which both allow feedback loops). The most popular form of state diagram is called the UML Activity Diagram because it is frequently used with UML class diagrams. The unified modelling language also includes two more forms: sequence diagrams and collaboration diagrams which both share some common features with activity diagrams.

Specification and Description Language (SDL)

The SDL is a specification language for specifying and describing the actions of reactive and distributed systems clearly and concisely. Both the graphical Graphic Representation (SDL/GR) and the textual Phrase Representation (SDL/PR) are identical representations with the same underlying semantics of the SDL. Models are typically displayed in the graphical SDL/GR format, with SDL/PR being mostly used for model exchange between tools. A device is described as a collection of interconnected abstract machines that are FSM. Structure, communication, behaviour, data, and inheritance are all covered by the SDL. Partitioning the mechanism into a set of hierarchies helps to understand component actions. Gates connected by channels are used to communicate between the components. Since the channels are staggered, contact is typically asynchronous; but, once the latency is set to zero, communication becomes synchronous. The SDL is a specification language targeted at the unambiguous specification and description of the behaviour of reactive and distributed systems. The SDL provides both a graphical GR (SDL/GR) as well as a textual PR (SDL/PR), which are both equivalent representations of the same underlying semantics. Models are usually shown in the graphical SDL/GR form, and SDL/PR is mainly used for exchanging models between tools. A system is specified as a set of interconnected abstract machines which are extensions of FSM. The SDL covers five main aspects:

structure, communication, behaviour, data, and inheritance. The behaviour of components is explained by partitioning the system into a series of hierarchies. Communication between the components takes place through gates connected by channels. The channels are of delayed channel type, so communication is usually asynchronous, but when the delay is set to zero (that is, no delay) the communication becomes synchronous. It allows tools to be automated for various tasks such as: simulating execution models with SDL-Simulator or compiling it into an executable with SLD2EXE.

Data Flow Model

The Data Flow Model in CPSs includes the following terminologies:

1. Source: A device that provides data to another device in a flow.
2. Destination: A device that receives data from another device in a flow.
3. Data Storage Device: Devices which store data before transmitting them to other devices.

A source cannot provide data without being connected with at least one destination and/or at least one storage device. Data are exchanged in a certain direction, between entities of the system or with external systems. The data flow also depends on the entities of the system. For example, if an entity has no functions related to data flow, it won't be displayed in a diagram of data flows, but it still will have input and output ports. An entity can be responsible for all inputs and outputs related to one type of data flow or just one input or output port. Entities can perform specific actions related to such type (e.g. logging information). Entities that deal with inputs and outputs of different types don't display ports as they have different sets of responsibilities:

1. Inputs are processed by the entity before being transmitted to the next entity downstream.
2. Outputs are generated by this entity after having received inputs from upstream entities.
3. Control Port is used to control the entity.

Tomasulo's algorithm, Kahn Process Networks, Synchronous data flow are some approaches incorporating data flow methods.

Tomasulo's Algorithm

Tomasulo's algorithm was developed by Vincent J. Tomasulo at IBM. Tomasulo's algorithm is a key feature of the IBM System/360 Model 91 (Babbage et al. 2021). It improved the speed of floating-point operations. The key idea of Tomasulo's algorithm is that every logical operation has a "physical" meaning, which refers to one or more physical operations on the various storage units in a computer system that needs to be carried out. A significant contribution to this design was its implementation of register renaming. The goal was to enable in-order execution when it was needed and out-of-order execution for higher performance, even if this means some level of re-computation in hardware and hence an increase in hardware complexity. Tomasulo's register renaming technique gave rise to a different class of data cache called associative caches because they are used not only as a repository for values but also as part of an indexing scheme. This type of cache has since been widely adopted by industry, particularly on RISC machines and multiprocessors with shared memory architectures. Associative caches are also called content-addressable caches (CACHE). They were invented by Robert Paddon around 1976 while working at IBM Yorktown Heights during the development of their 3090 mainframe computer project that never went into production due to its high cost per instruction cycle that could be achieved at the time. They were later implemented on vector processors for scientific computing workloads by Cray Research who sold their company to Silicon Graphics Inc (SGI). After the acquisition of SGI by Rackable Systems in 2007, they became part of their Apollo brand and were deployed on their storage systems for high-performance computing.

Tomasulo's algorithm requires that all registers be allocated dynamically because they are needed for the instruction currently being executed and also may be needed by a later instruction. Therefore, it is necessary to assign each register to some reservation station, which in turn must know whether the register is "owned" by any given thread of execution. There are two main types of renaming in Tomasulo's algorithm they are as follows.

Physical Register Renaming

Physical register renaming is the process of mapping all references to registers to a physical location that includes temporary values so that a hardware instruction can access them as if they were stored in regular registers (Sima 2000). This is done by transforming the virtual instructions into physical ones, then using a table of valid addresses and an indexing system to map these virtual addresses to the corresponding physical addresses.

Virtual Register Renaming

Virtual register renaming is an algorithm that maps logical registers to physical registers based on their usage to avoid cache misses and contention between multiple cores (Sima 2000). The algorithm maintains a virtual-to-physical mapping table that records all register assignments for every instruction so that a new instructions can find the appropriate free location when it is issued. It also deals with instructions that operate on several sources (e.g., ADD AL, BL). The algorithm uses the notion of the locality to predict which register(s) are likely to be used by a new instructions so that it can immediately allocate the appropriate space for it. The idea is that if an instruction operates on two locations (e.g., AL and BL), and those two locations are close together in memory, then it is likely that this same instruction will also use nearby registers as well (e.g., AH and CH).

Instructions in a system following Tomasulo's algorithm enter at one end of the machine and exit from the other, with reservations stations for specific execution units situated between them. When an operand of instruction needs to be calculated (e.g., a simple arithmetic calculation or a memory reference), then this operand enters one or more reservation stations from which it can leave when its calculation has been completed, and it no longer needs to store this value somewhere. If there is insufficient space in any particular reservation station, then some other unused reservation station will hold on to this result until space becomes available elsewhere. Since all instructions are scheduled without regard for how much work they need to do in parallel with each other. The opportunities for overlapped computation will arise naturally as long as there is enough hardware capacity overall.

An important issue here is that every such operand needs its own set of free registers so that it can both calculate its values and continue storing them somewhere else. If there are only one set of free registers available, then some operands would always have to wait their turn before entering into calculations themselves (since they would not have access even though earlier calculations had finished). This means that ideally, all computations should occur in parallel whenever possible; while Tomasulo's algorithm ensures maximum efficiency among simultaneously executing instructions as far as possible, nothing about Tomasulo's algorithm mandates or forces maximum-efficiency use out of time on offer, a condition known among computer scientists as "perfect scheduling". This distinction has implications both technical and economical: generally speaking, competition between software developers seeking greater speed versus those looking instead towards greater programmatic complexity generally favours software developers rather than consumers; but since physical hardware resources suffer resource contention too (with corresponding issues including heat dissipation), when hardware resources are finite then economic constraints may lead decision-makers into choosing less capable but cheaper chips over more capable but costlier ones even though these decisions run counterintuitively against engineering principles on paper (similar logic applies equally well across all industries: e.g., automobiles where sometimes cheaper plastics substitute for expensive metal). In these cases, performance can never get better than linear, whereas complexity scales exponentially.

The key differences between Tomasulo's algorithm and the score boarding algorithm include:

Register Renaming

Tomasulo's algorithm uses a hardware register file to hold speculative registers. This eliminates the need for hardware speculation and hence eliminates many limitations of score boarding.

Reservation Stations

Tomasulo's algorithm employs a number of reservation stations that can hold instructions ready for execution in any given cycle. There is one instruction each per execution unit, including floating point units, load/store units, integer arithmetic/logic units (ALU), branches and miscellaneous instructions such as those dealing with memory protection or cache management. This allows maximum parallelism in execution by eliminating some limitations of the scoreboard method (e.g., only two instructions can be executed at once).

CDB bus: The Common Data Bus is an extra-wide 64-bit bus on which all values are broadcast from all computational units to any required reservation station(s) whenever needed (Gromada and Pham 1993). This allows large blocks of data to be loaded from memory into registers without stalling the pipeline waiting for access to external caches or ALUs.

Kahn Process Networks

The Kahn process network model was first introduced by Kahn in 1963. Kahn's initial intention was to show that a system of "N" linear differential equations with N state variables could be reduced to an equivalent system of only one differential equation, hence simplifying analysis for such systems (Zhang and Zhang 2006). However, demonstrating how a single equation could represent any linear dynamic system with constant coefficients quickly leads to realising that this one equation, could also serve as the basis for what would later become known as the KPN model or process network. The KPN model is a modification of the Pollaczek-Khinchin theorem. A KPN consists of a set of deterministic sequential processes communicating through FIFO channels. Processes communicate asynchronously; one process writes data to the channel while another process reads data from the channel. This communication is accomplished through a dual-rail signalling scheme where each individual signal in the rail corresponds to a single bit, and both rails are used for communication: one rail being for sending signals and the other being for receiving signals. The first (sending) signal in a rail corresponds to the leftmost bit and the last (receiving) signal in a rail corresponds to the rightmost bit. The KPN model does not include synchronisation, nor does it guarantee determinism beyond sequential ordering requirements specified by input-output relations among processes constituting the system.

Synchronous Data Flow (SDF)

Synchronous Data Flow (SDF) is a limitation on Kahn process networks in which each process knows how many tokens it can read and write in advance. It is useful for modelling digital signal processing (DSP) routines. The SDF model is a broadening of the SDN model. It can be used to simulate any network topology as well as any network protocol's behaviour. A generalisation of the SDN model is the SDF model. It can be used to simulate any network topology as well as any network protocol's behaviour. In traditional Kahn process networks, a single global clock determines when each node reads and writes. SDF allows for multiple clocks, which can be asynchronous concerning one another. Processes can access shared data at the same time but may do so in any order they want. There are no assumptions about how much data will be read or written by each process in advance, processes may read or write all their tokens, none of them, or some other number. The SDF model does not limit the topology of the network; it can be used for networks where nodes communicate via message passing as well as networks where nodes synchronously update shared memory. SDF is similar to the SDN model in that both allow processes to access shared data simultaneously, but there are a few key differences. First, an SDN assumes synchronous execution, whereas SDF does not. Second, in SDN, each process has its own separate token buffer, whereas in SDF, tokens may be written to shared memory or may not exist at all, determined by the program. Third, since there are no assumptions about how many tokens will be read or written by each process in advance in SDF, it allows for variable-length token buffers as opposed to fixed-length buffers of size N. The tradeoff for this flexibility is that there needs to be more buffering space allocated for each node if a variable number of tokens can exist per node than if nodes had fixed buffers of size N. Finally, only one clock cycle may execute an operation on a given node at any given time while with SDN there can be several clocks executing operations simultaneously on different nodes; consequently, clock skew must also be taken into account when using SDF as opposed to simply assuming every node has its own local clock and using regular (non-real time) scheduling algorithms like first come first served (FCFS).

Discrete Event (DE) Model

DE is a modelling technique for systems that consist of many activities. The elements of the system are states. In DE modelling, state changes in the system correspond to occurrences, which can be external events or internal events such as tasks. These occurrences are categorised as arrivals, departures, and instances. Arrivals and departures are external events that trigger changes in the system's state. Instances are internal events that trigger changes in the system's state. In a cyber-physical system, these elements correspond to functions or tasks with their own states: for example, transmitting data over a channel is an instance event triggered by the arrival of a message to transmit; transmitting data is an instance event triggered by the availability of free bandwidth; and when no messages can be transmitted for a certain amount of time, then waiting for this interval is also an instance event triggered by the need to transmit data again. Verilog is one of the approaches in modelling a CPSs following the DE method.

Verilog

Verilog is an electronic device modelling hardware description language (HDL) most often used to design and to verify digital loops. It is also used for the testing of analogue and mixed-signal circuits and the construction of genetic circuits (Thomas and Moorby 2008). A hierarchy of modules consists of a Verilog architecture, in which the modules communicate with other modules through a set of declared input, output, and bidirectional ports. A typical module in Verilog may contain any combination of net/variable statements, concurrent and sequential statement blocks, and instances of other modules on its internal level (sub-hierarchies). Sequential statements are placed inside a begin/end block and executed in sequential order within the block. Due to the concurrent execution of blocks, a Verilog is considered a data-flow language.

Challenges in Modelling

Models are important in the design phase in model-based design and model-driven growth. They shape the requirements for systems and represent the evolution of the system design. They allow simulation and analysis, which can lead to earlier detection of design flaws than prototyping. Under certain conditions, automated or semi-automated processes may synthesise implementations from models. However, the inherent heterogeneity and sophistication of CPSs put all current modelling languages and frameworks to the test. A CPSs model includes models of physical processes as well as applications, computing platforms, and networks. Sensors, actuators, physical mechanics, computation, machine scheduling, and networks of contention and communication delays are all part of the feedback loop between physical processes and computations. Modelling such systems with acceptable fidelity is difficult because it necessitates the inclusion of control engineering, software engineering, sensor networks, and so on. Furthermore, the models usually include many heterogeneous components. Although these challenges are quite diverse for understanding, these are staged into six categories as follows.

Models with Solver Dependent and Determinant Behaviour

Physical processes are expressed as continuous-time models of dynamics, while computations are defined using state machines, data-flow models, synchronous/reactive models, and/or DE models in a CPS. Solvers that numerically approximate the solutions to differential equations are used in continuous-time models. The art of designing such solvers is well-established but far from easy. Integrating such solvers with discrete models is a newer challenge, and many existing tools have issues. One issue that may emerge is that even though the underlying structure being modelled is determinate, the action described by the model can be non-determinate. This implies that rather than defining a particular trait, the model describes a set of behaviours. This can happen when DEs are running at the same time, and the modelling language's semantics fail to define a particular action. Non-determinism like this will catch system designers off guard. Another issue is that numerical solver normally dynamically changes the step size they use to increment time, and the model's actions can be influenced by the step sizes chosen.

Designers, who barely have insight into the rationale for step-size selection, will be surprised once again. The next issue that can emerge is Zeno Behaviour, which occurs when an infinite number of events occur in a finite time interval. Zeno Behaviour can emerge as an artefact of simulation, but it can also reflect physical phenomena like chattering.

Component Consistency in a Model

Although a hypothesised model built in a virtual setting is initially useful, such test scenario models are often lost in operation. When they become more sophisticated and practical, the simplistic regression test becomes obsolete. There is no guarantee that the prototype model and the final design will fit if the model is left as a regression test. The final version would almost certainly be based on a replica of the test model, which will invariably differ from the test model. Worse, even though code generators are used to synthesise software from models, the software will always develop independently of the model, raising divergence. When a simple model transforms into a complex one, the same dilemma occurs since a single component in the simple model becomes several components in the complex one. How do we ensure that the various components develop in lockstep? Let's assume there's just one water tank, but in fact, a building could have multiple water tanks, and water must be exchanged between them, which necessitates consistent component evolution over time.

Un-linked Model Components

The more complex a model gets, the more difficult it is to verify that the relations between elements are right. The likelihood of errors increases as model elements are strongly intertwined. Unit errors, textual errors, and transposition errors are the three most frequent types of errors. When a port sends data in units other than those required by the receiving port, unit errors occur. The water level in litres is given by the output port, while the input port expects a value in gallons. A different water-tank level is given to a port that expects a full tank level is considered a semantic mistake. When relations are switched, such as when the water motor input flow and a tank level are reversed, a transposition error occurs. A type system does not notice any of these errors.

Model Interactions

Most of the models are based on assumptions and therefore overlook implementation specifics like the underlying mechanism and communication networks. These simulations inherently presume that data is measured and distributed in zero time, so device behaviour is unaffected by machine and network dynamics. Computation and collaboration, on the other hand, require time. It is arguable that modelling the dynamics of software and networks is needed to test a CPSs model. Implementation is entirely unrelated to implementation and, as a result, cannot be used in a functional model. Instead, a functional model and an application model should be able to work together. The latter allows for the discovery of design space, while the former aids in the development of control strategies. Interactions between these domains can be evaluated using the conjoined models.

Apportioned Models

Since CPSs is distributed, it necessitates methods that make it easier to combine components that are isolated. Modelling distributed systems adds to the challenge of modelling CPSs by adding problems including time differences, network delays, imperfect connectivity, the accuracy of machine state perspectives, and apportioned agreement.

System Diversity

The inherent heterogeneity and ambiguity of CPSs run across many of the above difficulties. CPSs, by contrast, combines various subsystems. These subsystems also use domain-specific simulation techniques, which can be very complex. Incorporating the resulting models to create comprehensive framework views becomes exceptionally hard.

Summary

Modelling is a vital part of problem-solving and managing a construction enterprise in the development of CPSs. Problem-solving and asset ownership imply that a model or a simulation can predict predictions about possible outcomes in performance, reliability, and sustainability. To be able to use Modeling or Simulation to improve construction CPSs, building science knowledge and information regarding the real systems should be known. Hence, building simulation is a vital part of the toolbox for asset ownership modelling, asset management, decision-making, and problem-solving. A simulation model is a vital tool for policymakers to predict the performance of the future Integrated Infrastructure Systems. This prediction is vital to possible actions, efficient public spending, and future sustainable development of the built environment. The key point of this chapter is that the future works on construction analysis and decision-making will depend on which types of models and simulation, whether built into, advisory or the product, will be used to facilitate the decision-making changes. Important things that will drive the future of modelling and simulation in construction are predictive models as fully automated online platforms and the growing capability of the modelling and simulation toolbox. More importantly, good design and model-building benefits from open-source development ideas, comparative tests, and user-centric techniques using a deeper understanding of modelling and simulation software's for CPSs.

References

AlBreiki, H. H. and Q. H. Mahmoud. 2014. Evaluation of static analysis tools for software security. 2014 10th International Conference on Innovations in Information Technology (IIT), 93–98.

Babbage, C., M.-G. H. P., Babbage, P. E. Y. Ludgate, L. T. Quevedo and L. Couffignal. 2021. Analytical Engines (pp. 7–123). https://doi.org/10.1007/978-3-642-96145-8_2

Bitter, R., T. Mohiuddin and M. Nawrocki. 2017. LabVIEW: Advanced Programming Techniques. CRC Press.

Brinson, M. and V. Kuznetsov. 2016. Qucs-0.0. 19S: A new open-source circuit simulator and its application for hardware design. 2016 International Siberian Conference on Control and Communications (SIBCON), 1–5.

Brooks, C., E. A. Lee, X. Liu, S. Neuendorffer, Y. Zhao, H. Zheng, S. S. Bhattacharyya, E. Cheong, I. I. Davis and M. Goel. 2008. Heterogeneous concurrent modeling and design in Java (Vol. 1: Introduction to Ptolemy II). California Univ. Berkeley, Dept. of Electrical Engineering and Computer Science.

Burks, A. W., H. H. Goldstine and J. Von Neumann. 1982. Preliminary discussion of the logical design of an electronic computing instrument. *In*: The Origins of Digital Computers (pp. 399–413). Springer.

Figueiredo, J., C. Vítor, J. Machado, F. Soares and V. Carvalho. 2021. Modelica Modeling Language as a Tool on Control Engineering Education: Simulation of a Two-Tank System. 6–11. https://doi.org/10.1109/tale.2014.7062602

Fritzson, P. 2014. Principles of Object-oriented Modeling and Simulation with Modelica 3.3: A Cyber-physical Approach. John Wiley & Sons.

Graham, S. and S. Marvin. 2001. Splintering urbanism: Networked infrastructures, technological mobilities and the urban condition. Psychology Press.

Gromada, J. and T. Pham.1993. Selection and demonstration of a common data bus monitor and analysis system. [1993 Proceedings] AIAA/IEEE Digital Avionics Systems Conference, 368–374.

Günther, U. L., C. Ludwig and H. Rüterjans. 2000. NMRLAB—Advanced NMR data processing in Matlab. Journal of Magnetic Resonance, 145(2), 201–208.

Jantsch, A. and I. Sander. 2005. Models of computation and languages for embedded system design. IEE Proceedings – Computers and Digital Techniques, 152(2), 114–129.

Khanna, A. and S. Kaur. 2019. Evolution of Internet of Things (IoT) and its significant impact in the field of precision agriculture. Computers and Electronics in Agriculture, 157, 218–231.

Kiel, D., J. M. Müller, C. Arnold and K.-I. Voigt. 2020. Sustainable industrial value creation: Benefits and challenges of industry 4.0. *In*: Digital Disruptive Innovation (pp. 231–270). World Scientific.

Labeodan, T., K. Aduda, G. Boxem and W. Zeiler. 2015. On the application of multi-agent systems in buildings for improved building operations, performance and smart grid interaction – A survey. Renewable and Sustainable Energy Reviews, 50, 1405–1414.

Lee, E. A. 2007. Computing foundations and practice for cyber-physical systems: A preliminary report. University of California, Berkeley, Tech. Rep. UCB/EECS-2007-72, 21.

Lee, E. A. 2008. Cyber physical systems: Design challenges. 2008 11th IEEE International Symposium on Object and Component-oriented Real-time Distributed Computing (ISORC), 363–369.

Li, H., C. Miao and X. Du. 2021. Radio frequency identification design and simulation using the VHDL-AMS language. 73. https://doi.org/10.1049/cp:20061238

Macker, J. P. and M. S. Corson. 2004. Mobile ad hoc networks (MANETs): Routing technology for dynamic wireless networking. Mobile Ad Hoc Networking, 9, 255–273.

Maksarov, V. V and A. E. Efimov. 2018. Simulation modeling of dynamic characteristics of machining in NI LabView software environment to improve processing technique of a rod component. IOP Conference Series: Earth and Environmental Science, 194(2), 22021.

Pop, A. and A. Cohen. 2013. Openstream: Expressiveness and data-flow compilation of openmp streaming programs. ACM Transactions on Architecture and Code Optimization (TACO), 9(4), 1–25.

Prowell, S. J., C. J. Trammell, R. C. Linger and J. H. Poore. 1999. Cleanroom Software Engineering: Technology and Process. Pearson Education.

Ptolemaeus, C. 2014. System design, modeling, and simulation: Using Ptolemy II (Vol. 1). Ptolemy.org Berkeley.

Ralston, P. A. S., J. H. Graham and J. L. Hieb. 2007. Cyber security risk assessment for SCADA and DCS networks. ISA Transactions, 46(4), 583–594.

Reyneri, L. M., M. Chiaberge, L. Lavagno, B. Pino and E. Miranda. 2000. Simulink-based HW/SW codesign of embedded neuro-fuzzy systems. International Journal of Neural Systems, 10(3), 211–226. https://doi.org/10.1142/s0129065700000193

Shi, Q., X. Ding, J. Zuo and G. Zillante. 2016. Mobile Internet based construction supply chain management: A critical review. Automation in Construction, 72, 143–154.

Sima, D. 2000. The design space of register renaming techniques. IEEE Micro, 20(5), 70–83.

Su, J.-H., J.-J. Chen and D.-S. Wu. 2002. Learning feedback controller design of switching converters via MATLAB/SIMULINK. IEEE Transactions on Education, 45(4), 307–315.

Thomas, D. and P. Moorby. 2008. The Verilog® Hardware Description Language. Springer Science & Business Media.

Walkinshaw, N., R. Taylor and J. Derrick. 2016. Inferring extended finite state machine models from software executions. Empirical Software Engineering, 21(3), 811–853.

Wheat, D. 2011. Arduino software. In: Arduino Internals (pp. 89–97). Springer.

Wolfe, N., C. D. Carothers, M. Mubarak, R. Ross and P. Carns. 2016. Modeling a million-node slim fly network using parallel discrete-event simulation. Proceedings of the 2016 ACM SIGSIM Conference on Principles of Advanced Discrete Simulation, 189–199.

Wu, T.-Y., B. Wang, J.-Y. Lee, H.-P. Shen, Y.-C. Wu, Y.-A. Chen, P.-S. Ku, M.-W. Hsu, Y.-C. Lin and M.Y. Chen. 2017. CircuitSense: Automatic sensing of physical circuits and generation of virtual circuits to support software tools. Proceedings of the 30th Annual ACM Symposium on User Interface Software and Technology, 311–319.

Yatskiv, I. and M. Savrasovs. 2021. Microscopic transport model animation visualisation on KML base. 3003. https://doi.org/10.1051/3u3d/201203003

Zhang, W. and X. Zhang. 2006. Modeling service interactions using Kahn process network. 2006 Seventh International Conference on Parallel and Distributed Computing, Applications and Technologies (PDCAT'06), 203–208.

Role of Cyber-Physical Systems in Smart Cities

Syed Saad, Wesam Salah Alaloul and Syed Ammad

Introduction

A smart city is a place where the use of digital technology in the built environment enables more livable, efficient, and sustainable cities (Toli and Murtagh 2020). A smart city may use technology to implement its goals for increased efficiency, economic development, sustainability, and equality. Smart cities can be exemplified by features such as self-driving cars, smart grids, Internet of Things (IoT) devices, and systems that reduce public transportation costs and make it easier for people to commute. These technologies have the potential to increase the efficiency of transport networks by reducing traffic congestion and travel times (Haque et al. 2013). A Smart city could also monitor its own energy use in real-time and dispatch technicians when problems arise (Solanas et al. 2014). It may also leverage data analysis, for example, through machine learning, to optimise energy production and consumption (Haque et al. 2013, Solanas et al. 2014). Cities have long been the hubs of industry, commerce, innovation, and culture.

In the United States, a major study funded by the Department of Transportation and published in September 2013 found that "Big Data" could enable the creation of 100 smart cities, with an average GDP growth rate of 0.5% (Pramanik et al. 2017). In China, a 2015 white paper by China's Ministry of Industry and Information Technology said its goal is to develop 100 smart cities by 2020 (Hu and Zheng 2020). Cities generate more than 70% of global GDP (Hu and Zheng 2020). Smart cities will leverage technology to drive social and economic development by improving the quality of life for their residents while reducing carbon emissions through sustainable management practices that protect natural resources. They will become home to digital innovation networks that produce new sources of wealth and foster socio-economic transformation by mobilising knowledge-based economic activities while tackling some of the most pressing challenges that cities face. Smart cities use digital technology to increase public safety, provide vital data for smart decision-making, and improve the quality of life. They will be economically competitive, environmentally sustainable, and socially inclusive. In a nutshell, smart cities are all about improving the quality of life by using technology to make the most of urban environments. From clean water and efficient transportation to improved education and better health, smart cities are addressing both challenges and opportunities for citizens in the digital age (Silva et al. 2018). By implementing smart technologies in our everyday lives, we can lead more sustainable lifestyles and maintain livable environments. Technology has the power to transform the way we work, how we commute, what our homes look like and how we learn. An intelligent city is designed to provide a safe, healthy and secure living environment for its citizens. As such, the technologies implemented will have a huge impact on the way people live and work. For example, many new homes are now built with electrical wiring that can sense when something goes wrong, or an object passes in front of a circuit breaker. That way, the power can be automatically cut off to prevent a potentially hazardous event.

Characteristics of Smart vs Traditional Cities

A smart city is typically equipped with large-scale embedded computing, enhanced data management, and significant networking (Gharaibeh et al. 2017). This creates a more livable environment that conserves resources and reduces pollutants in the air. A smart city usually includes advanced features like a smart grid, street lighting, transportation systems, and buildings sensors in the public domain. Smart cities are also designed to minimise congestion and delays for travellers by using data collected from public security cameras and predictive analytics. Whereas traditional cities typically focus on allocating resources in an efficient way that does not require technology. They are often constructed to resemble a geographical map with residential, commercial, and industrial zones. A key goal of a smart city is to make any task easier on the city's residents and thereby lessen their negative effects on the environment. A traditional city has typically aimed to do the opposite by moving tasks away from citizens as much as possible. Yet, even those living in traditional cities have found solutions for reducing greenhouse gasses and overall pollution, such as installing solar panels on public housing or providing more green space for public use. A traditional city usually does not provide the variety of public amenities that citizens need for their daily living (Miao 2003). While smart cities take care of water service requirements, recycling needs, garbage coordination, and electricity supply. Some salient characteristics of a traditional city include the following: open and heterogeneous architecture, barriers to vehicular traffic, significant public commuting or transit use, weak or absent borders between outside and inside areas, wide-ranging migration patterns, limitations on cars to slower speeds and pedestrian-highest land use, improvisation, and functional shortfalls create additional opportunities.

Some salient characteristics of a Smart city include the following: improves quality of life for residents, production of less carbon, efficient energy consumption, recycling water for maximum use of water resources, production of as much energy as it consumes, protecting social equality, resourceful and efficient use of materials and land, slow population growth, strong educational system, innovating future technology, better use of municipal space, planning for efficient use of resources, responsible infrastructure, and a sustainable future for future generations.

Smart Cities Perspectives

Economic Perspective

Economically, smart cities allow for more efficiency in the irrigation systems which means a decrease in water usage (Mohanty et al. 2016). It also means a better ability to reduce energy costs in the building, which lets more money go back into the economy. A smart city employs information and communication technology (ICT) to boost operational efficiency and productivity, it shares data with the public, and improves public offices and citizen welfare. The six pillars of smart city categorization are smart economy, smart environment, smart technology, smart lifestyle, smart people and smart government (Schipper and Silvius 2018). Table 7.1 below shows the components that these pillars hold.

Table 7.1: Components of smart city (Mardacany 2014, Schipper and Silvius 2018)

Pillars	Components
Smart economy	High growth rate, efficient finance system, high GDP, large investments,
Smart environment	Low pollution, environment protection, pleasant nature, sustainable nature management.
Smart technology	Inter connectivity infrastructure, advanced ICT infrastructure, green energy resources
Smart lifestyle	Quality of life, good health conditions, educational institutes, personal safety.
Smart people	Smart labor force, creativity, open-mindedness, high literacy level.
Smart governance	Entrepreneurship, sustainable banking, high productivity.

Having smart technology that includes street-level mapping software on smartphones, means that pedestrians in cities will now be able to find green spaces near them at any time (Green 2019). The city will also benefit from increased traffic and economic prosperity, these technological aspects help with an easier flow-of-traffic management, pedestrian safety, and inventory monitoring which stimulates business investments.

The economic system acts as an important component of smart cities in two ways. Firstly, every day the changing needs of people are prompting improvements to a city's labour market. As industries change and grow, migration to the city from surrounding areas is correspondingly on the rise (Henderson 2005). Secondly, close ties between smart technology infrastructure and higher income levels in many cities have created hubs for innovation that feed specialised companies and manufacturing outfits with local innovators that seek advanced resources (Komninos 2008). Access to those resources has opened up the development of a new middle class in these cities.

Social Perspective

People, in general, have mixed opinions on the implementation of smart cities around the world; some believe that it will lead to dependence on technology and increased urban poverty, while others see it as an essential part of society's future (Albino et al. 2015, Newman and Kenworthy 1999, Nikitas et al. 2017). Here are some advantages, people will be safer, cleaner, more energy-efficient, like improved traffic infrastructure and recycling programs that make city life easier to live in. On the other hand, with this type of technology, people will need to endure a high level of surveillance as time goes on to provide constant improvements and accuracy.

Perspective of Problem View

Many developing countries have a major problem because 80% of cities are not smart simply because the technology does not exist to create one (Hollands 2008). This technology demand can create new technological advances and jobs in the following sectors: transportation, power grid, sewage control, water infrastructure, home automation, and municipal buildings, areas where an influx of capital is sorely needed. Many people who work with smart city programs face a problem when fitting all citizens into socio-cyber physics (De et al. 2017). For example, some people are wealthier and own expensive homes and appliances, while others do not have access to this type of information at all. There is also the sense of loss in having a conversation with their spouse as they are on opposite sides of town, so they will have to find things that both enjoy talking about.

Security Perspective

Technology that deals with smart cities not only provides a better quality of life for an individual, but it also means more security. This is because surveillance camera footage, open educational data, and "intent sensing" technology enable a faster response to natural disasters and are quicker at identifying threats. Currently, sensors collect information on criminal activity and behaviour of individuals near an area that alerts the police when there is evidence for suspicion (Brayne

2017). Another threat that smart cities deal with people who try to commit crimes using social media sites since they have facial-recognition technology on these platforms which can compare photos to its database in order to identify criminals or those who are wanted for a crime (Abdullah et al. 2017).

Classification of Smart Cities

Universal Smart City

The universal smart city functions collectively to monitor, manage, and interact with its occupants in an efficient manner (Saba et al. 2020). These cities deploy the use of different virtual devices like video cameras, kiosks, or touch screens in public areas for improved infrastructure and for living quality to improve citizen satisfaction and set standards for others to follow. Universal smart cities provide convenience for professionals who take care of energy policies, water management, and medical treatments resulting in a globally sustainable future. Universal smart cities usually incorporate infrastructure type C in their smart city classification. One of the most popular Urban Planning Instruments is Integrated Solid Waste Management Plans that significantly decrease environmental degradation and promote long-term resource conservation efforts. Furthermore, they provide citizens with efficient water and energy management to manage the treatment, storage, distribution, and transportation of these resources.

Environmentally Friendly Smart City

Environmentally friendly smart cities actively try to reduce their carbon footprint by adopting green construction techniques and infrastructure (Lee et al. 2014). These cities use their technology to focus on other matters that affect our environment, like pollution, natural disasters, and smart city tech, to accommodate these issues. Having a system in place for reducing these environmental damages is good for the environment and promotes sustainability. Environmentally Friendly Smart Cities usually incorporate infrastructure type A in their smart city classification. One way they can do this is by becoming more inhabitant friendly through projects like the Copenhagen climate protection agreement with an audit that targeted emissions from power plants. Furthermore, it can actively work towards other green projects like installing bike lanes for bicycles to increase the use of cars that decrease emissions.

Digital Economy Smart Cities

Digital economy cities provide high-speed internet access and encourage digital infrastructure within companies and homes to promote corporate density (Malecki 2003). Type D refers to Data centres, fibre optics networks, data exchanges and perhaps wireless infrastructure, all of which allow tech-savvy citizens to enjoy fast wireless data connections and quick information retrieval. It is responsible for the production and distribution of data to enable future smart innovations. Digital economy smart cities usually incorporate infrastructure type D in their Smart city classification. One way in which they make this happen is by installing public Wi-Fi hotspots that provide people with high internet speed internet access and more bandwidth while increasing infrastructure capabilities. Furthermore, it can actively work towards other digital projects like more fibre optic cables to decrease overall costs within the city.

Green Urbanism Smart Cities

Green urbanism cities make use of sustainable building techniques that do not disrupt the natural environment (Ng 2019). These cities make use of technology to keep an intact ecosystem by converting underdeveloped land into green spaces instead of constructing more buildings. The public water supply or sewage treatment plants are linked with parks and recreational areas, allowing wildlife such as birds and bugs to flourish and thrive in the untreated spaces. Type A refers to programs that keep vegetation clean through proper cleaning on walkways and biking routes and maintaining lush surroundings to discourage littering. Green urbanism smart cities usually incorporate infrastructure type A in their Smart city classification. They make this happen to transform swampland into wetlands that clean surface water runoff through natural means. Furthermore, it can actively work towards other green projects like installing more bike share locations and painting auto-centric roads with darker coloured asphalt to delay temperature rises caused by heat waves.

Vibrant Virtual Cities

Vibrant virtual cities are those which utilise advanced, pocket-size technology to create individualised experiences. These cities provide an abundance of jobs in a digital society and use progressive transport concepts to solve current problems in congestion and connectivity actively. Type D refers to the invention of smart traffic lights to allow for enhanced vehicular travel speeds, high-speed phone networks that promote near-instantaneous data transfer, meta-data urban buildings with sensors capable of tracking pedestrians and vehicles nearby. Vibrant Virtual Cities usually incorporate infrastructure type D in its Smart city classification. One way in which they make this happen is by introducing new street technology that provides a sustainable alignment for other virtual devices to share, such as more roadside infotainment. Furthermore, it can actively work towards other green projects like installing more smart bus stations with tailored routes and cabin architecture that promote alternate transport designs.

E-Living Smart Cities

E-Living cities provide the rich experience of an in-person lifestyle from a remote location (Stevens 2011). These cities are pioneers in sustainable technologies like 3D printing by using the latest technology to provide virtual experiences and simulations that would otherwise take much more time and energy, like visiting an office. Type D refers to the use of digital spaces where businesses operate remotely or in a hybrid environment, using intermittent applications for e-health, IT support or temporary workforces. E-Living smart cities usually incorporate infrastructure type D in their smart city classification. One way in which they make this happen is through 3D printing filaments from recycled trash like petroleum hydrocarbons which are much cheaper than other alternatives. Furthermore, it can actively work towards other E-living projects by utilising virtual reality that provides leaders with the chance to examine potential future trends and dilemmas within the city.

Cyber-Physical Systems in Smart City Spaces (SCSs)

Cyber-physical systems (CPSs) in smart cities are vital for enhancing the quality of life of citizens. They include electric power plants, traffic and streetlights, traffic signals, parking sensors, waste management systems etc. These systems are interconnected and allow data to be collected, analysed, and transmitted to provide a safer environment for people. With respect to the spaces influenced by the CPSs in a smart city, these can be sub-divided into three categories, i.e., Cyber Space, Physical Space, and Social Space (Nayyar et al. 2020, Randhawa and Kumar 2017, Tiddi et al. 2020).

Cyber Space

A virtual environment is free of geographic boundaries in both breadth and depth. Additionally, this physical reality adheres to the logical predeterminations (codes) that allow for interaction among users. Via cyber space, people have unlimited possibilities to proactively generate or react. Combined with cybernetic principles, the term cyber space becomes known as a potential computational medium no longer hermetically sealed within simple four-walled confines but instead carried with us throughout every waking moment where we are essentially laptops on the go. Telegraph, radio, phone lines, and air navigation provide conduits by which messages convey impulses that travel between cyber-space entities. Thereby establishing synchronicity in these disparate universes as if there's some sort of universal consciousness spanning human civilisation to every star, we have yet located with advanced telescopes. Cyber Space has had a profound effect on the way we live our everyday lives. For example, communications with family can have a different tone and interaction possibilities now that communication is instantaneous. Computers can process and amplify sound with/without visual stimulation, technology can be used as the mediator of diagnosis for doctors in rural areas. To connect with hospitals with specialists and equipment which are not present locally. Statistics of crimes happening in modern cities have become more alarming as a result of greater connectivity due to mechanised mobility. Which reduces the distance from criminals and victims, some topics such as politics change their essence in a virtual space with a huge reach facilitated by information flow. For simplicity, we can say that cyber-space is an environment where highly info-literate people interact virtually. It is a reality where many perspectives, for one thing, might exist and can be shared or debated among different groups. This has been transforming society profoundly since the inception of this innovation because it is a new way for humans to socialise. The effects are subtler, which vary depending on the person. For example, people may be able to get lost in cyber space and forget to come back.

Physical Space

A Physical space is a physical area needed for an individual CPSs agent to function and exist (Bagheri et al. 2015). A CPSs involves a physical space because it must consider sensors, actuators and other macroscale subsystems that interact with the physical space. A physical space focuses on the three physical variables relevant for an autonomous agent. These variables are; proximity, presence, and awareness (Durand et al. 2011). Physical space is necessary to do several tasks in everyday life, such as gathering data, planning actions, and adapting actions. Key components of "physical space" within a cyber-physical system are as follows: Interaction > Environments > Human > Tools (Andersson et al. 2016, Trouche 2004). Acting Deliberatively such as, running a company, parenting, or operating machinery non-deliberatively. Reactive rules of adjustment can drive non-deliberative functions in moments when full deliberation is not possible, i.e., driving an automobile through rush hour traffic or ramping up production to meet increased demand without pausing to reassess. A physical space should be considered for any remotely controlled tool that interacts with the natural world. This includes autonomous drones, robotics, telepresence systems and remote sensors. Some terms that might be used to define the physical space are:

1. The Radius of Required Clearance.
2. The Radius of Required Protection.
3. Key Process.
4. Proprietary Resource or Resource Sensitive Area.
5. Area of Unknown or Unaccounted for Activities.

A physical space needs to be considered large enough for an agent to do whatever it ought to while at the same time considering the design and function of the environment. The area in which a human can act is called the working environment. Active work, such as running or climbing, generally falls into the need for a larger environment. Consider an agent who needs to run away from their enemy but cannot cross rubble. The physical space would not be ideal without considering what may happen in the different environments in which an agent is put. In conclusion, the physical space is crucial on whether an agent can take a full action, a limited action, and no action at all and so forth.

Social Space

To understand social spaces in CPSs, one must first examine the architectural implications. Within social constructs, this typically refers to the physical space and how it can impact human communities. In physical community spaces, such as a city square or small town's main street, its functions include gathering areas and living arrangements, traffic efficiency, and economic activities of any given area. Through architecture, humans can regulate urbanisation by increasing living capacity and permeable corridors to ease travelling within an urban zone. With the advent of social space, humans have adapted programming of these physical spaces to replicate human dynamics and needs, such as having preferences towards the safe neighbourhood. Some spatial issues come into play in this phenomenon and present new challenges as more people rely on programs to exist in physical spaces. The number of people who use a program increases along with an increase in different types of users to become members and share interests in the program's platform (Heiberger and Harper 2008); this creates a particular gate-keeping or filtering algorithms that represents particular social norms and makes different divisions in physical space. These algorithms can present particular interests of which program a person is in and akin to some aspects of life where one might be discriminated against because they are not part of certain programs, the situation may emerge where app users might exclude other people who use applications differently or who come from different backgrounds.

Social spaces do not just happen on the internet but may result from physical structures within the environment. For example, how structurally dense an urban area is may also affect the extent of planned social spaces in the indoor or outdoor form. It can be seen as a cultural ecosystem where, for example, CPSs spaces can provide both the technology tools for people to connect within a given culture and the symbolic frameworks that constitutes some digital culture expressions (Pauwels 2012). Social spaces are very much needed in this context where anthropologists identify how information and new identities circulate. Which does not substitute traditional (physical) social organisations but is, at the same time, often required for cultures to maintain. A person usually enters society by a process of socialisation that follows before being able to function in a pragmatic way within its communities. For the cybernetic level, this would be data such as computer programs and applications that follow that same model of transitioning from being an outsider to gaining acceptance or maybe an iconoclast totally rejecting the current regime. Irrespective of who or what, it seems essential for new actors to undergo a process of socialisation before being enlisted in the social order.

CPSs in Architecture and Technology in Smart City Spaces

Smart Grid Systems

The notion of a smart city tends to be interpreted in many ways; as such, there is no universal definition of what distinguishes a smart city. Particularly, the development and prudent usage of resources (energy consumption for buildings) and infrastructure (communications infrastructure) are fundamental in maintaining high standards of living while simultaneously minimising the strain on our two-dimensional cities. One example that needs systematical but appropriate considerations when applying smart systems in a city lies within the utility networks; cities operate utility networks with three distinct aspects (Naphade et al. 2011), i.e. distribution of water and wastewater, collection of the solid waste stream and production of electricity. Expectations are set for these utilities to increase efficiencies in consumption, collect data on incidents/special requests. In this scenario, there will be three different manners of how a city can realise a smart system in terms of utility networks:

1. The installation of sensors for monitoring the energy supply chains will enable the creation of a network in which information is shared and able to document the usage of energy more accurately so that energy suppliers can adjust according to power demands.
2. Smart meters will enable homes and businesses to behave more efficiently, reducing consumption through informing households on consumption data.
3. Developing an online customer grid, which is necessary since communication with electricity distribution providers tends always to be a topic fraught with problems where periods of downtime can lead to higher costs from emergency generators.

Water heater remote monitoring is another example of a smart grid in terms of utility networks. This can allow for more efficient measures and data collection and inform individuals via their smart meters when it might be necessary to do laundry to take advantage of the hot water stored under the nameplate capacity in colder months.

Internet of Things (IoT)

With IoT, infrastructure and devices can be monitored, managed, and controlled remotely (Kelly et al. 2013). During smart city projects, IoT has the potential of lowering the deployment costs associated with large-scale urban systems management. Cellular technologies (4G LTE or Wi-Fi) provides unique possibilities for cost-effective solutions that could cover broad distances with a minimum material deployment in densely populated areas. It is important here is to consider heterogeneous configurations where internet access is wireless (like cell phone networks), but where the control and management head-end might be wired (like a web browser or desktop application). Data privacy and security are two main areas of concern. A majority of smart city initiatives rely on public data streams such as traffic monitoring, air quality detection, and water management (Neirotti et al. 2014). As more city infrastructure is connected through IoT sensors, the use of this data is becoming more important to build better models to predict human analytics metric outcomes, from crime rates to traffic congestion. The problem with this approach is that certain user information may be inadvertently captured and used.

Cloud Computing

The CPSs adds extensibility to the algorithm using an extension bus, sensors, switches, and actuators. Federated Intelligence completes the IoT Chain by providing a system-level intelligence with cloud orchestration capability. A fundamental aspect of the industry transformation to Cyber-Infrastructure principles is the interoperability between stakeholders that bring different perspectives to the decision-making processes's security across industries. This Federation process requires complex technology infrastructure such as Cloud Computing Providers (CCP), next-generation architectures for modelling, simulation and big data analytics (Yang and Tate 2012). Governments/ administrative bodies can have a government's contracts with CCP to offer cost-effective IT solutions for selected projects. This solution also becomes scalable as it groups multiple customers. A smart city needs data to improve management activities and reduce pollution (Nowicka 2014). They utilise ICT infrastructure to monitor the environmental indicators and respond efficiently when a problem occurs. In order to have these systems, IoT has been developed, which integrates data processing and automates subsequent tasks using cloud computing (Stergiou et al. 2018). One example which is for system maintenance and includes collecting, and processing real-time data from sensors connecting to the cloud, then emailing alerts if an anomaly is detected in air quality or humidity levels. To achieve this, the system should have facilities to store the huge amount of data in the cloud processed via cloud computing so that they could present it in needed moments when an anomaly is detected.

Transportation

In a smart city, transportation is integrated with public and private transit systems. This allows for electric vehicles, reduced emissions, off-street traffic congestion, fewer accidents, and lower infrastructure costs. CPSs are used to automate the movement of physical cars with tiny nano-sensors embedded in asphalt or seams to guide vehicles in roadways. When deploying a smart city around public transit (commuter) routes, focus on institutional destination access like universities, research centres and key medical facilities (Batty et al. 2012). This will help reduce the need for private vehicle trips. A network of interconnected traffic signals and communication systems allows a city to track and manage its flow of cars (Goodall et al. 2013). Advanced traffic software may be available, or newer sensors could monitor real-time conditions on highways, city streets, or bridge/tunnel structures where space is limited. Speed limits adjust according to conditions; multi-lane acceleration systems let drivers switch from a stopped position without changing lanes, saving time. Sensors in the pavement help move cars slowly when they are clumped together to minimise emissions and air pollution (Bowie 2011). Apps like Google Maps provide step-by-step instructions for how long it will take drivers to complete a journey during rush hour periods (without congestion) as well as with a range of traffic delays (Liu et al. 2016). It warns drivers about accidents, hazards, and areas of road work construction ahead on the route. Route optimisation plans can be created by city staff or citizens and posted to keep the information up to date. Faster routes mean less congestion and pollution as urban mobility becomes more efficient.

Service-Oriented Smart City Mobility Applications

An example of service-oriented smart mobility applications implementing CPSs is a congested zone detection system (Elshenawy et al. 2018). This system utilises vehicular traffic data collected by sensors to deduce choke points in the city's traffic and report it back to Eco Motion, which then sends out a notification to people on the app who want travel alerts. This results in individuals being less reliant on maps for navigation and allows more imaginative solutions to be applied, like letting single drivers take turns being part of a specialised carpool. Pedestrian navigation is another service-oriented application that implements CPSs (Wu et al. 2011). This application collects the utility of Google maps and combines it with traffic lights to show time delays for every street. It has an interruption warning that notifies a person when they need to divert their route because of roadblocks caused by construction. The result of this system is less traffic congestion and an increase in the smoothness of navigation. The Google Maps application implements both navigation systems. Following are few examples of service-oriented smart city mobility applications implementing CPSs:

Safety Guide

Functioning as a digital guardian, this SaaS (Software as a Service) solution understands the complex, real-time changes on the road through vast amounts of data from different sources, including driver behaviour and traffic signal information. Considering various risks and driving conditions at each corner, it steers drivers to preferred routes before choosing their own mindlessly inefficient journeys.

City Mapper

This app interlinks travel and congestion management data sourced from more than 43,000 sensors in car tires, junctions, and electricity connections. Empowered by big data insights and the latest risk assessment techniques, it makes driving a tailor-made experience. The new 'C3DR driving plane' displays consumer's scores for different journeys across multiple modes of transport at once.

Via

Via uses analytics to predict congested time periods on area roads. The company uses advanced Bayesian statistics for freight movement, predictive modelling for parking, and cab demanded prediction for passenger travel. As a result, they can produce more efficient mobility for commuters.

Optimity

This system aims to reduce vehicle CO_2 emissions by replicating the most efficient vehicle movement within a city. The system organises pedestrian, bicycle, and transit traffic as efficiently as possible while minimising traffic accidents.

Future of CPSs in Smart Cities

Sustaining Low Carbon Smart Cities

The roles of CPSs in a low-carbon smart city are discussed and studied in the realms of sustainable technologies (Inderwildi et al. 2020). The need for building a smart, green low carbon city requires designing and integrating CPSs to make these changes. Smart sensors and control networks capture data that helps address specific sustainable purposes while providing user response by analysing this information. Innovations such as power grids with better distribution models may enable a greater use of renewable power sources. This brings about a discussion on CPSs being implemented in the building process. Sensors and control networks enable cities to better manage the demand for electricity instead of relying on fuels such as coal or gas to power large stations (Zhao et al. 2019). Green is decided according to how efficient and sustainable a solution is, such as the CPSs it uses. Smart built adaptive traditionally manage thermal and ventilation conditions automatically. The controller controls a subsystem that can adjust between heating and cooling to closely maintain the desired balance no matter what outside circumstances arise. Demand response allows utilities to respond quickly to increased demands for energy by taking load shed on a system level rather than an individual feeder outage. Storage that is green can meet short-term power demands like windmills or solar panels through mini-storage or battery usage. Apartment buildings can install smart controls for ventilation and heating that use sensors that predict current and future heat, limiting the draft coming into the building from breezes and outside air. Studies have shown that sensors are effective in delivering on-demand responses more quickly than a traditional CO_2 based sensor, which may not be accurate in predicting at lower concentrations (Morawska et al. 2018).

The internet of things (IoT) is one way to capture real-time CPSs data in order to retrieve information pertaining to sustainable initiatives within a smart city (Nagy et al. 2018). For example, optimising the movement of traffic across a city (like banning out-of-town drivers during rush hour) can help alleviate more wear and tear on infrastructure, reducing the carbon footprint each vehicle has to create minimal congestion. One company is doing this by analysing the information load from different apps such as Google Maps for iOS, Android and Chrome on the desktop to show how people are travelling in any given area and at what time of day based on their data from 311 calls or app usage. This data helps the city gather spatial data on CO_2 footprint to find the most optimal alternative. Using smart sensors and controllers has been shown to have a positive correlation with enhancing users' well-being (Lin et al. 2019). According to research in Oakland, California and Michigan, sensors that help improve air quality with more advanced filtration systems and higher efficiency heating help lessen asthma attacks in patients, respectively. The development of COBie has advanced living standards by providing greater comfort and safety to occupants. One design for the industry is called COBie-CO_2 building project. The power grid has been said to be one of the largest contributors to carbon emissions (Ding et al. 2019). The tricky part about this is maximising the use of renewable energy sources in a smart city. Renewable energy sources have not proven a reliable way to replace fossil-fueled power grids globally but are shown to cause less environmental harm due to their speed efficiency. Therefore, it is worth exploring what we can do via CPSs at a micro level, such as implementing better distribution models or increasing electrical grid efficiency by 70%, leading to renewable energy playing a greater role in the grid without contributing to CO_2 emissions. The future of CPSs in a green, low-carbon environment suggests continued and progressive changes occurring exponentially. As new means of sensing and computing technologies are created, old ways of implementing sustainable measures are also set to improve qualitatively when it comes to efficiency as well as sustainability characteristics (i.e., lower energy use). Hence, implementation of CPSs in smart cities furthers the potential for smart environmental design by layering complexities in sensing, layout and problem solving.

Urban Farming in Smart Cities

Urban farming relies on the concept of growing food in cities, to remain sustainable, and CPSs are used in inputting weather data to let the farmers know what days require more water (Tsiatsis et al. 2018). This public placement for urban agriculture is a necessity and a way for citizens to become closer to the technology that their city officials are using. It does this by ensuring access to the ability to provide for communities across different economic backgrounds since produce may not always be affordable or accessible in local grocery stores. Public places like this can also reduce the effects of food deserts. The physical world has its limits; therefore, we need the technology that the measurements can account for, and that is how CPSs works in agriculture. Whether there is a change in weather or a surplus of produce, the farmer stands to benefit when they know what to expect from their land before it happens. Systemically knowing is the key to a healthy and thriving society in smart cities using CPSs. The concept of urban farming in smart cities is a good example of the issues surrounding sustainable and healthy living in an increasingly dense population. Some technologies and programs help take care of many different aspects. Important factors in managing sustainability include knowing where food comes from, water scrubbing plants to remove pollution, and extensive resources for looking out for your potential food problems due to climate change, depletion, etc. Urban agriculture has been embraced throughout the United States as a way for nearby citizens to provide themselves with sustainable nutrition and provide support for the environment. A large part of smart cities is integrated agricultural initiatives because they are highly susceptible to climate change. Urban agriculture supplements food sources and helps reduce the environmental impact of farmlands where populations are outnumbering what the area can accommodate them. Some parts of the United States also saw extreme ups and downs that made it difficult for farming operations to succeed. Places like the CSA Queen Anne Farm attempted to keep water usage low for urban growth, but the variability in climate destroyed their plans under periods of drought. Another example of how CPSs can be used to benefit urban farms is the increased familiarity of people with the latest technological advancements. The rise in cyber-criminal activities in the late 1990s called for the need for a more remote access to information and, specifically, citizen interaction. It may not be as specific or precise, but the benefits outweigh some reliability concerns. Urban farming aims to help provide some relief in terms of food scarcity and starvation, which should have a one-on-one impact. There are more people than ever starving because they live too remotely for profitability or resources to be accessible. The people that still managed the most success with the CSA initiative, like Kiz Knapp Educational Center's farm, had less time at risk for vulnerability through public input. It shows how many benefits one can derive from a diversity of output when trying to be sustainable. Urban farming also reveals the importance of data in agriculture – whether that is precise climate information for the future or to know when irrigation should be done.

Summary

CPSs is part of the process for cities to become smart cities that want to be considered part of the smart revolution and have to be "built partially on substructures, technologies and data". These systems provide services related to data analytics and place them into interactive displays in public settings. A smart city is a city-scale system that consists of information and communication technology (ICT) systems in the fields of urban infrastructure, space, and transportation. CPSs consolidates a physical environment with computation activities that have been traditionally external or undone. CPSs is responsible for safeguarding the user's information, ensuring that data can be accessed only with privileges on a given system. For the best living possibility in intelligent cities, machines should behave like humans and vice versa. One major issue which is necessary to be addressed when developing intelligent cities is cybersecurity. Additionally, device-related risks such as the managing and securing of devices would also need to be implemented over their lifetime. Security for embedded systems should be a very important issue in both a smart city/intelligent building construction application area or when operating infrastructures domains, whether public or private. In short, Smart Cities are the future of humanity, which will be incomplete without CPSs in place.

References

Abdullah, N. A., M. J. Saidi, N. H. A. Rahman, C. C. Wen and I.R.A. Hamid. 2017. Face recognition for criminal identification: An implementation of principal component analysis for face recognition. AIP Conference Proceedings, 1891(1), 20002.

Albino, V., U. Berardi and R. M. Dangelico. 2015. Smart cities: Definitions, dimensions, performance, and initiatives. Journal of Urban Technology, 22(1), 3–21.

Andersson, N., A. Argyrou, F. Nägele, F. Ubis, U. E. Campos, M. O. de Zarate and R. Wilterdink. 2016. AR-enhanced human-robot-interaction-methodologies, algorithms, tools. Procedia CIRP, 44, 193–198.

Bagheri, B., S. Yang, H.-A. Kao and J. Lee. 2015. Cyber-physical systems architecture for self-aware machines in industry 4.0 environment. IFAC-PapersOnLine, 48(3), 1622–1627.

Batty, M., K. W. Axhausen, F. Giannotti, A. Pozdnoukhov, A. Bazzani, M. Wachowicz, G. Ouzounis and Y. Portugali. 2012. Smart cities of the future. The European Physical Journal Special Topics, 214(1), 481–518.

Bowie, J. M. 2011. Development of a Weigh-in-Motion System Using Acoustic Emission Sensors. Florida: University of Central Florida. Retrieved from http://purl.fcla.edu/fcla/etd/CFE0003581%0A%0A

Brayne, S. 2017. Big data surveillance: The case of policing. American Sociological Review, 82(5), 977–1008.

De, S., Y. Zhou, I. Larizgoitia Abad and K. Moessner. 2017. Cyber–physical–social frameworks for urban big data systems: A survey. Applied Sciences, 7(10), 1017.

Ding, N., J. Pan, J. Liu and J. Yang. 2019. An optimization method for energy structures based on life cycle assessment and its application to the power grid in China. Journal of Environmental Management, 238, 18–24.

Durand, C. P., M. Andalib, G. F. Dunton, J. Wolch and M. A. Pentz. 2011. A systematic review of built environment factors related to physical activity and obesity risk: Implications for smart growth urban planning. Obesity Reviews, 12(5), e173–e182.

Elshenawy, M., B. Abdulhai and M. El-Darieby. 2018. Towards a service-oriented cyber-physical systems of systems for smart city mobility applications. Future Generation Computer Systems, 79, 575–587.

Gharaibeh, A., M. A. Salahuddin, S. J. Hussini, A. Khreishah, I. Khalil, M. Guizani and A. Al-Fuqaha. 2017. Smart cities: A survey on data management, security and enabling technologies. IEEE Communications Surveys & Tutorials, 19(4), 2456–2501.

Goodall, N. J., B. L. Smith and B. Park. 2013. Traffic signal control with connected vehicles. Transportation Research Record, 2381(1), 65–72.

Green, B. 2019. The smart enough city: Putting technology in its place to reclaim our urban future. MIT Press.

Haque, M. M., H. C. Chin and A. K. Debnath. 2013. Sustainable, safe, smart—Three key elements of Singapore's evolving transport policies. Transport Policy, 27, 20–31.

Heiberger, G. and R. Harper. 2008. Have you Facebooked Astin lately? Using technology to increase student involvement. New Directions for Student Services, 2008(124), 19–35.

Henderson, J. V. 2005. Urbanization and growth. *In*: Handbook of Economic Growth (Vol. 1, pp. 1543–1591). Elsevier.

Hollands, R. G. 2008. Will the real smart city please stand up: Intelligent, progressive or entrepreneurial? City, 12(3), 303–320.

Hu, Q. and Y. Zheng. 2020. Smart city initiatives: A comparative study of American and Chinese cities. Journal of Urban Affairs, 1–22.

Inderwildi, O., C. Zhang, X. Wang and M. Kraft. 2020. The impact of intelligent cyber-physical systems on the decarbonization of energy. Energy & Environmental Science, 13(3), 744–771.

Kelly, S. D. T., N. K. Suryadevara and S. C. Mukhopadhyay. 2013. Towards the implementation of IoT for environmental condition monitoring in homes. IEEE Sensors Journal, 13(10), 3846–3853.

Komninos, N. 2008. Intelligent Cities and Globalisation of Innovation Networks. Routledge.

Lee, J. H., M. G. Hancock and M.-C. Hu. 2014. Towards an effective framework for building smart cities: Lessons from Seoul and San Francisco. Technological Forecasting and Social Change, 89, 80–99.

Lin, C., G. Zhao, C. Yu and Y. J. Wu. 2019. Smart city development and residents' well-being. Sustainability, 11(3), 676.

Liu, R., H. Liu, D. Kwak, Y. Xiang, C. Borcea, B. Nath and L. Iftode. 2016. Balanced traffic routing: Design, implementation, and evaluation. Ad Hoc Networks, 37, 14–28.

Malecki, E. J. 2003. Digital development in rural areas: Potentials and pitfalls. Journal of Rural Studies, 19(2), 201–214.

Mardacany, E. 2014. Smart cities characteristics: Importance of built environment components. IET Seminar Digest, 2014(15564). https://doi.org/10.1049/ic.2014.0045

Miao, P. 2003. Deserted streets in a jammed town: The gated community in Chinese cities and its solution. Journal of Urban Design, 8(1), 45–66.

Mohanty, S. P., U. Choppali and E. Kougianos. 2016. Everything you wanted to know about smart cities: The internet of things is the backbone. IEEE Consumer Electronics Magazine, 5(3), 60–70.

Morawska, L., P. K. Thai, X. Liu, A. Asumadu-Sakyi, G. Ayoko, A. Bartonova, A. Bedini, F. Chai, B. Christensen and M. Dunbabin. 2018. Applications of low-cost sensing technologies for air quality monitoring and exposure assessment: How far have they gone? Environment International, 116, 286–299.

Nagy, J., J. Oláh, E. Erdei, D. Máté and J. Popp. 2018. The role and impact of Industry 4.0 and the internet of things on the business strategy of the value chain—The case of Hungary. Sustainability, 10(10), 3491.

Naphade, M., G. Banavar, C. Harrison, J. Paraszczak and R. Morris. 2011. Smarter cities and their innovation challenges. Computer, 44(6), 32–39.

Nayyar, A., R. Rameshwar and A. Solanki. 2020. Internet of Things (IoT) and the Digital Business Environment: A Standpoint Inclusive Cyber Space, Cyber Crimes, and Cybersecurity (1st ed.). Florida: Apple Academic Press Inc. Florida, USA. Retrieved from https://www.taylorfrancis.com/chapters/edit/10.1201/9780429276484-6/internet-things-iot-digital-business-environment-standpoint-inclusive-cyber-space-cyber-crimes-cybersecurity-anand-nayyar-rudra-rameshwar-arun-solanki

Neirotti, P., A. De Marco, A. C. Cagliano, G. Mangano and F. Scorrano. 2014. Current trends in Smart City initiatives: Some stylised facts. Cities, 38, 25–36.

Newman, P. and J. Kenworthy. 1999. Sustainability and cities: Overcoming automobile dependence. Island Press.

Ng, M. K. 2019. Governing green urbanism: The case of Shenzhen, China. Journal of Urban Affairs, 41(1), 64–82.

Nikitas, A., I. Kougias, E. Alyavina and E. Njoya Tchouamou. 2017. How can autonomous and connected vehicles, electromobility, BRT, hyperloop, shared use mobility and mobility-as-a-service shape transport futures for the context of smart cities? Urban Science, 1(4), 36.

Nowicka, K. 2014. Smart city logistics on cloud computing model. Procedia-Social and Behavioral Sciences, 151, 266–281.

Pauwels, L. 2012. A multimodal framework for analyzing websites as cultural expressions. Journal of Computer-Mediated Communication, 17(3), 247–265.

Pramanik, M. I., R. Y. K. Lau, H. Demirkan and M. A. K. Azad. 2017. Smart health: Big data enabled health paradigm within smart cities. Expert Systems with Applications, 87, 370–383.

Randhawa, A. and A. Kumar. 2017. Exploring sustainability of smart development initiatives in India. International Journal of Sustainable Built Environment, 6(2), 701–710.

Saba, D., Y. Sahli, B. Berbaoui and R. Maouedj. 2020. Towards smart cities: Challenges, components, and architectures. Toward Social Internet of Things (SIoT): Enabling Technologies, Architectures and Applications, 249–286.

Schipper, R. and A. Silvius. 2018. Characteristics of smart sustainable city development: Implications for project management. Smart Cities, 1(1), 75–97. https://doi.org/10.3390/smartcities1010005

Silva, B. N., M. Khan and K. Han. 2018. Towards sustainable smart cities: A review of trends, architectures, components, and open challenges in smart cities. Sustainable Cities and Society, 38, 697–713.

Solanas, A., C. Patsakis, M. Conti, I. S. Vlachos, V. Ramos, F. Falcone, O. Postolache, P. A. Pérez-Martínez, R. Di Pietro and D. N. Perrea. 2014. Smart health: A context-aware health paradigm within smart cities. IEEE Communications Magazine, 52(8), 74–81.

Stergiou, C., K. E. Psannis, B.-G. Kim and B. Gupta. 2018. Secure integration of IoT and cloud computing. Future Generation Computer Systems, 78, 964–975.

Stevens, K. 2011. Knowledge mobilization for e-living: Horizontal and vertical networks for development. International Conference on Informatics Engineering and Information Science, 1–12.

Tiddi, I., E. Bastianelli, E. Daga, M. d'Aquin and E. Motta. 2020. Robot–city interaction: mapping the research landscape—A survey of the interactions between robots and modern cities. International Journal of Social Robotics, 12(2), 299–324.

Toli, A. M. and N. Murtagh. 2020. The concept of sustainability in smart city definitions. Frontiers in Built Environment, 6, 77.

Trouche, L. 2004. Managing the complexity of human/machine interactions in computerized learning environments: Guiding students' command process through instrumental orchestrations. International Journal of Computers for Mathematical Learning, 9(3), 281–307.

Tsiatsis, V., S. Karnouskos, J. Holler, D. Boyle and C. Mulligan. 2018. Internet of Things: Technologies and Applications for a New Age of intelligence. Academic Press.

Wu, F.-J., Y.-F. Kao and Y.-C. Tseng. 2011. From wireless sensor networks towards cyber physical systems. Pervasive and Mobile Computing, 7(4), 397–413.

Yang, H. and M. Tate. 2012. A descriptive literature review and classification of cloud computing research. Communications of the Association for Information Systems, 31(1), 2.

Zhao, H., P. Jiang, Z. Chen, C. I. Ezeh, Y. Hong, Y. Guo, C. Zheng, H. Džapo, X. Gao and T. Wu. 2019. Improvement of fuel sources and energy products flexibility in coal power plants via energy-cyber-physical-systems approach. Applied Energy, 254, 113554.

Threats, Security and Safety of Cyber-Physical Systems in Construction Industry

Khalid Mhmoud Alzubi, Wesam Salah Alaloul and Abdul Hannan Qureshi

Introduction

The construction industry is making a shift towards automation and digitisation due to the raised growth of communication and information technologies as well as the Internet of Things (IoT), machine learning, 3D printing, and big data. These technologies will transform the design, planning, implementation, and operation and maintenance of the construction projects, positively impacting the overall project productivity, cost, time, and quality (Mantha and Garcia De Soto 2019). Different organisations and research institutions are giving the development and research of cyber-physical systems (CPSs) a high level of interest due to the significance of such systems in developing and enhancing the different performance aspects in these organisations. CPSs security and privacy have been recognized to be a future frontier of concern for technology and a field that needs to be matured and stimulated in all industries, including in the construction industry (Thomas et al. 2015). As the implementation of CPSs is growing, challenges of security are also rising and need to be taken into consideration. Trust has been shown to affect technology implementation significantly. Technological trust can be defined as the belief that a given technology can support the individual in achieving their objectives in situations wherever they may be exposed to vulnerability and uncertainty (Lee & See 2004). However, many factors can affect trust formation, and several models have been proposed for increasing the trustability of adopting these new technologies. For instance, a trust model has been defined by (AlHogail 2018), wherein trust can be assessed throughout three dimensions of variables: social influence, product, and security. Social influence-related factors include social influence and community interest. While product-related factors include product reliability and functionality, ease of use, helpfulness, and the perceptions of user usefulness. The third dimension is security-related factors which include the user's perceptions of risks and product security. Sensor networks Security has to be considered in the context of control security and information security. Control security includes mitigating all attacks on system estimation and control algorithms and resolving all control issues in the network environment. While information security encompasses securing information during processing, large-scale data sharing, and data aggregation in the network environment (Cárdenas et al. 2011, Lu et al. 2013). Information security focuses on data protection, for example, by using encryption, while control security focuses on protecting the dynamics of control systems against any cyber-attacks (Lu et al. 2015). Also, control security are the security risks that could happen when an unauthorized person controls one system or device, also recognized as hacking. While information security is about unauthorized access to stored and retrieved data that may be utilized in an improper way. Attacks on CPSs can lead to a great loss in people's livelihoods, particularly on the cyber layer. Therefore, CPSs security is becoming a more important issue than ever and have to be considered in at the beginning of the design process (Ashibani and Mahmoud 2017).

Working in a digital environment makes the different industries significantly vulnerable to cyber-attacks (Xuan Li et al. 2018, Jie Liu et al. 2017). Construction is not exempted, and moreover, the complex chain of interactions, coordination, dynamics, and data exchange between several inter-connected construction project stakeholders poses unique productivity, performance, and security risks. A threat can be defined as an event or action that may happen intentionally or naturally and has the potential to harm people, information, and the environment (Hutchins et al. 2015). Whereas an attack is the action taken to harm people, information, and environment. Since attack and risk have closely related meanings, they might be confusing at times and used interchangeably. Finally, vulnerability is the state of being susceptible to an attack or the point of weakness that may be used for attacking (Hutchins et al. 2015).

General Threats of CPSs Application

Although a part of CPSs advantages, they are exposed to various cyber security and physical attacks, challenges, and threats, and this is due to their diverse nature, reliance on sensitive and private data, and large-scale deployment. As such, accidental or intentional exposures of these systems can result in high damage effects, which makes it critical to put in place solid security measures. However, this could lead to an unacceptable network overhead (Yaacoub et al. 2020). A highly secure system should provide protection mechanisms against the unauthorized withholding of resources and unauthorized modification of information and should be free from the exposure of sensitive and private information to a wide range of people. CPSs are exposed to attacks and failures on both the cyber and physical sides due to their complexity, dynamic, and scalability nature. Attacks like, man-in-the-middle, eavesdropping, and denial-of-service (DOS) can be directed to the cyber-infrastructure such as communication infrastructure, decision-making mechanisms, etc. or the physical components with the intent of stealing sensitive information or disrupting the system in operation. Some of factors that make CPSs easily exposed to security threats are adopting insecure communication protocols, making use of a large-scale network, heavy use of legacy systems, or rapid adoption of commercial off-the-shelf technologies (Gunes et al. 2014).

Physical Layer Threats (Perception Layer)

The main security threats of the physical layer (perception layer) are shown as follows (Yaacoub et al. 2020, L. Zhang et al. 2013).

Physical Attacks

Physical attacks are mainly about physical destruction for the perception of the node itself, information disclosure, leading to a lack of information, and so on.

Equipment Failure

Equipment failure loss performance or equipment reduction because of aging, external forces, or environment, and it operates as abnormal.

Line Fault

Line fault referring to the failure node power lines. For example, a line-to-line fault, which is a short circuit between lines, caused by the ionization of air, or when lines come into physical contact, which happens when two current carrying conductors in a three-phase system accidentally come into contact with each other. This fault may cause damage in systems.

Electromagnetic Leakage

Equipment radiates out the electromagnetic signal at work through the ground, signal lines, the power lines, and the lines itself.

Electromagnetic Interference

By unnecessary electromagnetic disturbances or signals, the receiver of useful electromagnetic signals encounters inverse effects, which leads to deterioration of a system performance, a device, or a channel of transmission.

Denial of Service (DOS) Attacks

DOS is the attacker by consumption of the network's bandwidth. It can cause it to stop providing services by the targeted system.

Network Layer Threats (Transmission Layer)

The main security threats of the network layer (transmission layer) are shown as follows (Yaacoub et al. 2020,Zhang et al. 2013):

DOS Attacks

The attacker of DOS forces the server to not be full, through a buffer, and not accept any new requests or use IP spoofing.

Routing Attacks

It means that an attacker forges routing to send forged routing information, which leads to the wrong route interference with the right routing process.

Control Network DoS Attacks

Control network DoS attack is one where the attacker causes the target system to cease providing service attacks using network bandwidth attacks.

Direction Misleading Attacks

After receiving malicious packet nodes, malicious nodes choose the wrong path to send by modifying destination address and the source, which will result in confusion of network routing.

Black Hole Attack

Malicious node adds the fake available information of the channel to the received route request packet.

Flood Attacks

By way of Distributed Denial of Service (DDoS) and Smurf, the data transport layer network server resources are exhausted, which will lead to it being unable to provide normal services.

Trap Doors

In this attack the network attacker sets "authorities" in the system of the data transport layer.

Sybil Attack

Sybil attack is a malicious node that can damage the system network through illegally appearing as multiples.

Wormhole Attack

Two or more malicious nodes jointly attack the number of hops among malicious nodes. Thus, it is easy to obtain the right way and then block data transmission or tap the subsequent data packet.

Information Layer Threats (Application Layer)

Major security threats of the application control layer are shown as follows (Yaacoub et al. 2020, Zhang et al. 2013):

Leakage of User Privacy

Because of secure data transmission, storage and presentation, personal information of users, accessing records and other private data are obtained by privacy collectors, and this situation will cause privacy leakage.

Unauthorised Access

Attacker in this case has unauthorised illegal access to the network data in the system.

Malicious Code

It is the code that has security risks. It can be seen as a malicious code in the broad definition of unnecessary code in the system.

Distributed Denial of Service

Sources attract a server network attacked by large numbers of DoS attacking. In the system network, at the same time, this will format a DDoS attacks by overloading the network to interfere or even block the normal network communications.

Privacy in Data Mining

The system of the application control layer mines massive amounts of user data.

The Control Command Forged Attack

The attacker forges control commands in the system of the application control layer to achieve the goal of undermining the purpose of the system or maliciously using the system.

Threats Specific to CPSs of Construction Industry

Various cyberattacks have already happened in the construction industry to damage operations, tamper with existing records, access unauthorized files, steal proprietary information (Mantha et al. 2021). In the construction industry most of the reported cybersecurity incidents can be classified as a data breach such as making data public, data that is stolen or destroyed, or modified data, wire fraud such as redirected payments, or property and service loss, or damage like a power outage. Few of the data breach incidents include jeopardized security due to the stealing of specification files and the plans of construction projects (Mantha et al. 2020). Also, B. Mantha et al. (2020) mentioned that ThyssenKrupp, which is a very well-known construction elevator and escalator manufacturer, also fell victim to a data breach, which lead to their sensitive and confidential trade secret information to be held by hackers. Also, a lot of tax details of construction workers and the social security numbers of a US-based construction company, Turner, were compromised due to data sharing through unsecured channels posing business-related risks (Waston 2018). In a similar incident, tax information of employees of a concrete construction firm was compromised as mentioned at (Mantha et al. 2020). Also, US-based construction management and general contracting firm, Whiting-Turner, suffered a data breach and lost health insurance, and the tax-related information of all its employees (Mantha et al. 2020). On the other hand, in Australia, hackers tried to steal the details and information about the workings of the one-arm bricklayer robot developed by Fast Brick Robots (Pash 2018). Economic risks were faced during the collection of deposits from applicants in the name of a well-known Japanese construction machinery manufacturer, Komatsu, (Waston 2018). Due to unwarranted payments and wire fraud, Konecranes and Marous Brothers Construction lost about 17.2 million euros and 1.7 million US dollars, respectively (Waston 2018, Sawyer and Rubenstone 2019).

Failures of CPSs

Given the various attacks, threats, and vulnerabilities that the CPSs suffer from, it is important to represent and highlight the main failures of CPSs. These failures can either be major or minor. Avižienis et al. (2004), presented a well- detailed explanation in this regard:

Timing Failure

This means that the timing of information delivery is interrupted or delayed (transmitted/ received too late or too early). This may cause data management issues and would affect the decision-making process.

Content Failure

This means that there is incorrect content of delivered information, which would lead to some functional failure of the system. Content failure can be either non-numerical (like alphabets, sounds, graphics, or colours) or numerical.

Silent Failure

It occurs when there is no message received or sent in a distributed system.

Sensors Failure

This means that the sensors are improperly functioning and would seriously hinder the decision-making process due to inaccurate information or bringing a CPSs to a sudden cut.

Babbling Failure

It occurs when the information is delivered, resulting in a system malfunction and operating in a babbling manner.

Service Failure

It happens when an error propagates through the service interface and affects its normal performance ability or/and decision making. This failure can either result in a full or partial CPSs failure and can permanently or temporarily affect it.

Budget Failure

It occurs when the implementing cost of CPSs exceeds the budget limit before ever reaching the testing level. This is mainly caused by poor estimating and budgeting.

Schedule Failure

It occurs when the schedule set for planning, evaluating, and testing for a given CPSs are not achieved due to additional testing, further upgrades, or inadequacy for the needs of users.

Consistent/Inconsistent Failures

A consistent failure happened when all CPSs users perceived a given service identically. While inconsistent failure occurs when all CPSs users differently perceive an incorrect service (Taylor 2010).

The Cost of Security Attacks

The cost of security attacks can be considered in different forms, and the main ones are highlighted as follows (Yaacoub et al. 2020):

Service Delays

CPSs may be prone to service delays, which may affect their performance and render them inactive until the issue is solved either by maintenance or backup.

Cascading Failures

Such as software bugs, sensor failures, or overheating of nuclear power plants, which can cause environmental catastrophes like the case of Chernobyl (1986) and Fukushima (2011), series of TransCanada Corporation's natural gas leakage and explosion in Canada (between 2000 and 2018), as well as similar incidents in the Mexico, US, China, and other countries, water pipeline incidents, oil spilling, blackouts, and flooding. Also, natural gas pipeline explosion in Belgium (2004).

Affected Performance

System delays due to a non-malicious (accident) event or malicious (cyber-attack) can gradually affect the performance of CPSs and cause it to operate in an abnormal manner which can surely affect the decision-making process.

Financial Losses

Malware attacks like the ransomware targeting of Industrial Control Systems (ICMs) can cause a massive loss of information beyond recovery if the ransom is not paid or if the backup is not maintained. This leads to large financial losses over the long and short term especially if the information is deleted beyond recovery. CPSs recover might take months and even years.

Additional Spending

Which may be required to tackle the attempts of advanced continuing threat and zero-day attacks, which require additional spending in terms of security protection in a defense-in-depth manner.

Loss of Life

It can be the result of electric shock, radioactivity, flooding, and fire due to intentional or hazardous acts.

Disclosure of Information:

It can impact CPSs businesses and business trades and put the privacy of users at risk of having exposed their personal information.

Threat Modelling

Threat modelling is an essential way to understand threats of cybersecurity and efficient action plans and devise effective (A shostack 2014, Al-Muhtadi et al. 2021, Bhushan et al. 2020, Ferrag et al. 2018). Threat modelling is the process of recognizing targeted assets, potential threats, vulnerabilities, and attackers (Bodeau et al. 2018). A simple example for threat modelling is when antivirus installed in a PC or a laptop by users to protect themselves from hackers trying to access personal data using a malware injection. That is, the sequence of events involved by hackers (whom) to get access to private information (why) using malware injection (how) into a PC or laptop (where). Several threat modeling methods such as threat categories of STRIDE, PASTA, OCTAVE, TRIKE, VAST, and HTMM have been developed. An overview is presented next along with limitations and advantages for each one.

Stride

It was created by (Kohnfelder and Garg 1999) and uses data flow diagrams

(DFDs), including the events, entities, and boundaries of the evaluated system. The STRIDE acronym refers to the threat categories of Spoofing Identity, Tampering with Data, Repudiation, Information Disclosure, DoS, and Elevation of Privilege. Although it is a mature threat modelling method, it requires an precise DFD as input and may not cover all scenarios for the construction industry (Khan et al. 2017)). For instance, the safety-related threats of incorporating new technologies cannot be modelled in this method, such as drones that can be used to monitor progress on sites.

Pasta

The PASTA acronym refers to Process for Attack Simulation and Threat Analysis, which is a comprehensive threat modelling framework. It involves various stakeholders and has seven stages. Although it is comprehensive, it is tiresome and requires domain-specific components like design flaw analysis and application dependencies (Ucedavélez and Morana 2015).

Vast

It was developed by (Agarwal 2016) and the acronym (VAST) refers to Visual Agile and Simple Threat modelling. Scalability is one of the main advantages of VAST; it can be implemented in large projects and organisations. However, one of the limitations is that it requires operational threat models and creating DFDs as the key steps.

Octave

It was suggested by the CERT (Computer Emergency Response Team) in 2003 (Alberts et al. 2003) and the acronym OCTAVE refers to Operationally Critical Threat Asset and Vulnerability Evaluation. It is the approach for risk management dependent on strategic assessment. Technology risks are out of scope of this model and only organisational risks are considered. Also, there is another thing that limits its implementation and that is the complex documentation required in this model (Deng et al. 2011).

Trike

It was initially developed as a security audit framework (Saitta et al. 2005, Stanganelli 2016) and it is similar approach with vague and complex documentation. Also, it is requires building a DFD as part of the modelling process.

Coras

It is model-based risk assessment methodology of a similar limitation of meagre documentation (CORAS 2000). In addition to that, it requires development of CORAS diagrams for modelling the threats (den Braber et al. 2007) and it can require the knowledge of Unified Modelling Language (UML) (OMG 2017).

Htmm

It was developed by the Software Engineering Institute in 2018, and the acronym (HTMM) refers to a Hybrid Threat Modelling Method. It is based on the combination of Security Cards, persona non grata (PnG) activities, and SQUARE (Security Quality Requirements Engineering Method) (Mead and Stehney 2005). However, it focuses on software systems and requires the knowledge of identifying PnGs and applying for security cards. PnGs are like consultants who identify plausible vulnerabilities in the system and suggests mitigation strategies to address these vulnerabilities. Security cards are a structured approach to developing checklists for users to identify sophisticated attacks. This is especially challenging for the construction industry stakeholders who lack the necessary skill and expertise.

Linddun

It is another method suggested in the literature (Deng et al. 2011, Wuyts et al. 2018) and the acronym (LINDDUN) refers to Linkability, Identifiability, Non-Repudiation, Detectability, Disclosure of Information, Unawareness, Non-Compliance. However, it primarily focuses on data security and privacy concerns, limiting its comprehensive applicability to the construction industry. For example, this method does not focus on threats related to a functional modification of construction equipment like a tower crane excavator that can cause significant damage to assets such as columns and facade and to construction personal like engineers and workers.

Undoubtedly, the construction sector can learn from the existing models, methods, and standards. Due to their unique communication structure and corresponding cybersecurity challenges in the construction project, the existing studies and standards do not correspond to all the lifecycle phases of a construction project.

The limitations and disadvantages of existing threat modelling methods and standards are (Mantha et al. 2021):

1. They focus only on data exchange security and on building systems in the built environment.
2. They neglect bidding, planning, design, and construction phases.
3. They might require domain-specific knowledge.
4. They are time-consuming and tedious.
5. They lack an approach where the construction-related threats, attackers, vulnerabilities, and assets are identified and mapped.

Construction CPSs Security Requirements

According to National Institute of Standards and Technology (NIST) guidelines (Monostori et al. 2016), ensuring trust between the Internet of Things (IoT) and CPSs should consist of several factors. This is because both IoT and CPSs are depend on security, safety, consistency, privacy, resiliency, dependability, reliability, coordination, and interaction, all of these are combined to form a trustworthy and well-designed system. A perfect CPSs mechanism is achieved if this condition is satisfied. In the following subsections, the CPSs security requirements are defined and discussed.

Privacy

In CPSs, a massive collection process for data is constantly taking place, which most people are unaware of (Belguith et al. 2018). Therefore, any person in construction or in any other industry has the right to know what type of data is being collected about them and to whom these data are being shared with, and this in addition to their right to access their own data. However, this also requires preventing unauthorized and illegal access to the personal data and information disclosure of the users (Kaaniche and Laurent 2017).

Dependability

Intelligent Physical World (IPW) ensures that the CPSs adaptive behaviour is accomplished to assure the right Quality of Service (QoS) and to bring higher dependability and through the adoption of fault-tolerance mechanisms in real-time. Dependability includes two other qualities, reliability, and safety. Safety is often an objective defined in terms of the goals of organisation (Monostori et al. 2016). This is because of the cyber-security risks, and negative impacts, where vulnerabilities can be exploited and compromised by a hacker, or because of CPSs failure. So, safety is a strong concern for IoT, CPSs and Internet of Cyber- Physical Things (IoCPT) users alike. While reliability is based on the capability to adapt with variable conditions to recover and overcome from any potential problems and disruption either based on physical and cyber-attacks, in addition to natural disasters (Monostori et al. 2016). Physical systems depend on proper functionality and timing. However, if there are any potential mismatches, uncertainty and unreliability can cause disruptions and problems for services of CPSs. Therefore, maintaining a high reliability requires decreasing the levels of uncertainty. In fact, to sort electronic components imperfect reliability, it is also recommended to perform algorithms for error-correction (Rajamaki et al., 2012). As a result, (Rajamaki et al. 2012) stated that behaviour of CPSs could be predictable by performing and implementing artificial intelligence /Machine Learning (ML) schemes.

Resiliency

To overcome malicious and accidental attacks, CPSs have to be resilient. Therefore, CPSs physical and logical systems are prone to cyber security vulnerabilities from a security aspect.

Interaction and Coordination

They are essential to ensure the security of CPSs operations in all-time. Also, interaction and coordination between physical and cyber system components are the key aspect in CPSs (Hu et al. 2016). In fact, the characteristics of the main physical world are based on the constant change of the system over time. While the characteristics of the cyber world are based on sequence series without temporal semantics. So, to maintain the interaction and coordination between physical and cyber system elements, two basic approaches are presented to study and analyses this problem. The first one is the "cyberising" the physical (CtP) aspect through the introduction of cyber interfaces and properties and into physical systems and the second one is the "physicalising" the cyber (PtC) where cyber-software elements are to be represented in real-time (Deshmukh et al. 2013).

System Hardening

System hardening can be employed to defend against a lot of threats. Therefore, it is highly recommended to insulate critical applications that lack the appropriate measures for security from any Operating System (OS) that is not trusted in order to boost the security of CPSs and IoCPSs. Deshmukh et al. (2013), analysed several trust-computing technologies with their applications in the CPSs field. According to (Almohri et al. 2017), such analysis included an Encrypted Execution Environment (E3), Trusted Execution Environments (TEE), Trusted Platform Module (TPM), and Secure Elements (SE), to increase the integrity of operation systems. This allowed the enhancement of CPSs by improving the integrity of the system. However, suppose the Graph-based optimization was put together with parameters and in this way it can provide a reasoning basis to guarantee overall system integrity (Almohri et al. 2016). Therefore, in order to increase the security level, it is very important to set the right privileges such as task-based, rule-based, and role-based, in addition to setting strong password complexity policies. Moreover, to reduce exposure to remote wireless attacks, this also includes removing any old unused accounts and unused ports. So, therefore CPSs nature must be taken into consideration before achieving any design.

Operational Security (OpSec)

OpSec was introduced in 1988 to guarantee personnel security, information security, and physical security (Brabant and Van Brabant 2000) through careful risk assessment, careful planning, and careful risk management assessment (Aven 2016). Its primary task is to guarantee operational efficiency by denying any unauthorised access to private or public information, hence controlling observable actions and information about a given CPSs, particularly in inimical areas and environments (Brabant and Van Brabant 2000). One of its main advantages is providing the means to develop cost-effective measures for security to ride a given threat.

OpSec includes five main steps to achieve this task:

Critical Information Identification

Identify the critical information that can effectively degrade the operational effectiveness of a CPSs or place it is potential organisational success at risk if this critical information has been targeted.

Threat Analysis

Includes recognising capabilities and potentials of an adversary to gather information, analyze, process, and use the needed information.

Vulnerability Analysis

Analyse if there are any gaps that could affect the operations of CPSs, and it includes studying the strengths of an adversary and the weaknesses of a given CPS. consequently, developing an imaginable view over how a potential adversary might exploit this gap in security to perform a security breaking.

Risk Assessment

Risks are assessed according to the combination of vulnerability and threat levels, depending on the degree of these threat levels (low or high levels). The assessment of Risk levels includes evaluating the cost of implementing the right security measures by ensuring a trade-off between the benefits balance and effective cost.

Appropriate Application Countermeasures

Once the trade-off between the benefits balance and effective cost is achieved in the earlier phase, then the appropriate countermeasures are developed to offer the desired protection of CPSs against these ongoing threats in terms of effectiveness, cost, and feasibility.

CPSs Security Challenges

There are many benefits for the adoption of security standards and measures when it comes to protecting layers, components, and domains of CPSs. However, despite these advantages, the application of these security measures can impact CPSs, and these impacts can be summarized as follows (Yaacoub et al. 2020):

Reduced Performance

CPSs security measures can be partially or fully affected by performing these measures if the balance trade-off between security and performance is not carefully taken into consideration. This can affect normal operations and requires more human interventions to assign domains and services manually.

Higher Power Consumption

It is a serious issue, essentially for battery-limited and resource-constrained end devices of CPSs. A higher power consumption means a higher cost to maintain and a shorter lifespan.

Transmission Delays

Data transmissions are prone to delays because of the additional process of encryption that is being added to hinder and stop the active and passive eavesdropping attacks. In spite of the protective feature that it offers, this is rejected in real-time CPSs.

Higher Cost

When security levels are high, then the computational costs will be high, which are not limited to the initial capital spending phase, but also include updates, training, and operational phases.

Compatibility Issues

Some of the employed security measures are not compatible with some CPSs and vice versa. This can be because of the firmware, or the software in use, Operating System, etc.

Operational Security Delays

There is always a training phase that precedes the full operational security mode upon the deployment of any security service. Thus, the service will be temporarily ineffective or basic and prone to attacks.

CPSs Security Solutions

A lot of effort was taken to manage and asses risks, specifically focusing on the security of the built environment and Building Information Modelling (BIM) data sharing. For example, a cybersecurity framework was developed by NIST for managing and accessing critical infrastructure. Although the NIST framework emphasizes detection and identification as primary steps for the management of cyber risk, which are the key components of threat modelling, it does not detail vulnerabilities and cyber threats in construction (NIST 2018). Due to that none of the studies employed and adopted these procedures during construction. On the other hand, the Publicly Available Specification (PAS) 1192-5, developed by the British Standards Institute (BSI), focuses on the security of information. It provides a framework to guarantee that the data and information is shared in a security-minded way. This is to enable the security and reliability of digitally built assets, taking into consideration that the stored data about built assets could be used by a person with malicious intent (PAS 1192-5 2015). Another regulation, namely GDPR and it refers to General Data Protection Regulation that was introduced in Europe in the year 2018 , requires improved cyber-security for the operators of essential services, including construction projects using digitally built environments, including intelligent buildings and digital infrastructure (GDPR 2018). Best practices were established and provided by these documents to improve the security of facility management and construction management practices. As mentioned and discussed previously, cybersecurity attacks and incidents still take place although companies considered these practices and standards suggested and introduced by the governments. This is due to a lack of continued understanding of the landscape of cyber threat. Attackers work relentlessly to find loopholes, faults, and weak-points in the existing systems and take advantage of the weak links. Therefore, as a part of the process of risk management, it is essential to continually evaluate security for any system.

Maintaining a secure environment for CPSs is not an easy task due to the constant increase of integration issues, challenges, and limitations of existing solutions, including the privacy, lack of security, and accuracy issues. Nonetheless, this can be mitigated by using different means including cryptographic solutions and non-cryptographic solutions.

Cryptographic Solutions

Cryptographic measures are mainly utilized to secure the communication channel from any unauthorized interception and access along with any active/passive attacks (Chandia et al. 2007). In fact, traditional cryptography approaches based on performing hash and cypher's function are not easy to apply to CPSs, including IoCPT, because of the constraints of size and power. As a result, the concentration must be limited to data security, and instead, it must ensure and maintain the efficiency of the overall system process alongside. Cryptographic solutions were classified by Yaacoub et al. (2020) based on fulfilling one of the following security goals: Availability, Confidentiality, Authentication, Integrity, and Privacy Preserving.

Non-Cryptographic Solutions

Several non-cryptographic solutions were also introduced and developed to eliminate and mitigate any possible malicious event or cyber-attack. This was done by implementing firewalls, Intrusion Detection Systems (IDS), and Honeypots. As a result, several researchers presented several solutions which are mentioned and discussed in the following subsections.

Intrusion Detection Systems (IDS)

Various types of IDS methodology are available because of the availability of several network configurations. Each IDS methodology has its own drawbacks and advantages when it comes to configuration, detection, placement in the network, and cost. In fact, the available approaches were designed mainly to detect specific attacks against specific applications, including Unmanned Aerial Vehicles (UAV) (Mitchell and Chen 2014b), Industrial Control Processes (Urbina et al. 2016), and smart grids (Sridhar et al. 2012).

The main four methods of IDS are signature-based, anomaly-based, behaviour-based, and hybrid-based.

Signature-based

Although this technique is very easy and fast to configure it is effective only for detecting known threats. Thus, it is ineffective against the detection of variants and new threats and shows weakness against them due to their matching signature remaining unknown and constantly updating its signature patches, encrypting services and polymorphic malware are examples of these threats. Regardless to its limited capability, signature-based IDS is very effective and very accurate against known threats (Liao et al. 2013).

Anomaly-based

This type compares the activites of the system instantly together with its capability to generate an alert when any deviation is detected from normal behaviour. However, such a detection technique suffers from a high false-positive rate (Mitchell and Chen 2014a). T.-H. Lee et al. (2014) suggested that energy consumption must be recognised as a parameter to analyse the behaviour of each node. Thus, defining a regular model for the consumption of energy for each route-over routing scheme and mesh-under routing scheme, where each node will monitor its own consumption. Thus, the IDS classifies the node as malicious and removes it when the node deviates from the normal energy consumption. Based on the evolving Spiking Neural Network algorithm Demertzis et al. (2017) presented in an advanced Spiking One-Class Anomaly Detection Framework (SOCCADF). And based on the author's findings, SOCCADF is highly suitable for difficult applications and problems with a massive amount of data. According to the author's results, SOCCADF has a higher performance at a very fast learning speed, with higher reliability, accuracy, and efficiency.

Behaviour-based

Behaviour-based can be identified as a set of thresholds and rules executed to define the expected behaviour of the components of the network, including both protocols and nodes. This approach can detect any intrusion as soon as the behaviour of the network deviates from its original behaviour. Behaviour-based provides a lower false-positive rate than anomaly-based detection and that is because it acts in the same way as anomaly-based detection with a slight difference from specification-based systems where a human expert is needed to manually define each specification rule (Mitchell and Chen 2014a). Therefore, no need for any training phase since they are implemented to operate instantly.

However, such an approach is not fit for all scenarios and may become error prone and time-consuming.

Hybrid-based

It is based on using specification-based techniques of signature and anomaly-based detection towards minimizing their drawbacks and maximizing their advantage. Raza et al. (2013) presented a hybrid IDS known as SVELTE, which offers the right trade-off between the computational cost of anomaly-based methods and the storage cost of signature-based methods. Krimmling and Peter (2014) combined anomaly and signature-based IDS approaches to cover and detect a wider attack range and tested their approach using the IDS evaluation framework that they presented.

Firewalls

Firewalls faced a rare use of employment in the CPSs domain because of the advancement of artificial intelligence and IDS technologies. Therefore, a small number were presented for firewall-based solutions. Jiang et al. (2017) mentioned the use of paired firewalls between manufacturing and enterprise zones to improve the cybersecurity of servers.

Honeypots and Deception Techniques

CPSs use deception which is a key defensive security measure to protect and hide their system which can be done using honeypots. However, other deceptive solutions also exist. For example, Antonioli et al. (2016) presented the design of a high-interaction, virtual, server-based ICS honeypot to ensure a cost-effective, realistic, and maintainable ICS honeypot that detects and captures the activities of attackers. Also, Duan et al. (2018) introduced a new framework called "CONCEAL" as a new deception and as a service paradigm that is scalable and effective. This was done by combining k-anonymity, m-mutation, and l-diversity. Where k-anonymity was used for fingerprint anonymization, m-mutation for address anonymization and l-diversity for configuration diversification. Another solution presented by Bernieri et al. (2018) called DDA (Deep Detection Architecture) to provide cyber-physical security for ISC. A cyber-physical simulation methodology was also exploited and presented to analyse the security modules under several attack scenarios. Moreover, DDA will be used into the IR 4.0 paradigm and widely used for the next ICS generation.

Security Solutions for CPSs in the Construction Industry

In the next subsections a list of the security solutions that can be applied to CPSs in the construction industry (Jain et al. 2012, Linares Garcia and Roofigari-Esfahan 2020):

Encryption

Due to the massive amount of information and data that is shared in open channels and publicly in the construction industry, encryption is a need for in construction CPSs. Encryption provides the ability to securely transfer data through these networks by avoiding sensitive information to be observed by malicious attackers and unauthorised access as well as hiding the original data. Also shared keys are a technique used within the context of encryption to provide the right keys to decode the encrypted information to the involved persons. In this way, information between stakeholders, sensors, and systems will have the right keys to decode encrypted data.

Communication under Security

CPSs components may need to collaborate automatically within secured networks. Therefore, a several devices have to be programmed to cooperate and effectively communicate regardless of the security measures placed in the system.

Data Aggregation

Data aggregation refers to when multiple CPSs components collect information within an information hub, and are then transferred this collected information outside or inside the system. Securing aggregated data is very important in CPSs networks because the aggregated data is desirable to attackers.

Summary

The construction industry makes a shift towards automation and digitization due to the increased growth of communication and information technologies as well as the Internet of Things (IoT), machine learning, 3D printing, and big data. These technologies will transform the lifecycle phases of the construction projects design, planning, implementation, and operation and maintenance, positively impacting the overall project productivity, cost, time, and quality. As the implementation of CPSs is growing, security challenges are also rising and need to be considered. Operating in a digital environment makes the construction industry significantly vulnerable to cyber-attacks. Several cyberattacks have already happened in the construction industry to negatively affect operations, tamper with existing records, access unauthorized files, and steal proprietary information. Given the various attacks, threats, and vulnerabilities that the CPSs domain suffers from, the main failures that could affect the implementation of CPSs in construction are: timing, content, sensors, silent, babbling, service, budget, Consistent, inconsistent, and schedule failures. These failures will result in delays, cascading failures, affecting performance, financial losses, loss of life, and disclosure of information. Several threats modelling was developed to understand cybersecurity threats and devise effective and efficient action plans like (PASTA, STRIDE, VAST, TRIKE, OCTAVE, CORAS, HTMM, AND LINDDUN). CPSs in the construction industry are required to fulfil privacy, dependability, consistency, resiliency, interaction, reliability, and coordination, to form a trustworthy and well-designed system. A lot of the security solutions for sensor networks can be applied to CPSs in the construction industry, like encryption solutions, communication under security, and data aggregation.

Despite their several advantages, CPSs in construction are exposed to several cyber and/or physical security attacks, challenges, and threats. This is because of their diverse nature, reliance on sensitive and private data, and large-scale deployment. As such, accidental or intentional exposures of these systems can result in catastrophic effects, which makes it critical to put in place solid security measures. The complex chain of interactions, dynamics, coordination, and data exchange between various inter-connected construction project stakeholders pose unique productivity, performance, and security risks.

References

A shostack. 2014. Threat modeling: Designing for security – Google Scholar. https://scholar.google.com/scholar?hl=en&as_sdt=1%2C5&q=Threat+modeling%3A+Designing+for+security&btnG=

Agarwal. 2016. Agarwal: Vast methodology: Visual, agile, and simple... – Google Scholar. https://scholar.google.com/scholar_lookup?title=Vast methodology%3A Visual%2C agile%2C and simple threat modeling. Various Interviews&author=A. Agarwal&publication_year=2016

Al-Muhtadi, J., K. Saleem, S. Al-Rabiaah, M. Imran, A. Gawanmeh and J. J. P. C. Rodrigues. 2021. A lightweight cyber security framework with context-awareness for pervasive computing environments. Sustainable Cities and Society, 66, 102610. https://doi.org/10.1016/j.scs.2020.102610

Alberts, C., A. Dorofee and J. Stevens. 2003. Introduction to the OCTAVE® Approach Approach. https://apps.dtic.mil/sti/citations/ADA634134

AlHogail, A. 2018. Improving IoT technology adoption through improving consumer trust. Technologies, 6(3), 64. https://doi.org/10.3390/technologies6030064

Almohri, H., L. Cheng, D. Yao and H. Alemzadeh. 2017. On threat modeling and mitigation of medical cyber-physical systems. Proceedings – 2017 IEEE 2nd International Conference on Connected Health: Applications, Systems and Engineering Technologies, CHASE 2017, 114–119. https://doi.org/10.1109/CHASE.2017.69

Almohri, H. M. J., L. T. Watson, D. Yao and X. Ou. 2016. Security optimization of dynamic networks with probabilistic graph modeling and linear programming. IEEE Transactions on Dependable and Secure Computing, 13(4), 474–487. https://doi.org/10.1109/TDSC.2015.2411264

Antonioli, D., A. Agrawal and N. O. Tippenhauer. 2016. Towards high-interaction virtual ICS honeypots-in-a-box. CPS-SPC 2016 – Proceedings of the 2nd ACM Workshop on Cyber-Physical Systems Security and PrivaCy, Co-Located with CCS 2016, 13–22. https://doi.org/10.1145/2994487.2994493

Ashibani, Y. and Q. H. Mahmoud. 2017. Cyber physical systems security: Analysis, challenges and solutions. Computers and Security, 68, 81–97. https://doi.org/10.1016/j.cose.2017.04.005

Aven, T. 2016. Risk assessment and risk management: Review of recent advances on their foundation. European Journal of Operational Research, 253(1), 1–13. Elsevier B.V. https://doi.org/10.1016/j.ejor.2015.12.023

Avižienis, A., J. C. Laprie, B. Randell and C. Landwehr. 2004. Basic concepts and taxonomy of dependable and secure computing. IEEE Transactions on Dependable and Secure Computing, 1(1), 11–33. https://doi.org/10.1109/TDSC.2004.2

Belguith, S., N. Kaaniche and G. Russello. 2018. PU-ABE: Lightweight attribute-based encryption supporting access policy update for cloud assisted IoT. IEEE International Conference on Cloud Computing, CLOUD, 2018-July, 924–927. https://doi.org/10.1109/CLOUD.2018.00137

Bernieri, G., M. Conti and F. Pascucci. 2018. A novel architecture for cyber-physical security in industrial control networks. IEEE 4th International Forum on Research and Technologies for Society and Industry, RTSI 2018 – Proceedings. https://doi.org/10.1109/RTSI.2018.8548438

Bhushan, B., A. Khamparia, K. M. Sagayam, S. K. Sharma, M. A. Ahad and N. C. Debnath. 2020. Blockchain for smart cities: A review of architectures, integration trends and future research directions. Sustainable Cities and Society, 61, 102360. https://doi.org/10.1016/j.scs.2020.102360

Bodeau, D. J., C. D. Mccollum and D. B. Fox. 2018. Cyber Threat Modeling: Survey, Assessment, and Representative Framework | The MITRE Corporation. https://www.mitre.org/publications/technical-papers/cyber-threat-modeling-survey-assessment-and-representative-framework

Brabant, K. Van and K. Van Brabant. 2000. Review practice humanitarian practice network formerly the relief and rehabilitation network operational security management in violent environments HPN. HPN Good Practice Review 8 Operational Security Management in Violent Environments. www.odihpn org.uk

Cárdenas, A. A., S. Amin, Z. S. Lin, Y. L. Huang, C. Y. Huang and S. Sastry. 2011. Attacks against process control systems: Risk assessment, detection, and response. Proceedings of the 6th International Symposium on Information, Computer and Communications Security, ASIACCS 2011, 355–366. https://doi.org/10.1145/1966913.1966959

Chae, S. and T. Yoshida. 2010. Application of RFID technology to prevention of collision accident with heavy equipment. Automation in Construction, 19(3), 368–374. https://doi.org/10.1016/j.autcon.2009.12.008

Chandia, R., J. Gonzalez, T. Kilpatrick, M. Papa and S. Shenoi. 2007. Security strategies for SCADA networks. IFIP International Federation for Information Processing, 253, 117–131. https://doi.org/10.1007/978-0-387-75462-8_9

CORAS. 2000. The CORAS Method. http://coras.sourceforge.net/index.html

Demertzis, K., L. Iliadis and S. Spartalis. 2017. A spiking one-class anomaly detection framework for cyber-security on industrial control systems. Communications in Computer and Information Science, 744, 122–134. https://doi.org/10.1007/978-3-319-65172-9_11

den Braber, F., I. Hogganvik, M. S. Lund, K. Stølen and F. Vraalsen. 2007. Model-based security analysis in seven steps – A guided tour to the CORAS method. BT Technology Journal, 25(1), 101–117. https://doi.org/10.1007/s10550-007-0013-9

Deng, M., K. Wuyts, R. Scandariato, B. Preneel and W. Joosen. 2011. A privacy threat analysis framework: Supporting the elicitation and fulfillment of privacy requirements.

Eequirements Engineering, 16(1), 3-32. https://doi.org/10.1007/s00766-010-0115-7. pdf

Deshmukh, S., B. Natarajan and A. Pahwa. 2013. State estimation in spatially distributed cyber-physical systems: Bounds on critical measurement drop rates. Proceedings – IEEE International Conference on Distributed Computing in Sensor Systems, DCoSS 2013, 157–164. https://doi.org/10.1109/DCOSS.2013.23

Duan, Q., E. Al-Shaer, M. Islam and H. Jafarian. 2018. CONCEAL: A strategy composition for resilient cyber deception-framework, metrics and deployment. 2018 IEEE Conference on Communications and Network Security, CNS 2018. https://doi.org/10.1109/CNS.2018.8433196

Ferrag, M. A., L. A. Maglaras, H. Janicke, J. Jiang and L. Shu. 2018. A systematic review of data protection and privacy preservation schemes for smart grid communications. Sustainable Cities and Society, 38, 806–835. https://doi.org/10.1016/j.scs.2017.12.041

General Data Protection Regulation (GDPR). 2018. An EPSU Briefing. *In*: epsu.org. Retrieved June 15, 2021 from https://www.epsu.org/sites/default/files/article/files/GDPR_Final_EPSU.pdf

Golparvar-Fard, M., S. Savarese and F. Peña-Mora. 2009. Interactive visual construction progress monitoring with D4A - 4D augmented reality – Models. Building a Sustainable Future – Proceedings of the 2009 Construction Research Congress, 41–50. https://doi.org/10.1061/41020(339)5

Gunes, V., S. Peter, T. Givargis and F. Vahid. 2014. A survey on concepts, applications, and challenges in cyber-physical systems. KSII Transactions on Internet and Information Systems, 8(12), 4242–4268. https://doi.org/10.3837/tiis.2014.12.001

Hu, F., Y. Lu, A. V. Vasilakos, Q. Hao, R. Ma, Y. Patil, T. Zhang, J. Lu, X. Li and N. N. Xiong. 2016. Robust Cyber-Physical Systems: Concept, models, and implementation. Future Generation Computer Systems, 56, 449–475. https://doi.org/10.1016/j.future.2015.06.006

Hutchins, M. J., R. Bhinge, M. K. Micali, S. L. Robinson, J. W. Sutherland and D. Dornfeld. 2015. Framework for identifying cybersecurity risks in manufacturing. Procedia Manufacturing, 1, 47–63. https://doi.org/10.1016/j.promfg.2015.09.060

Jain, A., K. Kant and M. R. Tripathy. 2012. Security solutions for wireless sensor networks. Proceedings – 2012 2nd International Conference on Advanced Computing and Communication Technologies, ACCT 2012, 430–433. https://doi.org/10.1109/ACCT.2012.102

Jiang, N., H. Lin, Z. Yin and C. Xi. 2017. Research of paired industrial firewalls in defense-in-depth architecture of integrated manufacturing or production system. 2017 IEEE International Conference on Information and Automation, ICIA 2017, 523–526. https://doi.org/10.1109/ICInfA.2017.8078963

Johnson, T. 2010. Fault-tolerant distributed cyber-physical systems: Two case studies. Retrieved from http://hdl.handle.net/2142/16191.

Kaaniche, N. and M. Laurent. 2017. Data security and privacy preservation in cloud storage environments based on cryptographic mechanisms. Computer Communications, 111, 120–141. Elsevier B.V. https://doi.org/10.1016/j.comcom.2017.07.006

Khan, R., K. McLaughlin, D. Laverty and S. Sezer. 2017. STRIDE-based threat modeling for cyber-physical systems. 2017 IEEE PES Innovative Smart Grid Technologies Conference Europe, ISGT-Europe 2017 – Proceedings, 2018-January, 1–6. https://doi.org/10.1109/ISGTEurope.2017.8260283

Krimmling, J. and S. Peter. 2014. Integration and evaluation of intrusion detection for

CoAP in smart city applications. 2014 IEEE Conference on Communications and Network Security, CNS 2014, 73–78. https://doi.org/10.1109/CNS.2014.6997468

Kohnfelder, L. and P. Garg (n.d.) Kohnfelder: The threats to our products – Google Scholar. 1999. Retrieved June 13, 2021, from https://scholar.google.com/scholar_lookup?title='The threats to our products'%2C Microsoft Interface&author=L. Kohnfelder&publication_year=1999

Lee, J. D. and K. A. See. 2004. Trust in automation: Designing for appropriate reliance. Human Factors, 46(1), 50–80. Human Factors and Ergonomics Society. https://doi.org/10.1518/hfes.46.1.50_30392

Lee, T.-H., C.-H. Wen, L.-H. Chang, H.-S. Chiang and M.-C. Hsieh. 2014. A Lightweight Intrusion Detection Scheme Based on Energy Consumption Analysis in 6LowPAN (pp. 1205–1213). Springer, Dordrecht. https://doi.org/10.1007/978-94-007-7262-5_137

Li, Xuan, C. Zhou, Y. C. Tian, N. Xiong and Y. Qin. 2018. Asset-based dynamic impact assessment of cyberattacks for risk analysis in industrial control systems. IEEE Transactions on Industrial Informatics, 14(2), 608–618. https://doi.org/10.1109/TII.2017.2740571

Liao, H. J., C. H. Richard, Y. C. Lin and K. Y. Tung. 2013. Intrusion detection system: A comprehensive review. Journal of Network and Computer Applications, 36(1), 16–24). Academic Press. https://doi.org/10.1016/j.jnca.2012.09.004

Lu, T., B. Xu, X. Guo, L. Zhao and F. Xie. 2013. A New Multilevel Framework for Cyber-Physical System Security. *In*: terraswarm.org. http://www.terraswarm.org/pubs/136/lu_newmultiframe_edge.pdf

Mantha, B., B. García de Soto and R. Karri. 2020. Cyber Security threat modeling in the construction industry: A countermeasure example during the commissioning process. https://doi.org/10.31224/osf.io/gn78a

Mantha, B., B. García de Soto and R. Karri. 2021. Cyber security threat modeling in the AEC industry: An example for the commissioning of the built environment. Sustainable Cities and Society, 66, 102682. https://doi.org/10.1016/j.scs.2020.102682

Mantha, B. R. K. and B. Garcia de Soto. 2019. Cyber security challenges and vulnerability assessment in the construction industry. Repozitorium.Omikk.Bme.Hu. https://doi.org/10.3311/CCC2019-005

Mead, N. R. and T. Stehney. 2005. Security quality requirements engineering (SQUARE) methodology. ACM SIGSOFT Software Engineering Notes, 30(4), 1–7. https://doi.org/10.1145/1082983.1083214

Mitchell, R. and I. R. Chen. 2014a. A survey of intrusion detection techniques for cyber-physical systems. ACM Computing Surveys, 46(4). Association for Computing Machinery. https://doi.org/10.1145/2542049

Mitchell, R. and I. R. Chen. 2014b. Adaptive intrusion detection of malicious unmanned air vehicles using behavior rule specifications. IEEE Transactions on Systems, Man, and Cybernetics: Systems, 44(5), 593–604. https://doi.org/10.1109/TSMC.2013.2265083

Monostori, L., B. Kádár, T. Bauernhansl, S. Kondoh, S. Kumara, G. Reinhart, O. Sauer, G. Schuh, W. Sihn and K. Ueda. 2016. Cyber-physical systems in manufacturing. CIRP Annals, 65(2), 621–641. https://doi.org/10.1016/j.cirp.2016.06.005

NIST. 2018. Framework for Improving Critical Infrastructure Cybersecurity, Version 1.1. https://doi.org/10.6028/NIST.CSWP.04162018

OMG. 2017. About the Unified Modeling Language Specification, Version 2.5.1. https://www.omg.org/spec/UML/About-UML/

PAS 1192-5:2015. n.d. Specification for security-minded building information modelling, digital built environments and smart asset management. 2015. Retrieved June 15, 2021, from https://shop.bsigroup.com/ProductDetail?pid=000000000030314119

Pash, C. 2018. How hackers and spies tried to steal the secrets... – Google Scholar. https://scholar.google.com/scholar?hl=en&as_sdt=1%2C5&q=How+hackers+and+spies+tried+to+steal+the+secrets+of+Australia's+one-armed+robot+887+bricklayer%2C&btnG=

Peng, Y., T. Lu, J. Liu, Y. Gao, X. Guo and F. Xie. 2013. Cyber-physical system risk assessment. Proceedings – 2013 9th International Conference on Intelligent Information Hiding and Multimedia Signal Processing, IIH-MSP 2013, 442–447. https://doi.org/10.1109/IIH-MSP.2013.116

Rajamaki, J., P. Rathod, A. Ahlgren, J. Aho, M. Takari and S. Ahlgren. 2012. Resilience of Cyber-Physical System: A Case Study of Safe School Environment. https://doi.org/10.1109/eisic.2012.10

Raza, S., L. Wallgren and T. Voigt. 2013. SVELTE: Real-time intrusion detection in the Internet of Things. Ad Hoc Networks, 11(8), 2661–2674. https://doi.org/10.1016/j.adhoc.2013.04.014

Saitta, P., B. Larcom and M. Eddington. 2005. Trike v.1 Methodology Document – Google Scholar. https://scholar.google.com/scholar?hl=en&as_sdt=1%2C5&q=Trike+v.1+Methodology+Document&btnG=

Sawyer T. and J. Rubenstone. 2019. Construction Cybercrime is on the Rise | 2019-05-08 | Engineering News-Record. https://www.enr.com/articles/46832-construction-cybercrime-is-on-the-rise

Sridhar, S., A. Hahn and M. Govindarasu. 2012. Cyber-physical system security for the electric power grid. Proceedings of the IEEE, 100(1), 210–224. https://doi.org/10.1109/JPROC.2011.2165269

Stanganelli J. 2016. Selecting a Threat Risk Model for Your Organization – Part Two. https://www.esecurityplanet.com/networks/selecting-a-threat-risk-model-for-your-organization-part-two/

Thomas, R. K., A. A. Cárdenas and R. B. Bobba. 2015. First workshop on Cyber-Physical Systems Security and PrivaCy (CPS-SPC): Challenges and research directions. Proceedings of the ACM Conference on Computer and Communications Security, 2015-October, 1705–1706. https://doi.org/10.1145/2810103.2812621

Ucedavélez, T. and M. M. Morana. 2015. Risk Centric Threat Modeling: Process for Attack Simulation and Threat Analysis. Wiley Blackwell. https://doi.org/10.1002/9781118988374

Urbina, D. I., J. Giraldo, A. A. Cardenas, N. O. Tippenhauer, J. Valente, M. Faisal, J. Ruths, R. Candell and H. Sandberg. 2016. Limiting the impact of stealthy attacks on industrial control systems. Proceedings of the 2016 ACM SIGSAC Conference on Computer and Communications Security. http://dx.doi.org/10.1145/2976749.2978388

Wuyts, K., D. Van Landuyt, A. Hovsepyan and W. Joosen. 2018. Effective and efficient privacy threat modeling through domain refinements. Proceedings of the ACM Symposium on Applied Computing, 1175–1178. https://doi.org/10.1145/3167132.3167414

Yaacoub, J. P. A., O. Salman, H. N. Noura, N. Kaaniche, A. Chehab and M. Malli. 2020. Cyber-physical systems security: Limitations, issues and future trends. Microprocessors and Microsystems, 77, 103201. https://doi.org/10.1016/j.micpro.2020.103201

Applications of Cyber-Physical Systems in Construction Projects

Khalid Mhmoud Alzubi, Wesam Salah Alaloul, and Abdul Hannan Qureshi

Introduction

Construction projects and the built environment are expected to be augmented by autonomous and connected systems to improve operations, productivity, comfort, safety, and communication. There is an essential need for an integrated approach to support the construction decision-making processes and to help in real-time project management and during the operation and maintenance of constructed facilities for intelligent real-time facility management (Shen et al. 2008). Thus, this integration will provide a way for taking the right decisions promptly by construction engineers and facility managers to improve productivity and efficiency. The adoption and integration of a CPSs technologies provides great opportunities to make the construction process more sustainable and intelligent (Anumba et al. 2010).

The application of CPSs in the construction projects will improve the way infrastructure and buildings are managed, built, and connected to other autonomous systems like transportation (Linares et al. 2019). Their integration via a CPSs aims to eliminate or decrease manual information gathering on the field and provide construction progress reports in real-time or minimize the time required for preparing the reports. It will save time for humans to focus on more aggregated-value and decision-making tasks (Correa 2018). Also, the benefits of CPSs implementation in construction projects includes the automation of simple and repetitive activities, increased modularization, increased productivity, increased safety, and the integration of future technology trends that enhance project outcomes (Linares et al. 2019).

Virtual prototyping wireless sensing technologies has been identified by research as having the ability to improve the construction delivery process: for example Building Information Modelling (BIM) has the potential to enhance the creation, exchanging, sharing, and management of construction information during the lifecycle of a project (Motamedi et al. 2009). Wireless sensors can collect data and store a wide range of real-time information from physical worlds. Many research projects have examined the use of Radio Frequency Identification (RFID), Global Positioning Systems (GPS), accelerometers, and other tracking technologies to track and monitor the movement of materials and personnel on the construction sites (Alshibani 2018, Joshua and Varghese 2011, Sherafat et al. 2020). Also, in recent years, several researchers have explored the integration of physical construction components and virtual models using several data acquisition technologies such as photographs, laser scanners and RFID tags. Some of these integration efforts and their limitations are briefly discussed here. Golparvar-Fard et al. (2009) explored the integration of digital cameras and Four-Dimensional Computer-Aided Design (4D CAD) to visualise progress deviations in construction projects. This approach involves superimposing the as-planned 4D CAD model into time-lapse photography and videotaping for collecting the as-built progress data. Bosche et al. (2008) integrating Three-Dimensional Computer-Aided Design (3D CAD) models and data from laser scanning for automated tracking of project progress. The approach enables an automated recognition of 3D CAD model objects from site data collected from laser scanning. The major drawback of the use of laser scan and digital photographs is that a number of images will need to be taken to fully capture the construction activities and further processing of the images is required, thus hindering access to real-time information. Also, digital photographs cannot be taken in bad weather.

Several researchers have utilized RFID tags for integrating the physical construction components and virtual models: Chin et al. (2005) investigated the use of RFID tags and 4D CAD for monitoring the progress in the supply chain management. In this study RFID were tagged on structural elements such as steel and curtain walls to track their status through the stages from the ordering to the delivery, receipt, and finally to the implementation stage. The status was captured in a 3D model to indicate progress status. Also, W. Hu (2008) developed an integrated RFID and 4D CAD model for tracking the construction components status. Construction elements like pipes, equipment, steel columns and beams are tagged with RFID passive tags, and an RFID reader is used to track their status from the manufacturing or fabrication plant to delivery, receipt, and finally to the construction site where they are installed. The disadvantage of the approach by Chin et al. (2005), Hu (2008) is that access to progress information is dependent on when the information is embedded into the tags by construction personnel. Motamedi et al. (2009) explored the use of RFID and Building Information Modeling (BIM) for lifecycle management for facility components. The authors proposed permanently attaching RFID tags to facility elements where the memory of the tags is populated with BIM information. There have also been attempts by the industry towards integrating the installation of precast concrete using BIM and RFID tags; the status of tagged precast concrete pieces was tracked from the fabrication to installation (Sawyer 2008). The pieces are identified using a RFID reader communication and Vela Systems Materials Tracking software installed in PC Tablet.

Various situations trigger the need for bi-directional coordination between the virtual model and the physical world in construction. For instance, tracking and controlling for construction resources, progress monitoring, safety management, workforce training, design changes, changes in-site conditions, and temporal conditions required for constructability. The next sections provide a detailed discussion for construction progress monitoring and process control, and safety management using CPSs.

Construction Progress Monitoring and Process Control

The special and dynamic nature of construction jobsites makes the use of traditional industrial monitoring systems impractical, labour incentive, and time consuming for the construction industry (Navon and Sacks 2007). Ineffective monitoring of construction resources and operations may lead to bad performance, reduce productivity, and project failure, whereas effective monitoring enables timely corrective actions for delayed operations and project success (El-Omari and Moselhi 2011). The absence of real-time information affects the ability of managers to monitor cost, schedule, and other performance indicators, which reduces their capability to manage the variability and uncertainty inherent in project activities and making timely corrective action (Zhang et al. 2009).

Effectively monitoring and controlling construction resources and components are very important aspects of management construction project. The monitoring of construction projects in a real-time manner is essential for ensuring that projects comply with budget, specifications, and schedule. It has been specified that integration between the physical construction world and virtual models can improve information and knowledge handling from the design phase to the operation and maintenance phase, hence improving the controlling and monitoring of the construction processes (Chin et al. 2005, Motamedi et al. 2009, Shen et al. 2008). With the recent development of robotics, computer vision, and the adoption of BIM, the collected data are integrated with project schedules, and BIM utilized to compare between the plan and actual status for completing the feedback of CPSs (Lin and Golparvar-Fard 2018). The direct application of CPSs in IR 4.0 scenarios is an enhanced controlling process (Sánchez et al. 2016). CPSs can provide broad controls over complex and large industrial processes through a heterogeneous network components architectures of sensors and actuators because CPSs integrates all the mechanisms to reach and maintain a synchronized state (Chen 2017). Also, in addition to the modern development of data collection technologies through mobile devices, laser scanners, tagged sensors, etc. in the construction industry (Ham et al. 2016, Han and Golparvar-Fard

2017), CPSs enable continuous progress updates by establishing the bidirectional communication cycle for efficient monitoring and controlling for construction projects. Data collection, operations and activities monitoring, and reporting are the main components of construction progress monitoring using CPSs.

Data Collection

The ongoing methods for construction documentation for operations have transformed into a paradigm shift due to the advent of high storage databases, accessibility of the internet, and in addition to high-resolution cameras. As a result, computer vision-based techniques and studies have grown increasingly and become popular with construction researchers to monitor and collect data for construction site activities. Also, the fast advances in battery, sensing, and aeronautics technologies, together with autonomous navigation methods and equipped low-cost digital cameras, have helped make Unmanned Aerial Vehicles (UAVs) more affordable, reliable and easy to operate (Puri 2005, Tatum and Liu 2017). UAVs can collect data by capturing many photos and videos, along with visual data processing methods, into 3D models; these platforms often perform construction site surveys and monitor construction progress (Ngadiman et al. 2021). Due to a UAVs small size and manoeuvrability, they can gather data from very low altitudes and cover the project at various heights and perspectives. UAVs with GPS technology are being used with predetermined waypoints to capture images from the same aerial perspective over time in order to track actual progress against planned construction progress (Tatum and Liu 2017). Routes are pre-programmed so that the UAVs can follow predetermined routes independently. Planning software allows routes, altitudes, speeds, and camera targets to be entered, and with some systems, landing can be achieved automatically. Also, equipped with appropriate sensors and camera technologies, UAVs provide an economic platform for obtaining topographical data. GPS-enabled UAVs automatically follow a GPS-controlled flight path planned. Using photographic systems which can provide high-resolution images, overlapping photos taken by the UAVs are put together in a mosaic which is then transformed into high-resolution 3D surface models that can be used for topographic mapping, volumetric calculations, or three-dimensional representations of job sites (Tatum and Liu 2017). Photogrammetry, which converts Two-Dimensional 2D images to 3D models using triangulation with high-quality photographs, is also being used. Combining photogrammetry with Lidar (light detection and ranging) technology, photos captured by UAVs allow the production of 3D building models, volumetric surveys, contour maps, and various other products.

Also, Mobile applications can be used for collecting construction data for monitoring construction sites. Mobile application used in remotely monitoring temporary structures requires a complete integration of sensing, data transmission, alarm display and/or alerts, and decision making. This integration requires the development of sensory modules, a wireless network, and mobile devices, and this combination provides for two-way data transmission between the sensory devices and actuators at the construction site and the system server in the site office (Moon 2017).

Progress Monitoring Techniques

The traditional methods for monitoring and collecting data highly rely on site engineers for conducting a job walk to document the progress status and other site notes, and these practices are costly, error-prone, time-consuming, and labour incentive and this results in a slow flow of information and ineffective decisions (Navon and Sacks 2007, Omar et al. 2018). A lot of studies have made valuable attempts to eliminate and reduce the limitations in traditional methods, by developing different systems and employing modern technologies and artificial intelligence to track, monitor, and analyse construction data (Arif and Khan 2020, Golnaraghi et al. 2019, Konstantinou et al. 2019, Petrov and Hakimov 2019). These systems often are equipped with various types of cameras and sensors and integrated with a computational platform that could perform autonomous navigation in a construction environment. These systems transform real-world construction sites into digital model representations. The point clouds generate 3D models, and these models represent the reality of construction sites. There are various available construction monitoring technologies, such as geospatial techniques (GPS and Geographic Information System (GIS), ultra-wideband (UWB), barcode, and RFID) and imaging techniques (laser scanning, vision-based, photogrammetry, and videogrammetry) (Pour Rahimian et al. 2020). Years of steady development in the construction industry, has led to a valuable innovation and this innovation is fuelled by BIM (Yang et al. 2021). BIM is believed to be a valuable technology for monitoring and controlling construction projects. BIM models are supporting progress monitoring by analysing the sequence of construction activities (Kropp et al. 2018, Yang et al. 2021).

Although valuable improvements are performed in the past decade, to automatically detect the progress in full-scale projects within the CPSs, it is still addressing as-built visibility issues, accounting for the lack of details in 4D BIM, and creating large-scale libraries of construction materials that could be used for appearance-based monitoring purposes (Lin and Golparvar-Fard 2020).

Cases for Applying CPSs in Monitoring and Controlling Processes

A monitoring system proposed by Han et al. (2016) is used to monitor and track the movement of a girder during hoisting on a cross-sea bridge in real-time. Smartphones are used by this system equipped with internal sensors to get the information of the girder movement and return an alarm message to the phone of the controller once the data exceeds a threshold, which indicates that the system is convenient and feasible. Also, the real-time monitoring feedback can provide significant information to operators so that an accurate decision can be made through hoisting when necessary. Another model proposed by Golparvar-Fard et al. (2015) for automated monitoring for progress using daily construction photographs where image-based 3D point clouds are generated and integrated with the BIM model. A machine learning method that utilizes Support Vector Machine (SVM) is developed to determine the state of progress. Also, cyber-physical systems have been deployed for real-time structural health monitoring of civil structure; structural health monitoring helps to prevent structural failures, such as bridges, cantilever beams and trusses (Hackmann et al. 2014).

Safety Management

Construction safety management has been a popular subject among researchers in recent years due to the high number of accidents in the construction industry. The variability and complexity of construction projects make safety management more difficult to implement compared to other industries. According to global statistical data, death accidents in construction are three times higher than average in other industries, also the injury rate is two times higher than the average of other industries (Sousa et al. 2014). Despite more awareness being obtained towards safety management in the recent years, the accident rate of the construction industry still high (Zhou et al. 2015). Therefore, the safety issues at the construction site are still a very important aspect of monitoring and supervision work of the construction stakeholders (Jin et al. 2020). The use of CPSs allows dynamics and changes in the physical world to be captured and reflected in the cyber world; also, changes and decisions in the cyber world can be communicated to sensors or actuators in the physical world for further actions. This bidirectional communication and coordination between physical and cyber worlds enables dynamic situations on construction sites to be continuously and timely monitored and analysed, and potential hazards to be proactively identified and prevented through decision-making (Wang and Razavi 2019). There are several benefits for implementing the CPSs technology in construction sites by providing timely solutions for many issues in the site. In construction safety management, the adoption of the CPSs in construction sites can actively respond to unexpected safety accidents and provide warning signals if there any hazards appear and effectively monitor and manage construction operations (Jin et al. 2020). When detecting a dangerous situation, it sends a message or signal to the workers in the site to take timely corrective actions for safety protection, and that will decrease the effects of accidents on the construction projects.

Safety Management Technologies

The CPSs reveal unsafe variables at the construction site using visualization technology (Guo et al. 2017) and information sensing technologies such as GPS, RFID, human behaviour sensors, gas sensors (Fu et al. 2020). Visualization technology solves the time-consuming problems of traditional methods for safety management by monitoring and analysing information related to worker behaviour and the jobsite environment with the help of location, alerting, and visualising technologies (Skibniewski 2014, Skibniewski 2014). Visualisation technology involves BIM, Virtual Reality (VR), and Augmented Reality (AR) (Guo et al. 2017).

The main aspects of visualization technology for monitoring construction safety are on-site worker behaviour, on-site environment monitoring, and information integration, analysis, and providing timely warnings (Guo et al. 2017). The following sections show the required technology for each aspect.

On-Site Worker Behaviour Monitoring

There are three types of unsafe behaviours involved on-site: coming near job hazard areas, incorrect operation, and misuse of personal protective equipment (PPE) (Guo et al. 2014); these behaviours can be recognised by monitoring the locations and motions of workers.

Sensor-based and Image-based techniques can monitor the workers' locations and motions. Sensor-based location technologies include Ultra-wide Band (UWB), RFID, Ultrasound, WLAN, and GPS (Guo et al. 2017). GPS, RFID, and UWB are the most widely used among location technologies. GPS is usually used outdoors to locate and track workers and equipment (Razavi and Moselhi 2012) because it provides 3D coordinates continually and is insensitive to weather and barriers. UWB can operate both indoors and outdoors and it is used to locate workers, equipment and materials (Aryan 2011). However, it is expensive when used outdoors due to the small signal cover (Cheng et al. 2011) therefore, it is more often used for indoor operations (Cheng et al. 2011, Teizer et al. 2013). By contrast, RFID has a higher signal cover range compared to UWB but weaker penetration ability; thus it is often used in indoor and outdoor environments where there are few barriers (Montaser and Moselhi 2014, Woo et al. 2011). The location technologies can also be combined to improve location performance and decrease their limitations. While image-based location technologies recognise 3D coordinates for workers depending on the position of two cameras and based on the known position of the cameras the worker position can be calculated (Brilakis et al. 2011, Park et al. 2012). Although image-based location technologies have an advantage over the sensor-based, that they do not require tags on the body of the worker, they can only locate workers locations within the range of camera view therefore they can be affected by occlusions. In summary, therefore, all the monitoring technologies for worker location cannot satisfy the whole requirements for monitoring workers in the construction site.

On-Site Environment Monitoring

A laser scanner can capture site information by analysing and identifying feature points in captured scans photographs it requires a large number of points to be analysed and transmitted and that will cause a time lag in providing the desired information (Cheng and Teizer 2013, Siebert and Teizer 2014). A smart scanning method has been developed to solve the problem of time lag by scans and dynamic objects in real-time by reducing the number of points required (Wang and Cho 2015). The position and posture of construction equipment are changing constantly through construction work, which makes monitoring equipment on-site very difficult. To solve this visualization technology has been employed by integrating sensor and laser scan technologies. For xample angular and linear displacement sensors have been applied to track the posture of a crane (Lee et al. 2012, Li & Liu 2012) and the collected data can be transmitted to a BIM model, which provides the safety officer or crane operator with real-time information to avoid any safety hazards. To summarise, while sensors can monitor the position and posture of equipment timely and accurately, image-based technologies can monitor both dynamic and static environment factors without need to install any tags.

Information Integration, Analysis, and Early Warnings

By analysing in real-time the working environment and positions and behaviours of workers, visualization technology can improve the performance of construction safety management. A virtual model represents the real-time status of a construction site which can help the safety offers to respond effectively and take the right decisions. For example, risks can be detected automatically and represented by different colours in the model (Ding and Zhou 2013), which can identify the risk in real-time. For equipment operators, visualization technology provides information about the working environment to prevent accidents caused by blind angles (Lee et al. 2012). Early warning signals, such as sound and vibration, can be sent to prevent accidents for workers. For example, calculating the distance between job hazards areas and workers and automatically judge if workers are within the hazards area or not (Guo et al. 2014).

Cases for Safety Management using CPSs

The CPSs detect unsafe practices and factors at the construction site using information sensing devices such as RFID, GPS, gas sensors, and human behaviour sensors (Fu et al. 2020). When a dangerous situation is detected, it sends a signal to the field workers in real time to let the staff make safety protections available to reduce the adverse effects of accidents on the construction site. Also, a virtual model of the scaffold system was developed where load cells, switch sensors, an accelerometer and a displacement sensor were used to acquire the data of a scaffold system in an experimental environment, and an Android mobile app was developed for human-machine interaction and, accordingly, the app was automatically activated with alarms if a risk of scaffold failure was identified (Yuan et al. 2016). In addition to the previous systems, a warning system was developed with information on workers' location and actions; this warning system can identify workers' unsafe status (e.g. falling from height, collision, etc.), automatically send warning messages to relevant workers and managers, and therefore improve the level of safety management on-site (Guo et al. 2014). Also, another approach has been proposed, a new way of preventing workers going into job hazard areas by equipping them with AR glasses to clearly see job hazard area boundaries (Talmaki et al. 2010).

Intelligent Transportation Management

Intelligent transportation refers to the advanced technologies of communication, sensing, control mechanisms, and computation in transportation systems to enhance safety issues, coordination, and services in traffic management with real-time information sharing (Gunes et al. 2014). Intelligent transportation facilitates transportation through sharing information using satellites and provides a communication environment among vehicles, the infrastructure, and passengers' portable devices (Gunes et al. 2014).

The intelligent transportation systems (ITSs) integrate pedestrians, vehicles, sensors, road-side infrastructures, traffic management centres, satellites, and other transportation system components by adopting different variations of wireless communication technologies and standards (Qu et al. 2010). ITSs of the future allows real-time traffic monitoring; increase in transportation safety and comfort through information exchange among traffic users; optimal traffic management; collision avoidance; and satellite-based technology to connect drivers, roads, and vehicles smoothly (Gunes et al. 2014).

With the integration of CPSs into infrastructures, vehicles, and roadways, ITSs can achieve driver assistance, collision avoidance or notification, improvements in travel time without fear of unexpected delays, reductions in congestion, and advanced control over infrastructure and vehicles for energy saving (Gunes et al. 2014). ITSs relies on sensors and embedded computer systems technology, cellular, wireless, and satellite technologies for vehicle-to-vehicle, vehicle-to-pedestrian, and vehicle-to- infrastructure communication to better manage complex traffic flow, safety, and extend situational awareness (Gunes et al. 2014).

Intelligent Crane Operations

The complex, dynamic, and continually changing nature of construction work has been recognized as an important contributor to the industry's high rates of injuries and fatalities. Tower cranes are a central component of many construction operations and widely used in construction jobsites for their efficiency. However, tower cranes and construction workers themselves suffer significant safety hazards from the natural sway of payloads. Cranes are arguably the most important type of machinery in most construction projects, commercial, residential, railway, bridges, and industrial plants. Crane operations present distinctive characteristics, compared to other machinery operations, with regard to temporal and spatial scales. The workspace of cranes covers most of the construction sites, particularly for tower cranes. Cranes are usually operating over the entire lifecycle of construction, responsible for most lifting activities. Intelligent crane operations refer to a computer-aided human-operated process.

An Intelligent Crane System (ICS) is expected to capture and detect the data for crane operations, analyse efficiency and safety conditions based on the captured data, and provide the human operator with the important information to improve decisions and to take corrective action in a timely manner. CPSs integrates computational resources with physical processes and establishes bidirectional coordination between cyberspace and the physical world. So, CPSs technology can be satisfied and provide the requirements for ISCs. CPSs allows for it to complete the loop of sensing, analysis, and feedback in real-time in the dynamic crane operation environment.

According to Fang et al. (2020), four main tasks expected from CPS-ICS: crane and load state sensing, work environment modelling and updating, safety and efficiency analysis and planning, and control feedback.

Crane and Load State Sensing

The first fundamental task in operations of an intelligent crane is to sense the payload and the states of the crane. Load moment indicator, which is a type of traditional crane computer system, mainly investigates the lift capacity of the crane in optimal conditions. It is essential to capture the crane motions in real-time to analyse the crane stability, capability, and interaction of the crane with the working environment. Basic requirements for technologies utilised to capture the cranes motions involve precision, accuracy, robustness, scalability, and are non-intrusive to the crane itself or other tasks related to the crane operation. The main technologies that are adopted for the crane task and load state sensing are real-time location systems (UWB, GPS, and RFID), computer vision, laser scanning, and kinematics analysis sensors (Fang et al. 2020).

Work Environment Modelling and Updating

This provides a model for the work environment and is the second major task for CPS-ICS. Manoeuvrability and lift capability of cranes can be greatly influenced by the spatial constraints in the working environment, particularly for mobile cranes because their workspace and location frequently change as the project proceeds. This will result in being very difficult for operators to be totally aware of constraints and the dynamic context of the work environment, accordingly this will result in operational inefficiencies and potential safety hazards. There are several technologies that are useful for modelling the work environment of crane like BIM, Laser Scanning, and Structure from Motion (SfM) technology (Fang et al. 2020).

Safety and Efficiency

The complex and dynamic environments of crane operation limit the human operator's ability to identify the safe situation and response to this situation and make the right decisions in a timely manner. In a CPS-ICS, once the physical status of the crane and the condition of the environment is detected and captured through the sensors, automatically the computer algorithms analyse the safety and efficiency situation in the operation and provide timely feedback such as warnings to potential risks and suggesting another lift paths (Fang et al. 2020).

Control Feedback

There are two modes for control feedback the first one is autonomous feedback which is limited to emergent brake and pay load stabilisation and the second one is the human-in-the-loop feedback (Neitzel et al. 2001, Ren et al. 2015). Most manoeuvring activities still need to be done by the human operator (Fang et al. 2020).

Girder Hoisting Monitoring

CPSs for hoisting monitoring using smartphones was proposed by Han et al. (2016) and this system uses smartphones equipped with internal sensors to detect the movement of the girder, which will be uploaded to a server, then returned to controller users. An alarming system will be provided on the controller phone whenever the returned data exceeds a threshold. The proposed system is performed to monitor the movement and orientation of a girder during hoisting on a cross-sea bridge in real-time. The results show the convenience and feasibility of the proposed system. The monitoring system consists of a collector programme installed on an iPhone (i.e., the collector) and a control programme installed in another iPhone (i.e., the controller). Additionally, a web server is used to gather the data collected by the collector iPhones and then return data to the controller. The controller sends instructions to a collector and observes the collected data. The collector collects monitoring data through its built-in sensors after receiving instructions from the controller and returns the data to the controller every 20 seconds. Once the current returned data exceeds a given threshold, an alarm will be triggered on the controller Phone, which then continues collecting and monitoring. The threshold can be set on the controller at any time according to operator experience and the requirements of the on-site conditions. Field monitoring results of two steel girder elements of a cross-sea bridge confirmed the convenience and practicability of the system. The dynamic acceleration and angle data of both hoisting procedures were collected and sent to a web server. The functions of sending instructions to the collectors and real-time monitoring can significantly enhance field hoisting monitoring capabilities.

Change Management

Virtual models have the ability to detect the variances of as-built and as-planned progress despite the complexity and the unique nature of the construction industry. The construction industry complexity comes from the several phases of the projects, and each of these phases requires several arrangements of specialized services, operations, and involvement of a lot of participants. The way to manage and coordinate the massive data and information amongst these participants is very important as this could affect the project success. The ability of keeping project participants involved and understanding of what is going on at every phase of a project, is essential for the successful completion of construction projects. Every member in the project team needs accurate and timely information about the progress and status comparison to the project plans so they can react quickly and take corrective actions. Also, when design and construction site changes occur, they should be shared between the project teams in a timely, accurate, and consistent manner so they react accordingly to reduce the risk of cost and time overruns and make the required documentations for the operation and maintenance phases. Thus, maintaining consistency between the physical construction and virtual models will enable on-site workers to effectively visualise and detect changes. Furthermore, the adoption and integration of these models will enhance the communication between the on-site engineers and the project managers in the office and provide them with real-time data from the construction site for effective decision making.

As-Built Information

As-built drawings are highly important to construction stakeholders for the purpose of renovations, demolition, and maintenance especially for critical hidden infrastructure services. Also, the as-built drawing represents a record of what was built and completed by the contractor. Sometimes the value of the final as-built drawings is commonly decreased because of not achieving it until the end of the project. This often results in high uncorrelated collections of incomplete and inaccurate information with limited ability for showing what was exactly constructed. This also results in the loss of chance to use constantly updated as-built models to manage ongoing work and identify if there are deficiencies in real-time to avoid rework. Effectively integrating virtual models and the physical construction will enable recordings of structural conditions to renovate, re-modelling, and historical restoration projects.

Operation and Maintenance

Several researchers have identified limitations in data transmission and communication among maintenance employees and the central management system which will result in a lower quality of transferred data, a lot of time for service processes, and ineffective capturing of component maintenance history. Linking the cyber components and physical components of a constructed facility will increase the ability storing and recapturing the required information for maintenance. This integrated approach can also provide remote access to the constructed facility to recognize and control the physical components in the building such as mechanical and electrical systems. This will promote sustainable practices in constructed facilities.

Challenges of CPSs Adoption

A lot of challenges faced the adoption of CPSs in any industry, including construction. The major challenges facing CPSs innovation are Dependability, Maintainability, Availability, Safety, Reliability, Robustness, Predictability, Accuracy, Compositionality, Sustainability, Adaptability, etc. (Gunes et al. 2014). Also, the shortage in supplying skilled and expert's workforce, professionals, knowledgeable experts, and trainers with a deep understanding of CPSs are expected to remain as a potential challenge in front of innovation, development, implementation and adoption of CPSs over the next few years. This is mainly because the field of CPSs requires integrating knowledge from multiple engineering areas with a right balance between theory and practice. Education and training in this field is challenging due to the depth of the required knowledge for the innovation, development, and implementation of CPSs. The adoption of the CPSs in different industries required different legislations instructions, and regulations for protecting data privacy, security for systems and personnel, as well as the testing and certification of CPSs. Moreover, considering that CPSs may span over different states or countries new legal terms and standards may be required to address the special requirements of CPSs (Törngren et al. 2015).

Cost

Cost is always a key consideration when deciding to apply new technologies to different scales of a construction project (West and Blackburn 2017). The scope and purpose of the project are essential in providing an adequate cost estimate for the application of CPSs. The cost of applying CPSs can vary depending on the level of sophistication, efforts and time utilized in developing the CPSs. The level of knowledge required to develop the CPSs can affect cost, and therefore, designing the CPSs for reuse can significantly reduce cost.

Benefits

There is a primary requirement for an integrated approach to support processes of decision-making in construction projects for improving project management activities by providing real-time data and information, also during the operation and maintenance activities of construction facilities for intelligent real-time facility management (Shen et al. 2008). Thus, this integration will enable construction stakeholders to make the right decisions in real-time to improve overall productivity and project performance. CPSs improves the efficiency, reliability, flexibility, autonomy, and self-healing properties while providing higher situational resiliency, robustness, awareness, and interoperability (Anumba and Roofigari-Esfahan 2020). Moreover, CPSs enable better communications, participation, collaboration, and control massive and complex systems. In addition, CPSs come up with opportunities for higher levels of remote access and connectivity. Also, CPSs provides several opportunities for skilled persons to design, develop, and deliver new systems, services, and devices.

Summary

The construction industry and the built environment are expected to be augmented by autonomous and connected systems to improve operations, productivity, comfort, safety, and communication. Over the last decade, the adoption of digital technologies has positioned firms involved in shaping the construction industry to take advantage of new technologies such as CPSs in improving the quality of construction facilities and the process of project delivery. There are many potential benefits of component-based CPSs in the construction industry. These benefits include access to real-time progress information which will help in quick decision making by the construction stakeholders in addition to the possibility for enhancing real-time communication and corroboration between jobsite and office employees. Another benefit of construction CPSs is that it can improve the facility management practices by enhancing the process of as-built documentation, which will aid in monitoring performance and controlling the constructed resources. Although, the capacity to actively control key components in the constructed facility after the construction stage, improved safety through monitoring the proactive hazard. There are various situations that trigger the need for bi-directional coordination between the virtual model and the physical construction. For instance, tracking and control for construction processes and components, progress monitoring, safety management, intelligent crane operations, as-built documentation, intelligent transportation management, sustainability practices, workforce training, design changes, changes in-site conditions, and temporal conditions required for constructability. Despite the benefits of applying CPSs in construction, a lot of challenges faced the adoption of CPSs in any industry, including construction which should be taken into consideration. Cost is always a key consideration when deciding to apply new technologies to different scales of a construction project. The cost of applying CPSs can vary depending on the level of sophistication, efforts and time utilized in developing the CPSs.

References

Alshibani, A. 2018. Automation of measuring actual productivity of earthwork in urban area: A case study from Montreal. Buildings, 8(12), 178. https://doi.org/10.3390/buildings8120178

Anumba, C. J., A. Akanmu and J. Messner. 2010. Towards a cyber-physical systems approach to construction. Construction Research Congress 2010: Innovation for Reshaping Construction Practice – Proceedings of the 2010 Construction Research Congress, 528–537. https://doi.org/10.1061/41109(373)53

Anumba, C. and N. Roofigari-Esfahan. 2020. Cyber-Physical Systems in the Built Environment. https://link.springer.com/content/pdf/10.1007/978-3-030-41560-0.pdf

Arif, F. and W. A. Khan. 2020. A real-time productivity tracking framework using Survey-Cloud-BIM integration. Arabian Journal for Science and Engineering, 45(10), 8699–8710. https://doi.org/10.1007/s13369-020-04844-5

Aryan, A. 2011. Evaluation of Ultra-Wideband Sensing Technology for Position Location in Indoor Construction Environments. University of Waterloo. https://uwspace.uwaterloo.ca/handle/10012/5883

Bosche, F., C. T. Haas and P. Murray. 2008. Performance of Automated Project Progress Tracking with 3d Data Fusion. https://pureapps2.hw.ac.uk/ws/files/785787/CSCE_2008_CO_449_Final.pdf

Brilakis, I., M. W. Park and G. Jog. 2011. Automated vision tracking of project related entities. Advanced Engineering Informatics, 25(4), 713–724. https://doi.org/10.1016/j.aei.2011.01.003

Chen, H. 2017. Applications of cyber-physical system: A literature review. Journal of Industrial Integration and Management, 02(03), 1750012. https://doi.org/10.1142/s2424862217500129

Cheng, T., M. Venugopal, J. Teizer and P. A. Vela. 2011. Performance evaluation of ultra wideband technology for construction resource location tracking in harsh environments. Automation in Construction, 20(8), 1173–1184. https://doi.org/10.1016/j.autcon.2011.05.001

Cheng, Tao and J. Teizer. 2013. Real-time resource location data collection and visualization technology for construction safety and activity monitoring applications. Automation in Construction, 34, 3–15. https://doi.org/10.1016/j.autcon.2012.10.017

Chin, S., S. Yoon, Y. S. Kim, J. Ryu, C. Choi and C. Y. Cho. 2005. Realtime 4D CAD + RFID for project progress management. Construction Research Congress 2005: Broadening Perspectives – Proceedings of the Congress, 331–340. https://doi.org/10.1061/40754(183)33

Correa, F. R. 2018. Cyber-physical systems for construction industry. Proceedings – 2018 IEEE Industrial Cyber-Physical Systems, ICPS 2018, 392–397. https://doi.org/10.1109/ICPHYS.2018.8387690

Ding, L. Y. and C. Zhou. 2013. Development of web-based system for safety risk early warning in urban metro construction. Automation in Construction, 34, 45–55. https://doi.org/10.1016/j.autcon.2012.11.001

El-Omari, S. and O. Moselhi. 2011. Integrating automated data acquisition technologies for progress reporting of construction projects. Automation in Construction, 20(6), 699–705. https://doi.org/10.1016/j.autcon.2010.12.001

Fang, Y., Y. K. Cho, C. Kan and C. J. Anumba. 2020. Cyber-Physical Systems (CPS) in Intelligent Crane Operations. Cyber-Physical Systems in the Built Environment, pp. 175–192. Springer International Publishing. https://doi.org/10.1007/978-3-030-41560-0_10

Fu, H., G. Manogaran, K. Wu, M. Cao, S. Jiang and A. Yang. 2020. Intelligent decision-making of online shopping behavior based on internet of things. International Journal of Information Management, 50, 515–525. https://doi.org/10.1016/j.ijinfomgt.2019.03.010

Golnaraghi, S., Z. Zangenehmadar, O. Moselhi, S. Alkass and A. R. Vosoughi. 2019. Application of artificial neural network(s) in predicting formwork labour productivity. Advances in Civil Engineering, 2019. https://doi.org/10.1155/2019/5972620

Golparvar-Fard, M., F. Peña-Mora and S. Savarese. 2015. Automated progress monitoring using unordered daily construction photographs and IFC-based building information models. Journal of Computing in Civil Engineering, 29(1), 04014025. https://doi.org/10.1061/(asce)cp.1943-5487.0000205

Golparvar-Fard, M., S. Savarese and F. Peña-Mora. 2009. Interactive visual construction progress monitoring with D4A-4D augmented reality models. Building a Sustainable Future – Proceedings of the 2009 Construction Research Congress, 41–50. https://doi.org/10.1061/41020(339)5

Gunes, V., S. Peter, T. Givargis and F. Vahid. 2014. A survey on concepts, applications, and challenges in cyber-physical systems. KSII Transactions on Internet and Information Systems, 8(12), 4242–4268. https://doi.org/10.3837/tiis.2014.12.001

Guo, H., Y. Yu, W. Liu and W. Zhang. 2014. Integrated appliation of BIM and RFID in construction safety management. Journal of Engineering Management, 28(4), 87-92.

Guo, H. L., W. P. Liu, W. S. Zhang and M. Skitmor. 2014. A BIM-PT-integrated warning system for on-site workers' unsafe behavior. China Safety Science Journal, 24(004), 104-109.

Guo, H., Y. Yu and M. Skitmore. 2017. Visualization technology-based construction safety management: A review. Automation in Construction, 73, 135–144. Elsevier B.V. https://doi.org/10.1016/j.autcon.2016.10.004

Hackmann, G., W. Guo, G. Yan, Z. Sun, C. Lu and S. Dyke. 2014. Cyber-physical codesign of distributed structural health monitoring with wireless sensor networks. IEEE Transactions on Parallel and Distributed Systems, 25(1), 63–72. https://doi.org/10.1109/TPDS.2013.30

Han, K. K. and M. Golparvar-Fard. 2017. Potential of big visual data and building information modeling for construction performance analytics: An exploratory study. Automation in Construction, 73, 184–198. https://doi.org/10.1016/j.autcon.2016.11.004

Han, R., X. Zhao, Y. Yu, Q. Guan, W. Hu and M. Li. 2016. A cyber-physical system for girder hoisting monitoring based on smartphones. Sensors, 16(7), 1048. https://doi.org/10.3390/s16071048

Hu, W. 2008. Integration of Radio-Frequency Identification and 4D CAD in construction management. Tsinghua Science and Technology, 13(Suppl. 1), 151–157. https://doi.org/10.1016/S1007-0214(08)70142-1

Jin, W., Y. Liu, Y. Jin, M. Jia and L. Xue. 2020. The Construction of Builder Safety Supervision System Based on CPS. Wireless Communications and Mobile Computing, 2020. https://doi.org/10.1155/2020/8856831

Joshua, L. and K. Varghese. 2011. Accelerometer-based activity recognition in construction. Journal of Computing in Civil Engineering, 25(5), 370–379. https://doi.org/10.1061/(asce)cp.1943-5487.0000097

Konstantinou, E., J. Lasenby and I. Brilakis. 2019. Adaptive computer vision-based 2D tracking of workers in complex environments. Automation in Construction, 103, 168–184. Elsevier B.V. https://doi.org/10.1016/j.autcon.2019.01.018

Kropp, C., C. Koch and M. König. 2018. Interior construction state recognition with 4D BIM registered image sequences. Automation in Construction, 86, 11–32. https://doi.org/10.1016/j.autcon.2017.10.027

Lee, G., J. Cho, S. Ham, T. Lee, G. Lee, S. H. Yun and H. J. Yang. 2012. A BIM- and sensor-based tower crane navigation system for blind lifts. Automation in Construction, 26, 1–10. https://doi.org/10.1016/j.autcon.2012.05.002

Li, Y. and C. Liu. 2012. Integrating field data and 3D simulation for tower crane activity monitoring and alarming. Automation in Construction, 27, 111–119. https://doi.org/10.1016/j.autcon.2012.05.003

Lin, J. J. and M. Golparvar-Fard. 2018. Visual data and predictive analytics for proactive project controls on construction sites. Lecture Notes in Computer Science (Including Subseries Lecture Notes in Artificial Intelligence and Lecture Notes in Bioinformatics), 10863 LNCS, 412–430. https://doi.org/10.1007/978-3-319-91635-4_21

Lin, J. J. and M. Golparvar-Fard. 2020. Construction progress monitoring using cyber-physical systems. *In:* Cyber-Physical Systems in the Built Environment (pp. 63–87). Springer International Publishing. https://doi.org/10.1007/978-3-030-41560-0_5

Montaser, A. and O. Moselhi. 2014. RFID indoor location identification for construction projects. Automation in Construction, 39, 167–179. https://doi.org/10.1016/j.autcon.2013.06.012

Moon, S. 2017. Application of mobile devices in remotely monitoring temporary structures during concrete placement. Procedia Engineering, 196, 128–134. https://doi.org/10.1016/j.proeng.2017.07.182

Motamedi, A. and A. Hammad. 2009. Lifecycle management of facilities components using radio frequency identification and building information model. Journal of Information Technology in Construction (ITcon), 14(18), 238-262. http://www.itcon.org/2009/18

Navon, R. and R. Sacks. 2007. Assessing research issues in Automated Project Performance Control (APPC). Automation in Construction, 16(4), 474–484. https://doi.org/10.1016/j.autcon.2006.08.001

Neitzel, R. L., N. S. Seixas and K. K. Ren. 2001. A review of crane safety in the construction industry. Applied Occupational and Environmental Hygiene, 16(12), 1106–1117. https://doi.org/10.1080/10473220127411

Ngadiman, N., M. Kaamin, M. Akmal, H. M. Nizam, M. Afnan, H. Johar, Muhammad and A. Roslin. 2021. Unmanned Aerial Vehicle (UAV) Visual Monitoring in Construction. *In*: Annals of the Romanian Society for Cell Biology (Vol. 25). http://annalsofrscb.ro

Omar, H., L. Mahdjoubi and G. Kheder. 2018. Towards an automated photogrammetry-based approach for monitoring and controlling construction site activities. Computers in Industry, 98, 172–182. https://doi.org/10.1016/j.compind.2018.03.012

Park, M.-W., C. Koch and I. Brilakis. 2012. Three-dimensional tracking of construction resources using an on-site camera system. Journal of Computing in Civil Engineering, 26(4), 541–549. https://doi.org/10.1061/(asce)cp.1943-5487.0000168

Petrov, I. and A. Hakimov. 2019. Digital technologies in construction monitoring and construction control. IOP Conference Series: Materials Science and Engineering, 497(1), 012016. https://doi.org/10.1088/1757-899X/497/1/012016

Pour Rahimian, F., S. Seyedzadeh, S. Oliver, S. Rodriguez and N. Dawood. 2020. On-demand monitoring of construction projects through a game-like hybrid application of BIM and machine learning. Automation in Construction, 110, 103012. https://doi.org/10.1016/j.autcon.2019.103012

Puri, A. 2005. A survey of Unmanned Aerial Vehicles (UAV) for traffic surveillance. Citeseer. https://citeseerx.ist.psu.edu/viewdoc/download?doi=10.1.1.108.8384&rep=rep1&type=pdf

Qu, F., F. Y. Wang and L. Yang. 2010. Intelligent transportation spaces: Vehicles, traffic, communications, and beyond. IEEE Communications Magazine, 48(11), 136–142. https://doi.org/10.1109/MCOM.2010.5621980

Ren, B., A. Y. T. Leung, J. Chen and X. Luo. 2015. A hybrid control mechanism for stabilizing a crane load under environmental wind on a construction site. Congress on Computing in Civil Engineering, Proceedings, 2015-January, 499–506. https://doi.org/10.1061/9780784479247.062

Sánchez, B. B., R. Alcarria, D. S. de Rivera and A. Sánchez-Picot. 2016. Enhancing Process Control in Industry 4.0 Scenarios using Cyber-Physical Systems. J. Wirel. Mob. Networks Ubiquitous Comput. Dependable Appl., 7(4), 41-64.

Saitta,P., B. Larcom and M. Eddington. 2005. Trike v.1 Methodology Document – Google Scholar. https://scholar.google.com/scholar?hl=en&as_sdt=1%2C5&q=Trike+v.1+M ethodology+Document&btnG=

Sawyer. 2008. Modeling Supply Chains. https://trid.trb.org/view/859177

Shen, W., Q. Hao, H. Mak, J. Neelamkavil, H. Xie and J. Dickinson. 2008. Systems integration and collaboration in construction: A review. Proceedings of the 2008 12th International Conference on Computer Supported Cooperative Work in Design, CSCWD, 1, 11–22. https://doi.org/10.1109/CSCWD.2008.4536948

Sherafat, B., C. R. Ahn, R. Akhavian, A. H. Behzadan, M. Golparvar-Fard, H. Kim, Y.-C. Lee, A. Rashidi and E. R. Azar. 2020. Automated methods for activity recognition of construction workers and equipment: State-of-the-Art review. Journal of Construction Engineering and Management, 146(6), 03120002. https://doi.org/10.1061/(asce) co.1943-7862.0001843

Skibniewski, M. 2014. Research trends in information technology applications in construction safety engineering and management. Frontiers of Engineering Management, 1(3), 246. https://doi.org/10.15302/j-fem-2014034

Skibniewski, M. J. 2014. Information technology applications in construction safety assurance. Journal of Civil Engineering and Management, 20(6), 778–794. https:// doi.org/10.3846/13923730.2014.987693

Sousa, V., N. M. Almeida and L. A. Dias. 2014. Risk-based management of occupational safety and health in the construction industry – Part 1: Background knowledge. Safety Science, 66, 75–86. Elsevier B.V. https://doi.org/10.1016/j.ssci.2014.02.008

Talmaki, S. A., S. Dong and V. R. Kamat. 2010. Geospatial databases and augmented reality visualization for improving safety in urban excavation operations. Construction Research Congress 2010: Innovation for Reshaping Construction Practice – Proceedings of the 2010 Construction Research Congress, 91–101. https:// doi.org/10.1061/41109(373)10

Tatum, M. C. and J. Liu. 2017. Unmanned aircraft system applications in construction. Procedia Engineering, 196, 167–175. https://doi.org/10.1016/j.proeng.2017.07.187

Teizer, J., T. Cheng and Y. Fang. 2013. Location tracking and data visualization technology to advance construction ironworkers' education and training in safety and productivity. Automation in Construction, 35, 53–68. https://doi.org/10.1016/j.autcon.2013.03.004

Törngren, M., R. Passerone, S. Bensalem, A. Sangiovanni-Vincentelli, J. McDermid and B. Schätz. 2015. Education and training challenges in the era of cyber-physical systems: Beyond traditional engineering. 2015 Workshop on Embedded and Cyber-Physical Systems Education, WESE 2015 – Proceedings. https://doi. org/10.1145/2832920.2832928

Wang, C. and Y. K. Cho. 2015. Smart scanning and near real-time 3D surface modeling of dynamic construction equipment from a point cloud. Automation in Construction, 49, 239–249. https://doi.org/10.1016/j.autcon.2014.06.003

Wang, J. and S. Razavi. 2019. TECHNOLOGY Peer-Reviewed for Safe Construction Sites. onepetro.org. https://onepetro.org/journal-paper/ASSE-19-02-41

West, T. D. and M. Blackburn. 2017. Is digital thread/digital twin affordable? A systemic assessment of the cost of DoD's latest Manhattan Project. Procedia Computer Science, 114, 47–56. https://doi.org/10.1016/j.procs.2017.09.003

Woo, S., S. Jeong, E. Mok, L. Xia, C. Choi, M. Pyeon and J. Heo. 2011. Application of WiFi-based indoor positioning system for labor tracking at construction sites: A case study in Guangzhou MTR. Automation in Construction, 20(1), 3–13. https://doi.org/10.1016/j.autcon.2010.07.009

Yang, A., M. Han, Q. Zeng and Y. Sun. 2021. Adopting Building Information Modeling (BIM) for the development of smart buildings: A review of enabling applications and challenges. Advances in Civil Engineering, 2021, 1–26. https://doi.org/10.1155/2021/8811476

Yuan, X., C. J. Anumba and M. K. Parfitt. 2016. Cyber-physical systems for temporary structure monitoring. Automation in Construction, 66, 1–14. https://doi.org/10.1016/j.autcon.2016.02.005

Zhang, X., N. Bakis, T. C. Lukins, Y. M. Ibrahim, S. Wu, M. Kagioglou, G. Aouad, A. P. Kaka and E. Trucco. 2009. Automating progress measurement of construction projects. Automation in Construction, 18(3), 294–301. https://doi.org/10.1016/j.autcon.2008.09.004

Zhou, Z., Y. M. Goh and Q. Li. 2015. Overview and analysis of safety management studies in the construction industry. Safety Science, 72, 337–350. Elsevier B.V. https://doi.org/10.1016/j.ssci.2014.10.006

Challenges of Cyber-Physical Systems Implementation in Construction Industry

Syed Ammad, Wesam Salah Alaloul and Syed Saad

Introduction

CPSs bring benefits of embedded computer system technology into the real world to generate a new class of applications (Marwedel 2021). Cyber-Physical Systems (CPSs) aim to make the cyber and physical realms more tightly coupled. It seems now that their opportunity for ensuring the effectiveness and maintenance of built facilities is being realised. The bidirectional accuracy of construction elements and their digital replicas is critical in these systems (Andersen and de Boer 2006). Social life has changed significantly as a result of the rapid advancement of technology. The embedded device information system substantially affects people's lives (Ash et al. 2004). However, since conventional embedded systems are closed and work poorly in terms of connectivity, power, extension, and other practical aspects, CPSs, which can compute, communicate, and control, has drawn the interest of many domestic and international scholars and academic organisations. CPSs have become the latest paradigm in the advancement of the information industry. The fourth industrial revolution (IR4.0) has been ushered in by the internet of things (IoT), which connects humans, systems, and data (Stăncioiu 2017). However, in technology cyber-physical networks, such as linked supply chains, Huge Data produced by many IoT devices, and business process control, cybersecurity have become a significant issue. Artificial immune mechanisms for IoT defense architecture, data mining/fusion in IoT enabled cyber-physical networks, and data-driven cybersecurity will all benefit from evolutionary algorithms combined with the other cognitive computing. In the industry 4.0 world, the Industry Internet of Things (IIoT) and the Industry Cyber-Physical System (ICPS) are becoming highly significant. A considerable number of sensing devices are now available, resulting in an avalanche of data, i.e., a large-scale wired network construction with data protection and access protocol problems (Dai et al. 2019). Data quality with significant noise when collected from industrial factories, adequate data storage, smart interconnection with cloud providers, and real-time analytics requirements are all issues that come with big data in real business.

In the construction industry, virtual models are becoming increasingly popular. As a means of coordination, alignment, and connectivity in building projects, virtual models have enormous potential (Sacks et al. 2010). Virtual models are also extremely useful for documenting as-built information. Despite their advantages, simulated models are often used only for modelling and tendering/bidding purposes. Extending these models to the design, processes, and repair stages of a facility's lifecycle will have a lot more value. Real-time bi-directional synchronisation between computer models and concrete structures is a great way to do this (Matthews et al. 2015). Computational tools are needed to closely incorporate the digital model and the physical construction so that improvements in one environment are instantly mirrored into the other to ensure bi-directional communication.

Also, with the introduction of Building Information Modelling (BIM), the construction industry is currently undergoing a transition in its conventional market processes (BIM) (Eastman et al. 2011). In an overview, BIM is a series of new processes for designing, planning, and constructing buildings built on 3D virtual objects that embody various building components and interdependencies. Today's majority of BIM implementations are concentrated in the building lifecycle's idea, construction, and planning stages (Arayici and Aouad 2010). Part of the explanation for this is that building operations are still heavily reliant on human labour. There is absolutely no complex connection between BIM models and actual development on-site during the project construction. It is critical to understand the importance of Industry 4.0 (I4.0) technology to construction while using the digitisation facilitated by BIM launch (Oesterreich and Teuteberg 2016). To overcome challenges developers, need to think seriously about security aspects inside their applications when developing CPSs for the construction industry (Alguliyev et al. 2018).

They need to choose appropriate tools and technologies to ensure the security of assets based on the physical, process, and communication layers in their applications. Also, hardware and software communication and systems integration can be challenging to design innovative sensors (mobile phone-based), devices to support the job site workers or risk map development. The following sections provide a brief insight into the discussion, and Figure 10. 1 illustrates the breakdown of the chapter. The breakdown starts with the introduction of challenges of CPSs implementation in the construction industry. In the next step streaming data in real time environment is further split into streaming data without real time constraints. And at last data collection is divided into sub section for better understanding of the breakdown.

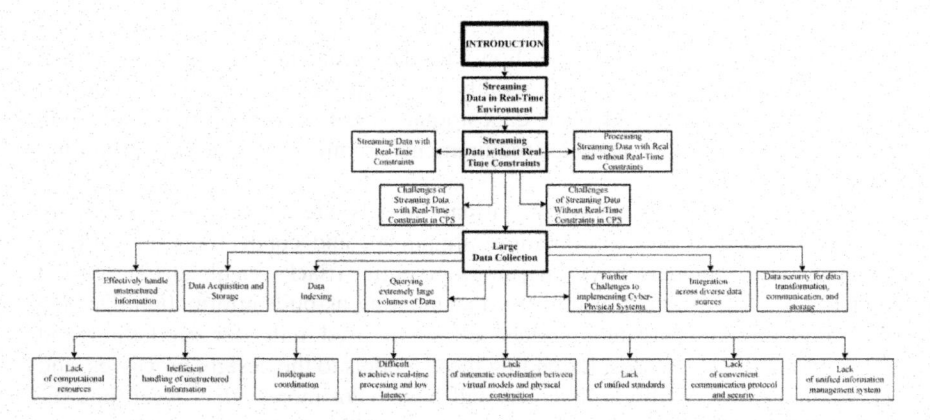

Figure 10.1: Chapter Breakdown

Opportunities and Challenges

Opportunities

CPSs increases a system's productivity, adaptability, dependability, liberty, and conscience qualities while increasing tactical awareness, stability, resilience, and interconnection. CPSs also improve the coordination, cooperation, and administration of big, complicated processes. And furthermore, CPSs allows for more connections and remote monitoring. Finally, CPSs offers a diverse range of possibilities for talented workers to design, implement, and deploy emerging technologies, networks, and applications (Jahromi and Kundur 2020).

Challenges

The primary obstacles to CPSs growth, advancement, and acceptance may be divided into three categories: educational, legal, and technological.

Aspects Related to Education: Qualified labourers, knowledgeable specialists, specialists, and academic instructors with a thorough grasp of CPSs are in high demand and will continue to be a key barrier to CPSs development, growth, and acceptance for at least the next few years. As a result, current curriculum systems should be developed and deployed under CPSs criteria (Zander et al. 2015).

Aspects Related to Legalisation: The implementation of the CPSs in various industries necessitates distinct laws and regulations regarding privacy protection, network, customer security, safety, responsibility, and CPSs conformity assessment. Furthermore, because CPSs may be spread across many cities, territories, and even countries, new regulatory norms and terminology may be required to expressly handle CPSs demand (Monostori et al. 2016).

Aspects Related to Technologies

The technological problems come in proportion from the differences between CPSs and established practices. For example, technical improvements are necessary for the creation of networks, interconnected, autonomous, and dependable systems that can safeguard CPSs safety, reliability, and cyberattacks (Linares Garcia and Roofigari-Esfahan 2020).

Streaming Data in Real-Time Environment

Streaming data is a type of real-time data that presents new information in a continuous stream (Ahmad et al. 2017). It is also known as high throughput data with high frequency and low latency. In a real-time environment, in the CPSs, there are two types of streaming data:

1. Streaming data with real-time constraints.
2. Streaming data without real-time constraints.

Streaming Data with Real-Time Constraints

This type of streaming data requires that the application responds to the arrival of each new event within a certain time called latency tolerance. For example, in the temperature data from a sensor, the application must respond within one second for each new reading.

Challenges of Streaming Data with Real-Time Constraints in CPSs

Handling Big Data for Streaming Data with Real-Time Constraints: Streaming data must be processed in real-time to meet its latency requirements. This requires much computational power. To handle streaming data with real-time constraints, the infrastructure must be able to process large amounts of streaming data within its latency requirements.

Handling Real-Time Constraints: Streaming data is generated in a continuous and often unpredictable manner. This makes it difficult for applications to handle real-time constraints. For example, in the case of streaming data from a sensor, if the application cannot process incoming data within its latency requirements, it will have to discard these events or buffer them. But this may lead to loss of real-time information, which will affect the operation of the system.

Handling High Data Rate: Streaming data is generated in a high frequency. To handle streaming data with real-time constraints, the infrastructure must be able to process large amounts of streaming data within its latency requirements at the same time.

Handling Large Data Volume: Streaming data may generate an enormous amount of data. To handle this data, the infrastructure must have a large amount of storage space and computational power.

Handling Data Asynchronously: Streaming data is generated asynchronously and may arrive at any time, making it difficult for applications to process them as they arrive. To handle streaming data with real-time constraints, the infrastructure must be able to process data asynchronously.

Handling Non-Linear Data Streams: Streaming data is generated in a non-linear manner. For example, in a temperature sensor, the temperature may rise or fall continuously with time. To handle streaming data with real-time constraints, the infrastructure must be able to process non-linear data streams.

Handling Corrupted Data: Streaming data is generated in a volatile manner. For example, if the sensor is placed close to a heater or air conditioner in the case of a temperature sensor, the temperature reading may change rapidly. To handle streaming data with real-time constraints, the infrastructure must be able to process corrupted data.

Handling High Throughput: Streaming data is generated at a high frequency and often arrives at a high rate. To handle streaming data with real-time constraints, the infrastructure must be able to process large amounts of streaming data within its latency requirements at the same time.

Streaming Data without Real-Time Constraints

This type of streaming data does not require that the application responds to each new event within a specific time (Golab and Özsu 2003). It is also known as "process data" because it is used for offline processing. For example, in the case of the temperature data from a sensor, the application must respond within a specific time to each new reading but not necessarily within one second, as in the case of streaming data with real-time constraints.

Challenges of Streaming Data without Real-Time Constraints in CPS

Handling Big data for Streaming Data without Real-Time Constraints: Streaming data must be processed in a batch mode to meet its latency requirements. This requires a lot of computational power. To handle streaming data without real-time constraints, the infrastructure must be able to process large amounts of streaming data within its latency requirements.

Handling Non-Linear Data Streams: Streaming data is generated in a non-linear manner. For example, in the case of a temperature sensor, the temperature may rise or fall continuously with time. To handle streaming data without real-time constraints, the infrastructure must be able to process non-linear data streams.

Handling Corrupted Data: Streaming data is generated in a volatile manner. For example, if the sensor is placed close to a heater or air conditioner in the case of a temperature sensor, the temperature reading may change rapidly. To handle streaming data without real-time constraints, the infrastructure must be able to process corrupted data.

Handling High Throughput: Streaming data is generated at a high frequency and often arrives at a high rate. The infrastructure must be able to process large amounts of streaming data within its latency requirements at the same time.

Processing Streaming Data with Real and without Real-Time Constraints

The challenges of processing streaming data with real-time constraints and streaming data without real-time constraints are as follows.

Storage and Data Management: Storage and data management are crucial for handling large amounts of streaming data that have real-time constraints and also for handling large amounts of streaming data that have no real-time constraints. To store a huge amount of streaming data, the infrastructure must have a large amount of storage and well-designed storage management policies. The storage system should be able to store the data so that it can provide pertinent data and answer the query from any of the available data when queried.

Data Management for Streaming Data with Real-Time Constraints: The infrastructure must be able to process data asynchronously and also be able to recover from failures. To handle streaming data with real-time constraints, the infrastructure must be able to recover from failures when the system cannot process data on time (Fernandez-Rodriguez et al. 2017).

Data Processing for Streaming Data with Real-Time Constraints: The infrastructure must process huge amounts of streaming data and cost-effectively manage their processing. To handle streaming data with real-time constraints, the infrastructure must be able to process huge amounts of streaming data and cost-effectively manage their processing (Ali et al. 2017). And it can process vast amounts of streaming data and manage their processing cost-effectively. To handle streaming data without real-time constraints, the infrastructure must be able to process huge amounts of streaming data and cost-effectively manage their processing.

Security for Streaming Data with Real-Time Constraints: Security is very important for handling streaming data with real-time constraints. To handle streaming data with real-time constraints, the infrastructure must process huge amounts of streaming data and cost-effectively manage their processing. But it is difficult and expensive to implement security for this type of data. Security for Streaming Data without Real-Time Constraints: Security is very important for handling streaming data without real-time constraints. To handle streaming data that has no real-time constraints, the infrastructure must be able to process huge amounts of streaming data and cost-effectively manage their processing (Khan et al. 2014). But it is difficult and expensive to implement security for this type of data.

Transport Protocols for Streaming Data: The infrastructure must process huge amounts of streaming data and cost-effectively manage their processing. This means that it must have the capability to process data at a high rate simultaneously. But this is difficult to achieve with current transport protocols such as TCP and UDP because they cannot provide such a high capability. This means that it must have the capability to process data at a high rate simultaneously. But this is difficult to achieve with current transport protocols such as TCP and UDP because they cannot provide such capability.

Large Data Collection

Data Acquisition and Storage

Data from multiple sensors are generated at a high rate and must be stored with minimal latency (Yu et al. 2004). For example, traffic-control systems collect hundreds of observations per second for each device in addition to the sensor's status.

Intermittent Events

Even if data are stored as generated, intermittent events can result in the dropping of samples and reduced sample length. This data may be needed later for post-processing of the results of a simulation or to support the adaptive real-time system (Viviroli et al. 2009).

Concurrency

Data flits in and out of cache memory depending on various factors (e.g., sensor data arrive at different rates). For example, outlier sampling is used when characterising a large population when faster sensors measure only a few devices over long periods. In contrast, more sensors may be collected across smaller sample periods for slow measurements.

Transience

Data can be highly transient and change so often that data from many trips may eventually need to receive similar treatment.

Large Runtimes

Once sub-sets are generated whose size and lifetimes change according to real-time priorities, these must be tracked. (e.g., Outlier sampling means those data in the lists for some of many subsequent sample periods are no longer valid). Large Run times are a worst-case input. Large run times are said in two ways and are either a high number of iterations where an incorrect operation is inputted or a significantly longer operation. Large runtimes can be defined as an input to a process, like a user input, that produces a very large, unintended result. Sometimes the input is an incomplete or an incorrect operation (like a multiplication operation with a small number), and the result is a division operation that may take minutes.

Alternatively, the input can be a large calculation, and the result takes a long time to compute. Working with IoT systems and real-time measures, chances of inputting large runtimes can increase. Having a process to limit the number of large runtime executions can be useful to prevent a system from crashing. These startup limits, when set, will restrict the number of iterations or calculations a process will complete. Typically, large runtimes are prevented by human action or other measures like implementing bound execution for a function.

Time Constraints

In addition to fixing a time for analysis upfront, more data may need to be collected over, say t seconds for metrics such as the average time of response to an event. This could be over a single period, across a finite timeframe, over infinitely many periods, or combining all three options. Stakeholders need to decide at what granularity this duration needs to be. The granularity should be as detailed as possible for the specific goal of the stakeholders. The time frame for the analysis should be finalised and the unit of time to be used during the analytic process (seconds, hours, etc.). An interpreter is advised to calculate the distribution of data for an object versus an average (i.e., variance). If inconsistency appears in the data, use statistical tests to investigate further.

Other Goals

Sensors may need primarily to exhaust their span of interest. They are not concerned with when this happens but may need to know they have enough time using various sampling strategies.

Sample Post-Processing

Processing methods of samples must be orchestrated so that relevant data are not lost permanently, and computation resources are not dissipated in a meaningless activity. Sample Post-processing is the process of analysing the result of a simulation as a sample taken from a probability distribution. It is often an optional stage of simulation and is sometimes referred to as one-step conditioning. It can be used to improve the accuracy of statistical data obtained from the simulation and help tell the difference between accurate and defective simulation results. To determine predicted probabilities from the simulation, it is often preferable to use sample post-processing instead of variance post-processing.

System Adaptation

The underlying physical system layout or resource allocation can change demand (e.g., due to traffic congestion due to bad weather or new policies). Adaptive responses depend on how the various data collected (e.g., sensor observations) were used by different actors in response to the ongoing system dynamics. The term "system adaptation" is the collective behaviour of adaptive human and machine elements operating together as individual agents and using the feedback data from the environment and other human and machine agents. In CPSs, system adaptation is the organised, coordinated response of existing CPSs agents to an inadequate or changing environment. System adaptation can be a consequence of System reconfiguration of existing agents and/or the introduction of new adaptive agents, resulting in dissolution (agent relegation). The result of system adaptation is a resilient and coherent CPSs that is responsive to future changes.

Privacy

Like most IoT applications, CPSs create sensitive data and records containing certain levels of personal information and metadata, distinguishing between individual activities and seeking to protect personal identity (Windley 2005). Special Interests: Interests may differ across teams or stakeholders, resulting in invariants of interest that are explicit. For example, the set of information about a given trip may be different for subway authorities vs operators or divisions within a government agency based on mandates to protect individual or corporate interests, which can span hardware/software and time. Such variants on interest may negotiate what and how data are collected, stored, manipulated or shared based on privilege (e.g., an emergency manager's need for historic vs real-time updates) and trust (among traditionally separated authorities above the device level: system, operator, agency).

Data Indexing

The indexing of large data in CPSs is susceptible to data redundancies, spatiotemporal variations, and other noise because of data volumes leading to the loss of temporal coherence (Thomson and Emery 2014). Automated indexing and applications for big data (particularly in CPSs) represent a statistical problem. It becomes necessary to ensure no information is lost or left out despite the unwieldy size. CPSs uses manufacturing processes despite having constraints peculiar to the particular products and components. Unlike other systems, human influence cannot be removed and removed from the given initial data; further variations also require modifications to introduce incidental changes over time. These facts call for non-robust algorithms that can address inexact queries at the lowest possible cost, such as range and nearest neighbour queries, yet maximally using indexed information, since frequent rebuilds are impractical due to high running costs. Decisions must also be made fast enough for their inclusion in feedback loops which are tight and at resolutions dependent upon the amount of data. The human user demands constant access over phenomenal amounts of data, requiring systems capable of generating useful responses in unknown correlated variables (Ho 2012). These characteristics present important distinctions about earlier methods and demand newer methods recommended for big data queries in CPSs. Although many advancements have been made in data handling for processing to combine treatment with artificial intelligence and the IoT, the large Scale CPSs

(LS-CPSs) increases data generated for constantly monitoring, which can be better understood. This "high-speed cycling scenario" is moving towards more real-time operations with the capability of accommodating further fast changes. This means that future constructions must accommodate data reorganisation by automatically relocating large amounts of relevant information, both internally and externally. Moreover, simulations present many challenges which require schema extensions for query answering; these feasible responses are expected to provide credible results within one order of magnitude of the total time needed for simulations (Halevy et al. 2006).

Querying Extremely Large Volumes of Data

Querying huge volumes of data issues in CPSs means, given the resource, issued queries, and an infinite result of that query (Búr et al. 2020). The focus of this type of issue in CPSs is whether it is a known form or not. An unknown greater volume of objects that need to be searched through in order to find the relevant information is one of the main disadvantages of using a manual search system. This seems to come from knowledge entropy such as large database, information extraction, and subject indexing. The researchers also attempted to treat the relationship between features of CPSs data in the query plan by considering three types of changes, which consider important changes which should be reflected by the generation of data in virtually anyway for visual appeals (Oztemel and Gursev 2020). The term query plan is defined concerning the process whereby an input device can approach some machines: a backup storage and retrieval points referred to as methods or accepted on systems in general, at Infobee.org in 2006. It requires a comprehensive reorganisation of the data to match resources and user queries that seek information or decision making. This will be considering the proposed changes that update tables with structure in representation to generate data. Finally, using the brute force computing approach by first using conventional text retrieval query methods (March and Hevner 2007).

The challenge regarding querying huge volumes of data issues in CPSs is fundamental that traditional large data retrieval algorithms and mathematics techniques do not apply effectively or are non-applicable to retrieve information of large sections (Zhou et al. 2019). This limitation leads to the development of statistical or graph-search methodology. Information spreading structurse generated from an exponential fashion have high probability structures used to reduce query tables where the content is needed uniformly, therefore creating a large query space (Agarwal et al. 2013).

The extreme view maintains a physical presence given the size of input collected heuristic programs, which are processing techniques that allow for painlessness and scale of enormous amounts of data involving querying an enormous volume of data issues in CPSs. Heuristic methods are data manipulation, and those that insert these rules may be sensitive to resource computation. To tackle problems querying in CPSs, generating and tabulating many database queries to be sent to the listed objects. The most effective approach for such an environment is specified in several articles. Many of them describe data space by techniques that either use uniformity optimisation technique or similarity transformations and statistical methods that have neighbourhood information with respect and deal with these queries up minimise the probability of information retrieval (Bandyopadhyay and Saha 2012).

Effectively Handle Unstructured Information

The challenges to effectively handle unstructured information in CPSs are diverse (Denker et al. 2012). The systems that keep track of the wider environment need an unstructured information model, flexibility to choose data sources autonomously, and predict what will happen shortly. To become much more intelligent than today's systems will require analysing the unstructured data gathered from a range of different sources and turning it into structured information containing insights about what might happen (Gruber 2008). With this kind of capability, it would be easier to anticipate conflicts and react to accidents while gaining a much better estimate of the risks that may be faced because incidents can be predicted and defended against. To cope with all these challenges, CPSs needs to handle the huge amount (volume + velocity) of unstructured data by unstructured sensor data and generate significant data streams onboard the system to process information in real-time and deliver great value. Requirements hard on CPSs and Artificial intelligence (AI) are because CPSs needs huge data and handle the huge volume of new sensor reading and new behaviour information that cannot be predicted. Therefore, many AI agents are required to be built to assist in CPSs, which communicate via messaging to perform actions. Particularly with AI technologies, bridging the IoT field things from CPSs seems promising (Calegari et al. 2021).

Integration Across Diverse Data Sources

The challenges to integration across diverse data sources in CPSs are addressed through two CPSs design guidelines: Context Isolation, which separates the concerns of data reading and creation from the use of context at runtime; and, Context Bindings, coordinated access to contexts through means like annotations (Rajkumar et al. 2010). Context Isolation improves the ability to test dynamic embedding of contexts, while Context Bindings provides an explicit explanation of context use for review. Both of these design guidelines are based on the principle that changes to the settings used for reading data must be tracked and analyzable separately from runtime contexts (Cheng and Garlan 2012). Together with a reference application, these guidelines demonstrate how a smarter CPSs can address diverse and sensor-based data sources transparently without sacrificing better safety or performance.

Data Security for Data Transformation, Communication, and Storage

Data security in a CPSs is a challenge that can be tackled from three different perspectives: data transformation, communication with outside systems, and data storage (Atat et al. 2018). While the security of these processes is essential from an information assurance perspective, rigorous correctness and strong dependability results are expected from the possible interactions between CPSs and the cyberworld. These two characteristics are challenging to establish together since security properties require errors to be detectable and tolerant, while robustness properties want the system or subset of its functionalities to remain working despite erroneous inputs or operations. For example, it will be shown how a complete change of input data is tolerated from an RPC-Service request without vulnerabilities. Moreover, message exposure when network nodes are already compromised means that only confidentiality/integrity must be secured to preserve the properties of these services for resilience management and fault isolation (Xiao et al. 2007). The details appear in the following sections.

Data Transformations

While the usual approach of compilers from high-level languages to low-level representations and operations. Which are performed by a computer, is hidden under programmer abstractions; both human developers and software can directly address these transformations. Today crypto transformers have gained some popularity in the software engineering community for the risk of supply chain attacks. Communication protocols are also known to contain subtle bugs or particular implementation issues that reveal private data or compromise integrity (Heberlein et al. 1989). Hence crypto-operations should be added to data processing loops and used by platforms (WH4S platform) that execute their operations on platforms and devices or in end-devices (which take care of R4S messages to transmit them, log events and actively filter infiltrations). A fully secure system cannot be automatically trusted. Transactions tend to increase in complexity as they flow through a network, increasing the opportunity for systems to process or misinterpret user-inputted data improperly. CPSs often do not use the latest computing technology as users with low salaries who buy new then break them are often at risk of being robbed, and the data they carry are also at risk of random noises. This suggests automatic ad-hoc security assessments of any IoT systems exchanging data with the system or even specific objects should not only be done from a computer science perspective but a needs-driven economical perspective (Cleland-Huang et al. 2014).

Communication

As cryptography is tracked to models for information exchange, definition and implementation are based on specific properties in the system environment. The logical environment also includes architectural choices and the applicability of trusted cryptographic implementations (Scriber 2018). However, the physical model depends on the temperature or pressure levels of devices available or available from repair stores to a device in the field, unless a highly dense off-the custodier environment can afford high-temperature alternating links. Angular locality and distances, alteration of bodies into which the components are placed are a few others. What may exist as one (because of algorithmic dependencies) proof in Toronto will be inherently unsuitable for distribution to Cleveland since distances are vastly different for the same country, for example.learning the things that exhibit specific failure biases and code-based quality issues in changes of environment or through failures is a challenging problem. Their solution will mean a significant effort to minimise data loss, isolate compromised resources and make risk management measures achievable by multiple devices with limited pocket budgets.

Storages

While most encryption and decryption implementations come with libraries and kernels pre-innovated to the quantum world, the superluminal speed required to power them access shares with classical conventional ciphering only partially. Not all data should be handled in every problem domain, so storage back stores must handle heterogeneous encoded cubes of transaction information that are to be stored, transmitted and processed in addition to the transformed data of individual entities. Implementation of such backup means considering both development (cache loaders, etc.) and validation steps in an IoT system. Because storing errors is an issue of high consequences in a platform used to isolate compartmentalised services. External interactions can either cause failure or enhance resilience (Scarfone et al. 2007).

Further Challenges to Implementing CPSs

Implementing Cyber-Physical Systems is like a glass half full or half empty, the same thing. It depends on the observer's point of view (Taha 2015). The establishment of CPSs depends on the progress of science and technology, which is the crucial basis for the development of CPSs. However, the development of CPSs is also the core of future scientific and technological progress and the key to the development of science and technology. Many challenges are implementing CPSs in the construction industry (Leitão et al. 2016). CPSs are dependent on the IoT. Under the premise of CPSs, the manufacturing industry and construction industry, such as in the manufacture of equipment, software, and machinery, are greatly dependent on the IoT. The construction industry is a field that is not conducive to the IoT in the first place, so it is not easy to implement CPSs in the construction industry. There is a lack of good security in traditional construction. In the construction industry, the safety of workers is the priority, and many construction workers are not familiar with security knowledge. As well as the construction staff does not have security awareness, it is challenging to implement CPSs in the construction industry. Few more challenges to implement CPSs are in the following sections (Ashibani and Mahmoud 2017).

Inefficient Handling of Unstructured Information

The construction process is a process of handling a lot of different kinds of information. Information about construction sites is very large. Most of the information is currently unstructured and stored in various formats, such as text, images, and videos (Soibelman et al. 2008). Information is also scattered in different formats, and some information is stored in paper documents. The unstructured information of the construction process is very difficult to manage, and it has not been used effectively. Inefficient handling of unstructured information makes the construction process unable to keep up with the rapid development of information technology. It is a big challenge for the construction industry to implement CPSs (Alaloul et al. 2018).

Inadequate Coordination

Although the construction process is very important for people's lives, the construction industry is not a high-tech industry. It is a very traditional industry. Therefore, it is not easy to implement CPSs in the construction process (Pilloni 2018). Most of the construction tools are designed by people, and the process is very manual. The coordination between the construction process and the design process is not smooth, and much information is lost. In addition, the construction process is a process that involves a lot of different departments, such as architecture, design, engineering, surveying, construction, legal departments, etc. There are a lot of information requirements between the different departments, and there is a lack of efficient coordination. Inadequate coordination makes it challenging to implement CPSs in the construction industry (Shih et al. 2016).

Difficult to Achieve Real-Time Processing and Low Latency

CPSs should achieve real-time processing and low latency. It should be able to process the large amount of information generated by sensors in real-time (Kang et al. 2012). In the construction industry, the construction sites are usually large, and there are many construction workers. In addition, the construction sites contain a lot of different types of equipment and machinery. The construction sites should process a lot of information. Currently, heavy construction equipment, such as bulldozers, can run at a low speed in a very short time. It could be said that low latency is achieved. However, it is very difficult for the construction equipment to achieve real-time processing. The construction equipment is usually used in a very large construction site, and it is difficult for the construction equipment to connect to the Internet (Bohn and Teizer 2010). It is also difficult for the construction equipment to achieve real-time processing and low latency.

Lack of Computational Resources

Lack of computational resources in CPSs describes that the strength of one system's performer could become unable to act as it would hope to. In this situation, it could send demands such as its desired level and or frequency. The power might be so weak, for example, that the home can't get these types of control over the system, and when that's the case, it is of little worth or exchange for it already from the start. A huge amount of information is generated and collected in the construction process, and the construction process requires a large number of computational resources. Nowadays, the construction process is still very manual. The construction equipment is not available, so it is difficult for the construction process to achieve real-time processing and low latency. It is challenging to implement CPSs in the construction industry.

Lack of Unified Standards

There is a lack of unified standards in the construction industry, so it is difficult for the construction industry to implement CPS. There are a lot of standards for construction, such as CAD (Computer-Aided Design), BIM, and CAM (Computer-Aided Manufacturing). These standards are related to the design, construction, and manufacturing industry, and they are not unified; they are not used in the construction industry.

Lack of Automatic Coordination between Virtual Models and Physical Construction

The construction process is a process of manual coordination. In the construction process, the information from the design process is only passed manually to the construction site, but the construction process cannot communicate with the design process in real-time, and the information cannot pass from the design process to the construction process in real-time (Ciribini et al. 2016). In addition, there is no coordination between the design and construction process, and the construction process is not able to automatically communicate with the design process. The design process cannot automatically change the design process according to the changes in the construction process, and it is difficult to achieve real-time processing and low latency (Ciribini et al. 2016). It is difficult to implement CPSs in the construction industry.

Lack of Convenient Communication Protocol and Security

The construction process is a manual operation process, and it is inconvenient to implement CPSs in the construction process. The IoT is an essential foundation for the implementation of CPSs, but it is very difficult to implement CPSs in the construction process because of the lack of convenient communication protocol and security. In addition, there is no unified standard in the construction process, and there is a lack of unified communication protocol, so it is not easy to implement CPSs in the construction process (Lilis et al. 2017).

Lack of Unified Information Management System

There is a lack of a unified information management system in the construction process (Gao et al. 2018). The design and construction process are not unified. The design process focuses on the design of a building, and the design process involves a lot of design information, such as design drawings, design documents, etc. The construction process focuses on the construction of a building, and the construction process is a process that involves a lot of construction information, such as building information models, construction drawings, etc. The lack of a unified information management system makes it challenging to implement CPSs in the construction industry (Ashibani and Mahmoud 2017).

Summary

There are challenges towards implementing CPSs in the construction industry, consider the ones listed as follows: First, there should be strong coordination between manufacturers of IoT solutions and standards bodies. This is a significant challenge for industries like manufacturing and software services, which already had a backbone for designing and implementing IoT-enabled devices/systems. Secondly, IoT technology should be flexible enough to deal with high amplitude events within construction sites and also have the capability for continuous (Fail-safe) monitoring capabilities during all expected landscape scenarios. There could be overloads, unexpected load growths, electrical expenses, and safety risks at the construction site as an example of large-amplitude events. In addition to that, national standards bodies also require draft processes in areas like risk management and digital security. The confidentiality of data must be addressed to ensure data protection, i.e., employees cannot copy and distribute information without permission etc. Thirdly, device management and authentication issues that might lead to disruptions in the operation and usage of these systems should be avoided. This can be achieved if proper guidelines are followed, and agreement reached upfront among manufacturers during the design of the micro-devices and leading to functional extensibility and digitisation. It is required that all parties involved in the process of production of the micro-devices are constantly secured and updated about the security of these devices. It is also required that there should be a contingency mechanism if these are not forthcoming from design to their end uses.

References

Agarwal, S., B. Mozafari, A. Panda, H. Milner, S. Madden and I. Stoica. 2013. BlinkDB: Queries with bounded errors and bounded response times on very large data. Proceedings of the 8th ACM European Conference on Computer Systems, 29–42.

Ahmad, S., A. Lavin, S. Purdy and Z. Agha. 2017. Unsupervised real-time anomaly detection for streaming data. Neurocomputing, 262, 134–147.

Alaloul, W. S., M. S. Liew, N. A. W. A. Zawawi and B. S. Mohammed. 2018. Industry Revolution IR 4.0: Future Opportunities and Challenges in Construction Industry. MATEC Web of Conferences, 203, 02010. https://doi.org/10.1051/matecconf/201820302010

Alguliyev, R., Y. Imamverdiyev and L. Sukhostat. 2018. Cyber-physical systems and their security issues. Computers in Industry, 100, 212–223.

Ali, M. I., N. Ono, M. Kaysar, Z. U. Shamszaman, T. L. Pham, F. Gao and A. Mileo. 2017. Real-time data analytics and event detection for IoT-enabled communication systems. Journal of Web Semantics, 42, 19–37.

Andersen, M. and J. de Boer. 2006. Goniophotometry and assessment of bidirectional photometric properties of complex fenestration systems. Energy and Buildings, 38(7), 836–848.

Arayici, Y. and G. Aouad. 2010. Building information modelling (BIM) for construction lifecycle management. Construction and Building: Design, Materials, and Techniques, 2010, 99–118.

Ash, J. S., M. Berg and E. Coiera. 2004. Some unintended consequences of information technology in health care: The nature of patient care information system-related errors. Journal of the American Medical Informatics Association, 11(2), 104–112.

Ashibani, Y. and Q. H. Mahmoud. 2017. Cyber physical systems security: Analysis, challenges and solutions. Computers & Security, 68, 81–97.

Atat, R., L. Liu, J. Wu, G. Li, C. Ye and Y. Yang. 2018. Big data meet cyber-physical systems: A panoramic survey. IEEE Access, 6, 73603–73636.

Bandyopadhyay, S. and S. Saha. 2012. Unsupervised Classification: Similarity Measures, Classical and Metaheuristic Approaches and Applications. Springer Science & Business Media.

Bohn, J. S. and J. Teizer. 2010. Benefits and barriers of construction project monitoring using high-resolution automated cameras. Journal of Construction Engineering and Management, 136(6), 632–640. https://doi.org/10.1061/(ASCE)CO.1943-7862.0000164

Búr, M., G. Szilágyi, A. Vörös and D. Varró. 2020. Distributed graph queries over models@run.time for runtime monitoring of cyber-physical systems. International Journal on Software Tools for Technology Transfer, 22(1), 79–102.

Calegari, R., G. Ciatto, V. Mascardi and A. Omicini. 2021. Logic-based technologies for multi-agent systems: A systematic literature review. Autonomous Agents and Multi-Agent Systems, 35(1), 1–67.

Cheng, S.-W. and D. Garlan. 2012. Stitch: A language for architecture-based self-adaptation. Journal of Systems and Software, 85(12), 2860–2875.

Ciribini, A. L. C., S. M. Ventura and M. Paneroni. 2016. Implementation of an interoperable process to optimise design and construction phases of a residential building: A BIM Pilot Project. Automation in Construction, 71, 62–73.

Cleland-Huang, J., O. C. Z. Gotel, J. Huffman Hayes, P. Mäder and A. Zisman. 2014. Software traceability: Trends and future directions. *In*: Future of Software Engineering Proceedings (pp. 55–69).

Dai, H.-N., R. C.-W. Wong, H. Wang, Z. Zheng and A. V. Vasilakos. 2019. Big data analytics for large-scale wireless networks: Challenges and opportunities. ACM Computing Surveys (CSUR), 52(5), 1–36.

Denker, G., N. Dutt, S. Mehrotra, M.-O. Stehr, C. Talcott and N. Venkatasubramanian.

2012. Resilient dependable cyber-physical systems: A middleware perspective. Journal of Internet Services and Applications, 3(1), 41–49.

Eastman, C. M., C. Eastman, P. Teicholz, R. Sacks and K. Liston. 2011. BIM Handbook: A Guide to Building Information Modeling For Owners, Managers, Designers, Engineers and Contractors. John Wiley & Sons.

Fernandez-Rodriguez, J. Y., J. A. Alvarez-Garcia, J. A. Fisteus, M. R. Luaces and V. C. Magana. 2017. Benchmarking real-time vehicle data streaming models for a smart city. Information Systems, 72, 62–76.

Gao, Z., L. Xu, L. Chen, X. Zhao, Y. Lu and W. Shi. 2018. CoC: A unified distributed ledger based supply chain management system. Journal of Computer Science and Technology, 33(2), 237–248.

Golab, L. and M. T. Özsu. 2003. Issues in data stream management. ACM Sigmod Record, 32(2), 5–14.

Gruber, T. 2008. Collective knowledge systems: Where the social web meets the semantic web. Journal of Web Semantics, 6(1), 4–13.

Halevy, A., M. Franklin and D. Maier. 2006. Principles of dataspace systems. Proceedings of the Twenty-Fifth ACM SIGMOD-SIGACT-SIGART Symposium on Principles of Database Systems, 1–9.

Heberlein, L. T., G. V. Dias, K. N. Levitt, B. Mukherjee, J. Wood and D. Wolber. 1989. A network security monitor. Lawrence Livermore National Lab., California Univ., Davis, CA (USA).

Ho, S. Y. 2012. The effects of location personalization on individuals' intention to use mobile services. Decision Support Systems, 53(4), 802–812.

Jahromi, A. A. and D. Kundur. 2020. Fundamentals of Cyber-Physical Systems. *In*: Cyber-Physical Systems in the Built Environment (pp. 1–13). https://doi.org/10.1007/978-3-030-41560-0_1

Kang, W., K. Kapitanova and S. H. Son. 2012. RDDS: A real-time data distribution service for cyber-physical systems. IEEE Transactions on Industrial Informatics, 8(2), 393–405.

Kavallieratos, G. and S. Katsikas. 2020. Managing cyber security risks of the cyber-enabled ship. Journal of Marine Science and Engineering 2020, 8(10), 768. https://doi.org/10.3390/JMSE8100768

Khan, N., Yaqoob, I., I. A. T. Hashem, Z. Inayat, W. K. Mahmoud Ali, M. Alam and A. Gani. 2014. Big data: Survey, technologies, opportunities, and challenges. The Scientific World Journal, 2014.

Leitão, P., W. A. Colombo and S. Karnouskos. 2016. Industrial automation based on cyber-physical systems technologies: Prototype implementations and challenges. Computers in Industry, 81, 11–25.

Lilis, G., G. Conus, N. Asadi and M. Kayal. 2017. Towards the next generation of intelligent building: An assessment study of current automation and future IoT based systems with a proposal for transitional design. Sustainable Cities and Society, 28, 473–481.

Linares Garcia, D. A. and N. Roofigari-Esfahan. 2020. CPS in other industries. *In*: Cyber-Physical Systems in the Built Environment (pp. 31–43). https://doi.org/10.1007/978-3-030-41560-0_3

March, S. T. and A. R. Hevner. 2007. Integrated decision support systems: A data warehousing perspective. Decision Support Systems, 43(3), 1031–1043.

Marwedel, P. 2021. Embedded System Design: Embedded Systems Foundations of Cyber-Physical Systems, and the Internet of Things. Springer Nature.

Matthews, J., P. E. D. Love, S. Heinemann, R. Chandler, C. Rumsey and O. Olatunj. 2015.

Real time progress management: Re-engineering processes for cloud-based BIM in construction. Automation in Construction, 58, 38–47.

Monostori, L., B. Kádár, T. Bauernhansl, S. Kondoh, S. Kumara, G. Reinhart, K. Ueda. 2016. Cyber-physical systems in manufacturing. CIRP Annals, 65(2), 621–641. https://doi.org/10.1016/j.cirp.2016.06.005

Oesterreich, T. D. and F. Teuteberg. 2016. Understanding the implications of digitisation and automation in the context of Industry 4.0: A triangulation approach and elements of a research agenda for the construction industry. Computers in Industry, 83, 121–139. https://doi.org/10.1016/j.compind.2016.09.006

Oztemel, E. and S. Gursev. 2020. Literature review of Industry 4.0 and related technologies. Journal of Intelligent Manufacturing, 31(1), 127–182.

Pilloni, V. 2018. How data will transform industrial processes: Crowdsensing, crowdsourcing and big data as pillars of industry 4.0. Future Internet, 10(3), 24.

Rajkumar, R., I. Lee, L. Sha and J. Stankovic. 2010. Cyber-physical systems: The next computing revolution. Design Automation Conference, 731–736. IEEE.

Sacks, R., L. Koskela, B. A. Dave and R. Owen. 2010. Interaction of lean and building information modeling in construction. Journal of Construction Engineering and Management, 136(9), 968–980.

Scarfone, K., M. Souppaya and M. Sexton. 2007. Guide to storage encryption technologies for end user devices. NIST Special Publication, 800, 111.

Scriber, B. A. 2018. A framework for determining blockchain applicability. IEEE Software, 35(4), 70–77.

Shih, C.-S., J.-J. Chou, N. Reijers and T.-W. Kuo. 2016. Designing CPS/IoT applications for smart buildings and cities. IET Cyber-Physical Systems: Theory & Applications, 1(1), 3–12.

Soibelman, L., J. Wu, C. Caldas, I. Brilakis and K.-Y. Lin. 2008. Management and analysis of unstructured construction data types. Advanced Engineering Informatics, 22(1), 15–27.

Stăncioiu, A. 2017. The Fourth Industrial Revolution "Industry 4.0". Fiabilitate Şi Durabilitate, 1(19), 74–78.

Taha, A. F. 2015. Secure Estimation, Control and Optimization of Uncertain Cyber-Physical Systems with Applications to Power Networks. Purdue University.

Thomson, R. E. and W. J. Emery. 2014. Data Analysis Methods in Physical Oceanography. Newnes.

Viviroli, D., M. Zappa, J. Gurtz and R. Weingartner. 2009. An introduction to the hydrological modelling system PREVAH and its pre- and post-processing-tools. Environmental Modelling & Software, 24(10), 1209–1222.

Windley, P. J. 2005. Digital Identity: Unmasking Identity Management Architecture (IMA). O'Reilly Media, Inc.

Xiao, Y., V. K. Rayi, B. Sun, X. Du, F. Hu and M. Galloway. 2007. A survey of key management schemes in wireless sensor networks. Computer Communications, 30(11–12), 2314–2341.

Yu, Y., B. Krishnamachari and V. K. Prasanna. 2004. Energy-latency tradeoffs for data gathering in wireless sensor networks. IEEE INFOCOM 2004, 1. IEEE.

Zander, J., P. J. Mosterman, T. Padir, Y. Wan and S. Fu. 2015. Cyber-physical systems can make emergency response smart. Procedia Engineering, 107, 312–318. https://doi.org/10.1016/j.proeng.2015.06.086

Zhou, P., D. Zuo, K. M. Hou, Z. Zhang, J. Dong, J. Li and H. Zhou. 2019. A comprehensive technological survey on the dependable self-management CPS: From self-adaptive architecture to self-management strategies. Sensors, 19(5), 1033.

Index